Huai Xuan Collection

Su Yan 俗言
Customary Words

Xia Xue Ti Hang 下學梯航
The Long Arduous Way of Learning the Simple Things

Yu Cheng Tang Jia Xun 豫誠堂家訓
Yu Cheng Tang Family Precepts

Xue Sheng Ren Ju Liang 學聖人局量
Learning the Sages' Capacity for Forgiveness

By Liu Yuan 劉沅

plus Liu Yuan Sheng Ping 刘沅生平
Life of Liu Yuan

Copyright © 2016 by Yaron Seidman

All rights reserved. No portion of this book may be reproduced, stored in a retrieval system or transmitted in any form or by any means—electronic, mechanical, photocopy, recording, scanning or any other—except for brief quotations in printed reviews, without the prior permission of the publisher.

NOTE: Every effort has been made to ensure the information contained in this book is complete and accurate. However, neither the publisher, nor the authors, are engaged in rendering professional advice or services to the individual reader and no portion of this book is intended to diagnose, treat, or cure the individual reader. Neither the publisher nor the authors shall be liable or responsible for loss, injury, or for the damage allegedly arising from any information or suggestion in this book.

Su Yan *Customary Words*; Xia Xue Ti Hang *The Long Arduous Way of Learning the Simple Things*; Yu Cheng Tang Jia Xun *Yu Cheng Tang Family Precepts*; Xue Sheng Ren Ju Liang *Learning the Sages' Capacity for Forgiveness*; plus Liu Yuan Sheng Ping *Life of Liu Yuan*

Compiled and translated by Y. Seidman
The Long Arduous Way of Learning the Simple Things:
Y. Seidman with Vita Revelli

Published by: Hunyuan Group Inc.
Greenwich, Connecticut, USA

Email: info@hunyuan.org
Website: http://www.chineseclassics.org

ISBN 978-0-9891679-4-9

1st Edition (August, 2016)
Printed in the United States of America

Image credits: Liu family

Translator's Note

Liu Yuan, a Confucian scholar, educator, healer, an exemplary son and a model parent, lived at the end of the 18th and first half of the 19th centuries in Sichuan, China. Liu believed in bridging gaps between religions and people. He expounded on the common goodness possessed innately by all people and the need to rediscover it when obscured. His life synopsis follows this compilation.

Amongst many of Liu Yuan's works, this compilation brings forth several exemplary titles at the heart of his teachings, including a doctrine which campaigns for his belief in an innate goodness in people, later named the Huai Xuan doctrine.

The task of translating texts from a different time and place requires bridging not only language and culture, but even more so, transporting an old mindset into a modern one. In many cases, respected customs of earlier times are not respected anymore, linguistic craft unique to one language sounds awkward in another. This, naturally, poses a challenge to the translator and the reader. The Huai Xuan doctrine promotes innate goodness of the person; the human. It transcends geographical borders and cultural differences as it brings together all humanity. However, to teach goodness it refers to the current culture and common customs, simple words and accepted ideas. Thus, rather than only to a selected few, it reaches to every person living in those times and that culture.

Connecting past and present, the idea behind this common human phenomenon shines through when cultural and linguistic differences are overcome and the essence sought. It depicts the way that the full human life is lived in realms both material and spiritual, visible and invisible. In its core, there is 'finding center', the daily practice which may lead to a long and healthy life while spreading harmony everywhere.

Finding center and properness, with time, yields boundless energy flowing from a universal center, bypassing and minimizing the obstruction caused by own heart's selfish tendency and boundless material desires. This, when successful, results in a person propagating goodness in the world effortlessly. The force to propagate such goodness stems from a quality termed 'heaven nature', an infinite source of power unleashing 'heart goodness' and collectively named by Liu Yuan 'Heaven Nature Heart Goodness'.

In return for spreading such goodness, having a big heart and selflessly caring for others, this compilation of translations for the modern times of the teachings of the Huai Xuan is dedicated to Liu Baigu, Liu Yuan's great grandson.

Putting in words the Huai Xuan heart is not an everyday task, therefore all omissions and errors in translation or interpretation are entirely due to the translator's shortcomings. One can only hope to accomplish something good!

In Connecticut the summer of 2016

Yaron Seidman

Liu Yuan's Calligraphy

Contents

English

Customary Words — 1

The Long Arduous Way of Learning the Simple Things — 161

Yu Cheng Tang Family Precepts — 183

Learning the Sages' Capacity for Forgiveness — 189

Life of Liu Yuan — 199

Chinese

Su Yan 俗言 — 227

Xia Xue Ti Hang 下學梯航 — 283

Yu Cheng Tang Jia Xun 豫誠堂家訓 — 291

Xue Sheng Ren Ju Liang 學聖人局量 — 293

Liu Yuan Sheng Ping 刘沅生平 — 299

Customary Words

Liu Yuan

劉沅

Translation and
Commentary
Yaron Seidman
孟亞倫

©2016 Hunyuan Research
Institute
www.hunyuaninstitute.com

Table of Contents

1. The first requirement is to respect heaven and earth, father and mother

2. Keeping oneself flawless comes first

3. In order to cultivate, one must first be proper and sincere

4. If one wants to be sincere and wants to be proper, one must first forbid licentiousness

5. Why does one become like the animals as soon as one violates by way of licentiousness

6. Why does one shorten one's life and sever one's offspring as soon as one violates by way of licentiousness

7. One should carefully learn from father, mother, teacher and friend how to sever licentiousness

8. After abstinence of sexual desires is mastered and one follows the Dao of the *Great Learning* then one can begin using propriety to regulate emotions

9. Dao of the *Great Learning* is not limited to the obvious Dao of humans but also it aspires to equal the sages and equal heaven; it prevents disease and prolongs life; it prevents hunger, cold and sufferings

10. In the *Great Learning,* for sincere intention and proper heart, one must first fear the mandate of heaven; therefore one should not immediately prohibit discussion about misfortune and fortune, spirits and ghosts

11. The basis of Dao is in the *Proper Place of Center* Zhong Yong. However, since the meaning of these two words was not clear to

the earlier literati, people thereupon viewed the sage in a lofty manner, viewing Dao as unreachable, and so the practice of aspiring to become the sage and become heaven was not practiced anymore

12. Serving father and mother – including brothers

13. Respecting equally father and mother. One cannot distinguish father as important and mother not. Filial piety to one's father naturally means filial piety to one's mother; the forefathers mistook the *Classic of Rites*. One must discern it clearly

14. Serving the monarch

15. Source of political integrity, scholars and selecting talent for government service must account for this first, only then is it a real talent

16. If the three cardinal relationships of social order are not proper then the five kinships are not proper. Therefore the superior one cultivates himself

17. Monarch and minister must act as the sage

18. Cultivate talent, treat the wise courteously and cultivate the scholarly, it is the urgent task of the country and of the family

19. Dao takes place with daily practice of human relations, and yet fulfilling this Dao is rare. It is because the path is separated into heart and True Nature, customary and sagely not conforming, one must differentiate it clearly and practice it vigorously

20. In order to teach, one must first nurture. Later generations find it most difficult to dwell in nurturing. One must act according to circumstances, the authority should lie with the monarch, parent and teacher

21. If responsibilities are heavy for monarch and parent, then the task should go first to the teacher. If one does not practice the Dao of the *Great Learning* then certainly it is difficult to seek the teacher

22. If there is a sagely teacher then there are his sagely disciples. To become sagely is not extremely difficult. The ancient literati mistook it for something far and removed, they caused future generations obstacle and waste. Be sure not to mistake for the sake of their error

23. Dao is not beyond human emotions and the innate law of things. Therefore each person can do it. However, one must use heaven principle in order to assess it and it must conform to the times

24. Human emotions and innate law of things cannot be separated from the common custom. One should not praise the past and condemn the present, nor look lightly at customs of the ordinary people

25. Sorting and Reaching is the skill of nurturing both inside and outside. When saying that this means to reflect outward, it teaches people to probe into the root of external things, this means that there is knowledge with no moral scruples. It is to pursue the trivial and forget the essential

26. To nurture Qi and not move the heart is the proper heart of the *Great Learning*. If one does not understand this principle he argues against Buddha and Laozi, his false argument is his crime against the truth and he eradicates "understand the heart and observe True Nature" and "cultivate truth and nurture True Nature". The correlation of heart and Qi, the wide difference of proper and sincerity, nobody knows

27. The myriad affairs begin in the heart. The myriad principles converge in True Nature. Preserving heart and nurturing True Nature and then human relations can be controlled and practiced. The truth of Buddha and Laozi is nothing else than heart and True Nature. If one refutes this and loses the truth of preserving and nurturing then it is not the real thing

28. The accomplishment of heart and True Nature is the root of daily human interactions. If one erroneously explains Sorting, Reaching, Sincerity and Proper of the *Great Learning*, and he doesn't know the truth of Buddha and Laozi being the same as Confucius, he separates it to many different paths, each with his own heterodoxy, then the scripture is not the proper truth. How can the common people follow it excitedly?

29. Loyal and filial come first in practicing virtue. Yet from antiquity until today, the mistakes are many. One must follow the original meaning of Confucius and Mencius, then he becomes a survivor and not a dead follower, loyal and filial then present with distinction

30. In order to find a loyal official, one must look amongst filial children. One must carefully study cases in the history annals describing loyalty with no filial piety or filial piety without loyalty in order to prevent people from suspecting that loyal and filial contradict each other

31. Being not clear about the correct Dao and having many hypocrites was always the reason, since ancient times, for the country to be in chaos and to perish. One should urgently correct this

32. The Dao of Great Learning encompasses everything, swipes clean everything; it is easy to know and easy to do. If above it

becomes a teaching and below everybody practices it then there is no worry under heaven

33. Only if Dao is centered for current times can every person do it. If it is looked at as lofty then it leaves a legacy of trouble with the family and country. From ancient times until today it was always like this. What a pity!

34. Words convey the Dao. Yet, Dao's meaning is worn out by words. One must first practice it in person and therefrom compose words, sayings and books. Then Dao is not overgrown with weeds

35. The words "having emotion in the world" everybody knows. However, they don't differentiate it clearly nor act upon it energetically. Instead, people act contrary to Dao

36. The numerous words of the sage all sum up to one principle. The principle is what heaven and human share in common

Customary Words Preface

Sages did not write books in order to become famous. Some were more, some were less [famous].

They [simply] followed their duty and wrote them.

They self-cultivated and wrote books about their experience in order to instruct the masses. People treasured it and then Charge, Plan, Lesson, Mandate,[1] *Changes* and its commentary,[2] poetry, *Historical Documents*, among others, came about.

From Fu Xi and Shennong to Kings Wen and Wu, the system of the sages matured, the method for human's cultivation was [by then already] complete.

Confucius cultivated further enlightenment into the midst of this road; masters Zeng Zi, Zi Si and Mencius further advanced his lead. The scope of works from antiquity until today on this topic cannot be measured. Throughout the generations, Confucian scholars, one after the other, compiled works. They desired to become one school of thought, yet even though they quoted Confucius and Mencius, they abandoned the guidelines and dangerously sank.

Now, I don't know, but because I have read books for many years, I have my own opinions; therefore, I annotated, in detail, the lost books of Confucius and Mencius. I called them "*Common*

---

[1] These four terms are styles of chapters in the *Shu Jing Book of Historical Documents*.
[2] *Yi Jing Book of Changes*

Explanations" because they describe the common Dao of heaven, the common path of earth and the common affairs of people that are knowable by everyone.

And since children labor hard in their complexity, I also put forth *"Children Questions"*, *"Correcting Errors"*, *"Guiding the Novice Practitioner"* and *"Honest Words of the Ancient Great Learning"*. This allows them to be clear and intelligible.

Now, books are many and they make one perplexed and so it was necessary to gather up the main points and weave them together. Therefore, with devotion, and not being afraid of the labor of words, I calculated it like this in order to instruct my household, otherwise how would I dare publish it? Noblemen of good taste, I esteem your pardon.

The 4th year of Xian Feng Reign, Jupiter is at Jia Yin, first month of the lunar year, Zhitang wrote this at the age of 87.

Dao should be performed diligently. It is not with words and letters.

Because there are many books and the actions people take are too few, I have no choice but to write this article. It is not that I want to contend the forefathers and it is also not that I have the slightest desire for fame. I am very old and my children are still immature. I have no alternative but to commit to their inheritance. This is the wish of Zhitang.

Customary Words

By Liu Yuan of Shuang Liu

From Fu Xi and Shennong to Confucius and Mencius – they were all sages, yet their affairs were not the same, how so?

[It is because] the times they lived in, the positions they occupied and their generation's customs were not the same.

The sage created ceremonial rites according to prevailing customs. Above, he performed rituals and music; below, he delivered words and deeds and they all achieved proper center. Therefore he was able to regulate and bring to completion the Dao of heaven and earth. He assisted what is appropriate to heaven and earth in order to influence the people.

Since the burning of the books,[3] written works became precious and the number of books increased daily. Many authors have expounded on the Dao of the sages; however, many are disorganized and miss the mark; confused are the majority.

They did not attain the truth of the sage.

The followers revered the sage but did not realize that with his heart, the sage penetrated the innate laws of things to the extreme. [Yet] if his sense of the natural law of things did not conform to Dao, then the sage used heaven principle to take a middle road.

He would neither follow nor transgress the customary; he conformed to proper center, which was the propriety of the time. How can one say that none of the current customs can be followed?

---

[3] Burning of the books during Qin dynasty in 213 B.C.

The customary [way] says that the human body endures countless calamities in the world. For the same reason, Confucius says that heaven and earth's True Nature is precious for the person. If one has a body, one needs to embody heaven's nature and only then can one be regarded as a human being. Ordinarily, people say that one should maintain the kind heart of heaven's nature.[4]

The kind heart of heaven's nature is what sets the human apart from the animals and beasts. The difference between a human and an animal is just with this little bit. Therefore it is called "slight". If the common people lose it then they become like the animals. The nobleman preserves it and so he becomes like the sage.

In later times, from Shun, Yu, Tang and Wen, all through to Confucius, they were people who preserved this "slight". They were all sages.

One can see that to be a sage means to be a human.

Every person has the kind heart of heaven's nature. Every person can do it. Every person can learn how to be like the sage and so it is said: "Every person can be like Yao and Shun."

Since the ancient literati talked about the Dao in a muted way, spoke of the sages in a lofty manner, and transmitted too many books, people had no way to ask for proper guidance. Therefore, I have no alternative but to use common language and explain it to children and juniors as follows:

---

[4] 天理良心

1. The first requirement is to respect heaven and earth, father and mother

Shu Jing states: "heaven and earth is the mother and father of the myriad things."

Common saying: The human body is a micro heaven and earth. It is the result of kindness of heaven and earth, father and mother.

Every person knows that, so how come intentions and actions do not give heed to the kind heart of heaven's nature? Father and mother gave birth to my body, heaven and earth granted me the human principle. If there is no heaven and earth then one cannot attain this human principle. If there is no father and mother, from where could one get one's body? Therefore heaven and earth, father and mother are called the Four Greats.

Since ancient times, sages and men of virtue served heaven as if serving their parents and served their parents as if serving heaven. If there is evil in any single thought, the physical parents may be deceived, but heaven and earth will not be deceived. Raise one's head and see heaven, bow one's head and see earth;[5] if one violates heaven's nature it is like violating and going against one's father and mother. Father and mother must hold responsible a child who lacks filial duty. How could heaven and earth fail to hold responsible a person who lacks heaven's nature?

---

[5] This sentence also means yearn for heaven and bow one's head in submission to earth.

With great care, King Wen revered the monarch in heaven. Confucius said: "know thy heaven in myself." This is neither wishful thinking nor crazy talk; it is basically viewing heaven and earth as I view my father and mother. People of the world don't know that heaven and human are one Qi. They claim that heaven's Dao is lofty and distant, divinities obscured. They are deceived by this thought and thus fail to know reverence. Over time, all their thoughts become like this. They disappoint the creation's kindness of heaven and earth, father and mother, missing the correct principle of human conduct. Day by day they degenerate to become like the animals, where their human heart becomes corrupt and their customs evil. Everywhere under heaven and in succession they encounter many troubles and mishaps.

The four words "heaven's nature kind heart" are the foundation of the human, they are the cause for the line dividing corruptness and generosity. One cannot stop talking about it, not even for one day. The *Great Learning* and *Proper Place of Center* describe: "Exercise caution in one's private life." They talk of ten eyes and ten hands to prevent leaking in the roof. It illustrates that a human has to show consideration to heaven's nature.

The ancient literati were afraid that people will abandon the meaning of being human and flatter ghosts and spirits and so they avoided speaking of ghosts and spirits. They only said that they were afraid that people know of ghosts and spirits. Now ghosts and spirits are the divine being of Yin Yang, while heaven and earth are the ancestors of Yin Yang. Therefore respecting ghosts and spirits means respecting heaven and earth, or what is called "fearing heaven's decree". If one does whatever one wants, ignoring heaven, absentminded of ghosts and spirits, then how can one have a revering heart? How can one control and set free one's heart?

Some suspect that if one believes in ghosts and spirits, then there must also be talk of misfortune and fortune; and if one talks about misfortune and fortune, then with all affairs he will aim to avoid misfortune and seek fortune. Thus, things that he should do, he would not do.

This is why the ancient literati did not talk of misfortune and fortune. People do not know that to respect heaven and earth is not like seeking to avoid misfortune or attain fortune. All affairs begin from the heart; if the heart is neither respectful nor sincere then it is apparent in one's words and actions. How can one then reach to goodness with no evil? What the heart thinks, people cannot tell; however, spirits of heaven know it. Therefore, with every single thought that rises, one must expel evil and adhere to goodness and then one can face heaven and earth and his father and mother.

Human beings are the happiness of heaven and earth, father and mother – so how can there be poverty, suffering and untimely death? Heaven and earth hold the power of misfortune and fortune, therefore avoiding misfortune and attaining fortune has its conventions. It is thus said: "Benefit is lucky, following the perverse is unlucky, accumulating goodness is a celebration, accumulating what is not goodness brings calamity."

Heaven and human are one Qi mutually connected. The ultimate of understanding is with this one principle, so how can one take a conventional view or recklessly explain the great Dao.

The sage restrained himself with every thought, as he was afraid to offend heaven and earth. In exactly the same way, he was afraid to offend his father and mother. One must have this approach first and then one can join with heaven principle, then one can be a human being.

His motive was not about misfortune and fortune. Yet he helped subsequent generations through the use of misfortune and fortune. The *Book of Changes* uses "auspicious, inauspicious, regret and worry" to teach people and Confucius often advocated this book. Later Confucian scholars did not know the meaning of heaven and human linked together; they did not understand Confucius's explanation of cultivating and overturning.[6] The disciples refrained from mentioning ghosts and spirits, misfortune and fortune and simply just used the principle to teach people that serving father and mother like heaven is good, and that serving heaven and earth like father and mother is even better.

---

[6] Confucius explained that when a tree is upright heaven cultivates it, when a tree is crooked heaven overturns it. This meant that if one was proper heaven gave him life naturally, if one was crooked heaven would destroy him.

If the principle is mistaken then where can one cultivate one's body[7] and achieve virtue, where can one see the invisible and hear the soundless?

Thus if one wishes to be a human being, if one wishes to avoid calamity, then one must place respecting heaven and earth, father and mother first.

Yaron: In Huai Xuan doctrine and for Liu Yuan, a living person, in addition to the physical body, has two components: heart and heaven's nature.

Heart is an instrument separating energy from unity; its expression is emotions. Heaven's nature is a thread of life carried through generations from parents to their children. It is also called the heaven's nature in me. Respecting and fearing heaven is about this heaven's nature, it talks about understanding the one thread of life inside the human being.

Heaven's nature is inside the heart, not the heaven one sees outside as the sky. Heaven inside the heart is constant and unchanging, unlike the emotions separating outward and fluctuating. Being filial to one's parents relates to the heart, by making one's emotions proper but it also relates to heaven's nature, recognizing the transmission of life from my parents to me.

---

[7] "Cultivate one's body" throughout the text has the double meaning "cultivating the physical body" and "cultivating the self".

Initially, before birth, it is an embryonic heart full of kindness given by the parent's heaven's nature. After birth, the heart separating from heaven's nature animate the physical body to move, act and react, and without it there is no life possible. Heart full of emotions and desires one easily understands, however, heaven's nature within the heart is understood experientially, through sustained and diligent practice.

2. Keeping oneself flawless comes first

When Confucius speaks of the Dao of *Great Learning* it references self-cultivation as the foundation. Mencius also says that after one cultivates one's body then all under heaven becomes peaceful.

In all the sages' teachings there is no additional Dao other than self-cultivation.

Naturally, if one does not have an enlightened teacher then one must err. Not only do Buddhist and Daoist monks lose the truth of Buddha and Dao while generating many absurdities, also what the Confucians generate is something other than the proper principle of Confucius and Mencius. Alas, the self-cultivation skill from beginning to end is described in the *Great Learning* and yet the Song dynasty Confucians altered the *Great Learning*, selfishly lying, and thereupon when people use it they are at a loss.

To cultivate one's self, one must keep one's self flawless.

Mencius said: "What is a grand affair? Selflessly serving one's parents is grand. Keeping what is grand? Keeping one's self is grand. Ones who do not err themselves and are able to selflessly serve their parents, I have heard of them. Ones who err their own self and selflessly serve their parents, I have never heard of those."

Confucius says: "Within the creation of heaven and earth, humans are precious" and "father and mother become whole and they give birth to it, for a child to become whole he returns to it, it may be called filial piety."

With every stroke one does not dare to forget one's father and mother, with every word one does not dare to forget one's father and mother; everything converges on this one principle.

The Dao of keeping oneself flawless means that every thought is within heaven's nature, with every affair there is cautiousness, guarding one's body and cultivating one's self is all in their midst. Zeng Zi's fear and trepidation, proceeding with extreme caution, in every action exterminating desire and addiction, eradicating lust, revering virtue and correcting evil, these actions are also included within.

The practical application of this effort is nothing other than nurturing both movement and stillness, cultivating both the root and the branches.

If one abides by the Great Learning and one attains the meaning of keeping one's self flawless, then at the higher realm one can aspire to equal the sages and heaven. Next to that, one can aspire to equal virtuous persons and longevity, prolonging one's life and expelling illness.

Later followers thought that all kinds of odd things are part of the meaning "keeping one's self flawless". Therefore they said, "The benevolent enjoys longevity, with great virtue one must enjoy longevity." Confucius, even though saying the words, why didn't he continually think of it?

Since the sages' transmission was lost, people leaned toward nurturing heart and didn't know that to be content, one needs to serve heaven. They leaned toward absorbing Qi and didn't know that one puts one's physical body into practice in order to fulfil one's True Nature. Like this, the Daoists and Buddhists guarded their heart as if it was the teaching of the Buddha; they manipulated Qi in order to attain eternal life. The Confucians were similarly inflicted; they wanted to follow True Nature, but instead distanced themselves from it. Some were able to attain the skin and shell but obscured its principle; they didn't understand the meaning of keeping one's self flawless, so how could they have attained the sincere body?

Alas, when humans are oppressed they become untidy.

Since ancient times, the wise and foolish, the one who cultivates or the one with shortcomings, they all had different tastes and were earnest for material reasons.

Heaven's solid strength is not the same as the nature of heart, thus it returns and conveys, to extreme depth, benevolence without deficit. The sage cultivated his body, studied and taught others in order to rectify the heartache of the finite worldly lifespan. Dao therefore is most revered and precious and one cannot stop learning it, not even for a brief moment. The sage is thus the filial son of heaven.

Since the ancient literati misunderstood, the sages' Dao became like a pie in the sky. Those seeking to be like the sages and the virtuous were unable to redeem this good fortune. Sad!

Yaron: "Flawless" means to emphasize heaven's nature within the heart. The heart brings forth heaven's nature by being dutiful and loyal. It guards it by minimizing selfish desires. The flawless action is everyday and not distant and lofty. For example, if the heart is unhappy, irritated and angry, resolving it to become content is a flawless action. In fact, as soon as the slightest wish to become content and resolve the unhappy feeling sets off, heaven's nature is already expressing, the human heart in that moment is flawless.

3. In order to cultivate, one must first be proper and sincere

Heaven and earth is summed up as this one principle: When principle Qi is condensing, eternal and infinite, has no competitor, not mingling with other things, not waxing and waning, continuing or discontinuing then it is called sincerity. The human being attains the proper principle and proper Qi from Heaven and earth and then he has life; if he is able to embody this principle in his own body then it is called the sincere body. The sage reaches the pinnacle of this sincerity and it is then called the "pinnacle of sincerity under heaven".

When an ordinary person doesn't deceive his heart nor turn his back on principle [8] this then is the method for achieving a sincere body.

However, one must first make clear what is the principle and what is true or false.

What conforms to principle is proper and what does not conform to principle is evil. When the principle is proper and one does it with a true heart then it is a sincere body. The ordinary person's heart often floats astray. If the heart floats astray how could one cultivate his body? Therefore one should perform diligently the four sentences "if it is not propriety don't look at it". [9] These four sentences Confucius uses to preserve the good heart. One should

---
[8] Principle means heaven's nature that exists inside the heart.
[9] This is the first sentence of the four: if it is not proper don't look at it, don't listen to it, don't talk it and don't act upon it.

pursue it at every moment and, over time, one will be able to remove evil and see the proper. About the idea of becoming a sage one should be just and honorable, not deceiving or swindling. Make an effort! Make an effort!

Yaron: To be proper means to follow the principle with every word and action. To be sincere means to embody the principle, to make the principle one's nature and naturally express it in all actions. Proper means to correct errors, sincere means to have no errors. One is first proper and then one becomes sincere.

4. If one wants to be sincere and wants to be proper, one must first forbid licentiousness

Mencius says: "Human's difference from animals is slight."

The slight difference is the kind heart of heaven's nature. Kind heart and heaven's nature is a joint concept. Generally speaking, when one does things conforming to principle and one's heart is peaceful then this is a kind heart without obscurity.

When an affair is not conforming to principle and one insists on doing it, either doing it without realizing it is wrong, or knowing perfectly well it is wrong and still doing it, then after one does it, and when in between sleep and wakefulness, the heart surely is not at ease.

The kind heart is then obscured.

This thought of the kind heart possibly becoming not peaceful is the seed that a human must plant endlessly. It is the foundation of the sage and the virtuous person.

One takes advantage of the initial movement of this thought, using it to repent the distressed heart, aspiring to have this no more.

One affair is like this and then every affair is like this.

One gradually does it like this until it becomes habit, then naturally one delights in goodness and disdains from evil.

All sorts of evil thoughts are easy to extinguish; however, "licentious desire" – these two words come about inside the blood and Qi, most easily do they make one lose his head and disdain the principle, also they are the most difficult to cut off.

Now, the boundary separating humans from animals is exactly in this place. Zealously, one must discharge a courageous heart, think of the clear spirit in heaven, as if one's father and mother are standing in front of one, see other people's wives and daughters as one's own older and younger sisters, not leer or think of them; like this, how would one dare a disorderly action. One takes a bad thought and, with a sword, severs it; thus, one does not become like the animals. Then one can see a filial person, a loyal minister, one can enjoy wealth and honor and good fortune.

People in the world, in not preventing this one thought, forfeit the kind heart and become like the animals; furthermore, because of this slip of one thought, their life is shortened and their future generations severed.

Poverty, disease and hardship are all due to erring with "licentious desire". Therefore, when children are sixteen or seventeen, one must be sure to teach them how to forbid and guard in order to cut off the main culprit, this is the action of virtuous parents and teachers. The following text explains it in detail.

Yaron: When life propagates as pure expression of principle then it continues unfolding far into the future. Desire for male-female relations ensures future human life. Licentiousness is a selfish desire seeking to propagate life from its branches and not from its root. It influences a person to err in all other aspects of life. Life's expression gradually loses its root. Life, instead of nurturing from heaven's nature feeds on heart desire.

5. Why does one become like the animals as soon as one violates by way of licentiousness?

Human is of the Luo[10] species. At the beginning of the primal chaos, the human was born without clothes or a way to hide himself. Without dwelling to shelter from wind and rain, not knowing which things are edible, he perished from drought, frost, hunger and poison; he did not yet know how to be a human.

Without clothes he was just like the animals, he ate vegetation and all sorts of things and grew hair all over his body. Heaven gave birth to a sage and he manufactured clothing and then people became different from the animals; they then had shelters to dwell in, the five grains to nurture their lives. Only then did humans attain security.

Now, since man and woman are the proper principle of Yin and Yang and only too easily can illicit sexual relations, for this a wedding ceremony was established to allow each to have a husband and a wife so they can continue from the ancestors further down to their children and grandchildren. Therefore the *Book of Rites* says: "Within the human Dao, the grand marriage is most important. The sage taught the proper five kinships and about man and woman he said 'they have a difference'. Now animals also have a rooster and a hen, a cow and a bull and they also bear offspring; however, they don't have a difference between their male and female."

---

[10] One of the five species, Luo literally means naked, without feathers or scales.

The *Book of Rites* says: "if there is no difference, there can be no righteousness; it is then the Dao of the animals." Zhuan commentary states: "If there is no difference between male and female, it is then animals." *Book of Rites* states: "Only animals have no rites, therefore father and son gather doe."

If man and woman make illicit sexual relations outside of the family structure then they are like the animals. Heaven and earth, father and mother, give birth to me, their accomplishment is my person. If I have this single drop of evil desire then I lose my person; it is a great lack of filial piety, how can one then have virtue or accomplishment? How can one have a name in this world? How can one thus have dignity to look at one's father, mother and one's ancestors? How can one thus face one's wife and children?

The ancients said: "if one does not forbid licentiousness then one is just like the dogs and pigs, one cannot avert meeting the butcher's slaughter. A great disaster coming upon a troop of soldiers often happens because the evil persons in their midst are too many; how can one not be fearful of this?

Yaron: Sexual desire between committed partners encourages a unification of principle and body; it fulfills the need to continue heaven's nature in this world. Random sexual desire toward people other than a committed partner prevents proper action and sincerity. Even though sexual desire itself is similar, different applications either create or destroy human life.

6. Why does one shorten one's life and sever one's offspring as soon as one violates by way of licentiousness

What makes a person a human is entirely within the four words "kind heart heaven's nature." The person violating with licentiousness has a brief moment of pleasure, but entirely does not think about the fact that I have older and younger sisters, that I have a wife and a daughter. If my older or younger sister, wife or daughter is stained by that other person, can I be reconciled? That person that stained my sister, wife or daughter, how can I tolerate him?

Even when my sister, wife or daughter walks on the street and there is a man leering at them, I still cannot tolerate him. Moreover, if he violates one of my relatives, how can I have mercy on him? I might hate or kill him, anything is possible. But if you take this thought and you turn it over and think, "when I violate the man's wife or daughter, isn't she human too? The illuminated spirit of heaven and earth, will it forgive me or not?"

Therefore, violating with licentiousness often ends in shortening one's life, or at least severing future generations. Even if we cultivated well in the previous incarnation and the ancestors have a legacy of virtue, if I force myself to do these things during my lifetime then my descendants will certainly not benefit from it.

To an extreme, my wife, daughter, son and grandchildren will have to pay for my actions. Try to look at people around you and you will see that this does not deviate a hair's breadth.[11] So how can we not collect our thoughts and realize that if we offend with licentiousness then we are willing to implant an infinite seed causing misfortune and entering the realm of the animals?

Yaron: Licentiousness toward another person's wife, daughter or sister is caused by a selfish heart willing to hurt others. A cruel heart does not express heaven's nature. Liu Yuan explains that when the heart does not express heaven's nature then it equals the person not being fully alive, the punishment is already there.

---

[11] Meaning, it is perfectly accurate.

7. One should carefully learn from father, mother, teacher and friend how to sever licentiousness

Father and mother must be clear regarding the principle; they should abstain from desires and cultivate the body. Even when they are home, husband and wife should not make rash remarks, or be lax with laughter. Behavior and speech in the lady's private quarters and sleeping area should have its rules; it should not reveal improper behavior. Sons and daughters should be guarded from the age of seven or eight, they should be taught that boys and girls should not sit together, and should not be lured by strangers. They should be finely taught to have a sense of humility, properness, kindness, goodness, respect and reverence. When they reach to the age of fourteen or fifteen, more attention is needed; they should then be taught the difference between a human being and a beast. Show them that from ancient times until today, men of honor demonstrate these qualities. Teach them to be sincere and considerate. If they move to another city to follow a teacher they must choose a person who is proper and clear about the principle. They must not travel or reside with a small-minded, improper person.

Sons and daughters should guard well the door of the inner chamber; female relatives who lack integrity should not cohabit the same residence. When selecting a son-in-law, he must be honest and considerate, benevolent and compassionate, coming from a family with propriety and righteousness; it should not be an issue of rich or poor. When the father and mother are proper and they teach the son and daughter to be proper too, then from childhood onwards it becomes a habit and over an extended period of time it becomes natural.

Contemporary people want to marry when they are sixteen or seventeen and immediately they want to have children. When they become fathers and mothers, they can't tell right from wrong with all the regular daily affairs. So how can they be fathers and mothers who teach children and grandchildren? Alas, the public's moral integrity is daily deteriorating and the human heart has difficulty returning to its proper place.

Confucius said: "first know how to be a son, then you will know how to be a father." If one is unworthy as a child or grandchild, how can one later assume the responsibility of a parent?

The teacher is as important as the parent and monarch. Regardless of one's trade, a person must have a teacher to teach him. If the teacher is improper, then even if that person was a good son and a good brother he will still become spoiled by that teacher. In addition, if the teacher is crooked then one's fellow students also become crooked. Every day as they get together they speak carelessly and act perversely. It is hard to fully explain the scope of this problem. When sons and brothers often see and hear crooked things and contract bad habits then they become unworthy and, until the end, they turn corrupt with no possibility to recover. When parents claim that their children are unworthy, they fail to recognize that the mistake was their own.

And so, if one does not have an enlightened teacher then one cannot fully grasp the principle of ethical relations, cardinal righteousness, moral cultivation and properly conducting oneself in society. In addition, selection of a teacher should be done by one's father and mother. If the father and mother are not proper themselves, then how could a son and brother choose correctly an enlightened teacher?

Now, who is an enlightened teacher? It is one who possesses a kind heart and clearly understands and is able to explain the eight meanings of filial piety, brotherly love, loyalty, trust, propriety, righteousness, honesty and humility. It is one able to demonstrate these values in their own family.

Thus, father, mother and a teacher are a lifelong root of good or evil, of fortune or misfortune. If one is a father, mother or a teacher, one must constantly self-cultivate and have humility. Confucius said: "If one makes oneself proper, how could one not make others proper? If one cannot make oneself proper, then how can one make other people proper?" Mencius said: "if one does not act with Dao, one cannot act with Dao toward one's wife and children; if one causes others to act with no Dao, one then cannot bring Dao to one's wife and children."

Countless monarchs, parents and teachers, in later generations, were extravagant and self-righteous, not cultivating their self. Followers often assumed the duty of loyal officials and were willing to sacrifice their life and yet many were treated unjustly. Such people[12] are so unworthy that their misfortune is beyond words.

---

[12] Speaking of the uncultivated monarchs, parents and teachers.

In the world, people often overlook things because it is customary. If the three cardinal guides of social order[13] are not proper, how could people hope for the five kinships to have proper place and for principle to have its proper measure?

Yaron: Parents and teachers give to children and students. The responsibility lies with the parent and teacher to transmit well and, in turn, promote good fortune. Self-observing and reducing selfish desires bring the parent and teacher closer to heaven's nature and then the transmission promotes good fortune.

---

[13] The three cardinal guides of social order are ruler-subject, parent-child and husband-wife.

8. After abstinence of sexual desires is mastered and one follows the Dao of the *Great Learning* then one can begin using propriety to regulate emotions

Since antiquity, the sage used propriety to teach people. He did not rely entirely on rules and laws but, rather, advocated diligent effort in body and mind.

Books from the era before Yao and Shun were lacking and disloyal so Confucius deleted and arranged the books and decided what comes down from Yao and Shun. In the beginning of the Charge of Yao, there is praise for Yao's virtue: "admire clarity, gently think, calm calm".

Admire means to be respectful. Respectful inside speaks of being still and nurturing this heart, while respectful outside speaks of inspecting and controlling words and actions. Over time, the person's will becomes like the spirit, the principle becomes clear and so it is described as "admire clarity". The human heart cannot stop thinking and thinking, often going astray; when it goes astray then there is no calm. With Yao's admiring clarity, the heart is proper and the body cultivated and whatever thinking comes about, it is naturally in order and sequence, conforming to propriety, therefore it is called gently thinking. Calm calm means that one is calm and then even calmer, embodying the natural way easily and fluently.

These six words explain explicitly the teachings of the sage.

The sages' words are thousands and thousands and yet the essence of all of them is summed up here.

"Sincere intention, proper heart, cultivated body" from the *Great Learning* is the meaning here. The Dao declined in the Spring and Autumn period and Confucius only taught it privately to his disciples. The monarch and ministers didn't understand the meaning and thereupon followed different paths of fame and gain, law and punishment, poetry and prose. The myriad styles of learning increased daily.

The Dao of *Great Learning* was on the decline and Confucius thought that future generations would not receive this transmission and so he asked Zeng Zi to write this one article. But Zeng Zi was worried that people will not know how to grasp this essence and so he started explaining it with "sincere intention" and, from that, he extended it into five articles.

From the Qin and Han dynasties, the compilation of Confucius and Mencius was widely circulated. This book was highly revered and its followers many but still they were not able to exploit its meaning to the fullest.

The Song dynasty Confucians heavily emphasized this text but did not reach to its true effect. With a one-sided view, they tampered with the original text. Zhen Xishan followed and propagated it, so while Zhuzi's version of the Great Learning circulated throughout time, no one was giving attention to the original text of Confucius.

In *Commentary of the Book of Rites Compilation by Imperial Orders Qin Ding Li Ji Yi Shu* the *Ancient Great Learning* is still extant. Truly, not daring to include something that is not of the sages' truth, I explained it plainly in *Honest Words of the Ancient Great Learning*. Very delicately I pointed out the meticulous work needed. However, Zhuzi's altered version had already become so popular that when scholars saw my work they inevitably felt astonished and disdained.

Unsurprisingly, the sage's original book explained the principle; it afforded people something to follow. To study the sage but not follow the accomplishments of the Dao of *Great Learning*, then how could one cultivate one's body? If one is not cultivated then how could one "improve oneself in order to improve others?" It is a must to have this measure.

Moreover, the sage talked about heaven, what he said surely is about heaven's nature, so how can one take the writing left behind and amend it, take the sage's text and rashly alter it, rashly explain it?

In the world now, wanting to study the sage, where could one find accomplishment?

I therefore took the *Great Learning* and delicately explained its words. Peasants know that one uses Dao to cultivate one's body and that one cannot be unworthy toward one's parents and monarch.

So what is the Dao of cultivating the body? Remove material desire in order to purify the heart, research the principle in order to attain perfect knowledge.

With pure heart and few desires, quiet the heart often and nurture spirit, pursue the heart of letting go and accumulate that of profound forgiveness, this is called "stopping at ultimate goodness".

The heart floats and moves easily and is most difficult to quiet and still. Therefore, in normal times one must persevere with respect; one must seek to conform to principle with words and actions, movement and stillness.

If the heart does not conform then one must restrain it; if it does conform then one must embolden it.

With every thought, one must neither deceive nor pardon oneself.

Persist like this and then goodness-Qi becomes abundant and will-Qi pure; Mencius calls it "collecting of righteousness generates Qi".

Zeng Zi, accordingly, began the transmission with an article about sincere intention. He took Confucius's many words and ideas and fully applied them within "sincere intention." Sincere intention means to inspect movement.

When there is no affair to deal with then one gathers one's heart to center without a single thought arising, the myriad causes brushed aside, extremely empty and extremely still, it fosters the spirit and Qi interdependence, quiet with no desire. This is the accomplishment of Mountain Stopping, the Dao of reaching center; it is preserving stillness.

The *Book of Historical Documents* says: "calm stopping", the *Book of Changes* says: "mountain stopping", the *Book of Poetry* says:

"stillness stopping" and therefore Confucius says: "stopping at ultimate goodness."

Stopping at goodness is the center of heaven and earth. The human body exists with heaven and earth together, knowing this is the way in, the ability of the heart to dwell here. Knowing heaven, self-reflecting and transforming the mysterious explains heaven's ability with ease.

What Zi Si said: "The Dao of heaven and earth can be summed up in one sentence" is this meaning.

Now, since ancient times people did not dare divulge the sages directly, assuming them to be the mystery of heaven and earth and worried that people will view them irreverently. However, if one didn't have an enlightened teacher to explain, then regardless there was no use.

In Kun hexagram, Confucius says: "The monarch establishes etiquette in the Yellow Bell, sitting in a proper position, with perfection in his center extending to his four extremities, reaching to his enterprises, perfection to the extreme."

In Gen hexagram he says: "Stopping in his place, when it is time to stop he stops, when it is time to go he goes, movement and stillness do not lose their proper time, his Dao is glorious." These descriptions are all derived from the principle of "stopping at ultimate goodness". Mencius says: "replenishing it is called perfection, replenishing and it has glory is called great."

What makes the person alive is Qi; spirit is the master of Qi, while the heart is the illuminating spirit of the human. What is called "the good heart is difficult to attain while the hateful heart is easy" means Qi and material are continually involved with each other. First there is Qi and then there is material, and as soon as there is material, Qi is in difficulty.

Heart is the divinity of Qi and blood; Qi and blood cannot be too busy, otherwise how can the human heart be pure with principle? Therefore one must nurture the vast Qi and over time one can stop moving one's heart. The vast Qi is not something outside the Qi in "Qi and blood", and yet in reality it is not the same as the Qi in "Qi and blood". Its accomplishment reaches to the spirit; Mencius makes the analogy of "firm and great" and he calls it "vast", speaking of its accomplishment.

Now, its body has no concepts like sound or smell so Buddha and Laozi call it "empty void", the origin Qi in "empty void" talks about the thing itself, while "vast" talks about its accomplishment. These are not two different things.

Confucians avoid speaking of "empty void" since they think that "its virtue cannot be revealed" so how could it be grand? What is recorded in heaven can only be imitated. How can virtue not be revealed in what is called "majestic"?[14] Majestic has the meaning of profound and far-reaching, of being indescribable, which makes "empty void". In literature, "majestic" and "heaven's grandeur"

---

[14] "Majestic" is composed from repeating twice the word dignified mentioned in the prior sentence.

mean the same, as they are purely about heaven's nature. The human heart cannot attain or see it.

How could one see if virtue exists in one's own heart? Therefore, it is said: "virtue that is not revealed." To speak of heart's virtue creates the perception that virtue is an object, conversely, it is said "to perceive myself is heaven; amongst all people there is none who can know me," wouldn't it be nonsense?

In addition, regarding nurturing heart method, if there is no empty void nourishing and cherishing, then one passes to and fro in hesitation endlessly. How does one learn about the practical meaning of the three words in the *Great Learning* "fixed, stillness, calmness"?

One must know stopping and then one is able to reach "fixed, stillness, calmness". Zhu Zi takes "ultimate goodness" and aligns it with external things, claiming that one can know ultimate goodness via these external things. Like this, how could one reach "fixed, stillness, calmness"? When this point's logic becomes clear then how could one still follow Zhu Zi and turn one's back on Confucius?

Only when one knows the center of heaven and earth, seeks the heart of letting go and stops in this proper place, if one perseveres with one's will and doesn't allow explosive Qi, for a long time, then one's heart confusion slows down until it reaches "fixed".

After it is "fixed" for a long time then spirit becomes calm, Qi becomes quiet and then it becomes "stillness". Once in stillness for a long time, then body and heart reside in "calmness". With "calmness", desires become fewer every day while heaven's intention unfolds daily.

Probing into principle makes it easy to differentiate and then to ponder. When one ponders, it causes one's heart to reveal itself, for what he sees or hears, external affairs cannot disturb one's heart; his words and actions, movement and stillness conform to proper etiquette, this is "being able to attain."

Confucius brings forth "stopping at ultimate goodness" as the important aspect in the *Great Learning* and he specifically points out its sequential effect. They clearly misread it; causing people to pursue external things, they described it as "exhausting the principle in all things." They did it like this while thinking that they could see everything in a clear light and have the entire application of the heart understood by all.

If there is no internal teaching of "nurturing True Nature,"[15] and one relies solely on one's eyes and ears for understanding, then how can one reach "fixed, stillness, calmness"?

More so, how can one achieve "pondering" and how can one "attain"? Just as "loyal and dutiful is ultimate goodness," who does not know this? Yet, very few people are able to be loyal and dutiful, so how can they talk about "fixed, stillness, calmness"? If teaching our own bodies and heart is not done and instead we cause people

---

[15] True Nature Xing 性 is within the Heart Xin 心. Heaven's nature Tian Li 天理 that is within the heart is what makes True Nature.

to have an exaggerated concern with external things without an end, then the sage's words become a pie in the sky.

The human heart is hard to restrain, the principle is hard to understand, without "stopping at ultimate goodness" one cannot preserve the heart, without "empty void" one cannot generate the "Vast Qi", and if like this one wishes to remove the evil heart and return to proper principle then this becomes absolutely impossible.

Therefore, if one wishes to forbid licentiousness, to know how to guard the body and make the body sincere, and other such affairs, then one must follow the Dao of the *Great Learning*. Everybody can know the Dao of the *Great Learning*; everybody can do it. This should not be sought outside of this body. Why would it become only for the scholarly? How could one desire that people thereby just squawk about studying Dao?

Yaron: Stopping at ultimate goodness simply means to not follow a desirous heart. A heart with little desire generates life for oneself and for others; it propagates no harm. Doing no harm and reaching to heaven's nature inside the heart make the person then attain the ultimate point, become a human.

9. **Dao of the *Great Learning* is not limited to the obvious Dao of the human but it also aspires to equal the sages and equal heaven; it prevents disease and prolongs life, prevents hunger, cold and sufferings**

The human attains the proper center Qi of heaven and earth, this Qi is principle and the origin of this principle Qi is Taiji.

When one attains this Taiji before birth, it is a lump of spirit Qi that can't be named nor its form described; it is completely unadulterated so-called "True Nature of heaven's mandate". When the baby is in the mother's womb[16] it cannot smell or hear,[17] it does not yet have the physical body,[18] it is entirely a lump of principle Qi, and therefore Mencius says: "True Nature is goodness."

When the human physical body is formed[19] and the baby exits the mother's abdomen, the nine orifices open, the seven emotions discharge, the center Qi of pre-heaven is now scattering, having difficulty to come back together, it separates and has difficulty to merge back together, and at this point the pure True Nature changes into a human heart which is diverse and confused. Now, after birth, the human heart is all about desire disposition, the attraction to material things, and therefrom it loses its properness. Thus Confucius said: "True nature, it gets close to it."[20]

---

[16] At conception.

[17] Also translates "there are no smells and sounds".

[18] Also translates "does not have yet the hundred bones".

[19] Also "the skeleton is formed".

[20] The human heart, ruled by desires, can get close to True Nature if desires are restrained, but it can never become completely without desire, therefore it only gets close to it.

The sage used doctrine to teach people that they need to remove selfish desire for material things[21] and, with that, reach to the clarity of heaven principle.

Internally preserving and nurturing and then one reaches to "stopping at ultimate goodness", externally inspecting and then sincerity coexists alongside likes and dislikes.

With all these, preserving spirit and nurturing Qi[22] is the main thing. Spirit is heart, spirit is the master of Qi and therefore one must persevere with one's will and not unleash one's Qi. However, this Qi is the vast Qi of the universe and not the Qi coming from breathing. Heart is a divine movement allowing perception; it is not the pre-heaven True Nature.

Preserving heart and nurturing True Nature means preserving the heart that has perception and nurturing the formless True Nature.

The principle at this point becomes very fine and pure; if there is no enlightened teacher then it cannot be transmitted.

Confucian scholars have evaded words by Daoist priests; they avoided speaking of spirit Qi. They didn't know that if a person doesn't have spirit Qi then they can't live and if heaven doesn't have spirit Qi then it can't take place. However, spirit Qi has the classifications of pre- and post-heaven; one should not mistake the two for the same thing.

---

[21] The Chinese words 格去物欲 is an expansion on the *Great Learning* term Ge Wu 格物. Song dynasty neo-Confucians explained the term Ge Wu as sorting out phenomena in nature, but Liu Yuan explains the term as eradicating the desire for material things, an inward reflection and not an external observation.

[22] Liu Yuan points to the similarity between the Daoist technique of preserving spirit and nurturing Qi to the Confucian technique of preserving heart and nurturing True Nature.

Pre-heaven spirit Qi is what makes heaven, heaven. When the human attains it, it is True Nature. Sun, moon, stars and constellations – this is the spirit shining of heaven and earth, while wind, clouds, thunder and rain is the true Qi of heaven. However, the author of the scattering of spirit Qi and the origin of this spirit Qi, one cannot attain or glimpse at, and so it is called the record of heaven; it has no sound or smell.

Now, the Dao of heaven and earth finds its root with the formless and each and every one of its manifestations is its application.

The human attains the principle of heaven and earth and so they live; what we call "life" means stopping at this spirit Qi.

Heart is spirit and one can't see one's own heart, so how could one see heaven's nature within the heart? Preserving heart and nurturing True Nature causes the Qi of one origin to replenish and gradually transform into spirit. This is not an empty void.[23]

Confucians don't speak of spirit but they do talk of heart, but how is the heart not the same as spirit? How can principle not be rooted in formless?

Principle governs Qi and Qi carries principle. If one departs from Qi then where can principle be? Thus being without sound and smell is the root of Dao.

Within formless, "nurturing stillness" is the skill that brings about centre. Purifying of illusion [24] means an unadulterated heaven principle without a shred of selfish thought. Extinction means

---

[23] Referring to the Buddhist concept of void.
[24] The Buddhist practice of mind purification.

keeping silent without moving until there is no selfish desire whatsoever.

So how is the truth of Buddha and Lao Zi an external principle?[25]

Buddhist monks and Daoist priests misunderstood and the Confucians didn't bother to investigate. They didn't know that those were methods of nurturing heart and instead they thought that they just abandoned human relations.[26] How is that not accusing falsely? Only cultivating heart and True Nature reach to the divine of spirit Qi.

Therefore, preserving heart and nurturing True Nature is the same as preserving spirit and nurturing Qi.

If spirit Qi becomes strong and solid, how will it not be possible to extend life? Accumulating righteousness and generating Qi too is not the same meaning as the practices of the Daoist priests, rather it is nurturing ordinary spirit and ordinary Qi, inside preserving and nurturing, outside performing human relations, then both the root and the branches are cultivated, the vast Qi of the universe fills between heaven and earth; like this, it can really serve its purpose and therefore longevity is in its midst.

Confucius said: "the benevolent has longevity, with great virtue one must enjoy longevity." He also said: "heaven helps that which conforms." When virtue is pure then spirit moves and heaven

---

[25] Foreign to Confucians.

[26] Daoists speak of mysterious spirit and nurturing Qi, Buddhists about void and purifying illusion, Confucians about True Nature and correcting the heart, but in reality these are similar in practice and understanding. Confucians denounced the monastic or hermit as simply abandoning human relations, not realizing renunciation to be an internal practice of inspecting movement.

follows, from heaven comes assistance and only auspiciousness without bad luck, how could one become destitute worrying about encountering hardships or being unable to avoid calamity? Confucius said: "heaven generates virtue in me, how could Huan Tui capture me?[27] If heaven didn't destroy this culture how could the Kuang people have their way with me?" As for the meaning of this principle, unfortunately, the earlier people didn't reach to this heaven-human principle and instead, in a trivial fashion, avoided Buddha and Lao Zi's words. They only knew good and bad luck, regret and worry, good fortune inherited from the parents, calamity that unfolds long after the bad deed took place, sages who all talk absurdities – how can one not be perplexed by all this?

Yaron: The fetal heart of feeling unity and happiness, being one with its mother, becomes different upon birth. The person now finds difficulty feeling the unity with nature. It artificially appears to one as if one is separated from everyone and everything; I am here and you are there. However, by observing thoughts and desires it affords, gradually, to glimpse at heaven's nature and unity; our connectedness to all things. For example, a person who feels irritated and angry with others, yet, upon self-reflection, may feel compassion, love and sympathy. Their heart can change from a dichotomous to an infant-like heart that is truly happy.

---

[27] As Confucius traveled through the state of Song, Huan Tui heard of it and with soldiers tried to hurt Confucius.

10. In the *Great Learning*, for sincere intention and proper heart, one must first fear the mandate of heaven, therefore should not immediately prohibit discussion about misfortune and fortune, spirits and ghosts

Heaven is only one principle. Principle is formless yet Qi has a trace.

The sacred aspect of principle and Qi is called ghosts and spirits.

Heaven is vast and earth solitary. What dictates them is principle and Qi; when the transformation is unpredictable, it is ghosts and spirits.

Human exists within the frame of heaven and earth. This heart that attains the properness of heaven and earth is Heaven-and-Earth-Heart. When a thought moves and it conforms to heaven's nature then it conforms to heaven's heart; if a thought goes against heaven's naturethen it antagonizes heaven's heart. Like this, accumulating over time, the difference between good and evil becomes great.

Those who conform to heaven prosper while those who antagonize heaven perish.

What kind of heart is heaven's heart? Conforming to principle and it gets close to it,[28] then this brings good fortune; not conforming to principle and heaven is far from it, then this brings ill fortune. Ghosts and spirits are the sacred aspect of heaven and earth, dominated by principle and Qi.

---

[28] Restraining desire, leading the heart to become closer to True Nature.

If one uses goodness to seek heaven it is like throwing a rock onto the water, if one uses evil to seek heaven then it is like throwing water onto a rock. This is a natural principle and not a supernatural event.

Therefore, in regard to ill and good fortune, it comes down to seeking one's own body and heart. It is not "defying principle and at the same time lovingly praying to the heaven's spirits". The *Book of Changes* teaches people by using "good and bad luck, regret and worry" because human emotions naturally gravitate toward "fearing misfortune and seeking fortune." It is demonstrated by the appearance of fortune and misfortune. One should know, however, that good and bad luck are generated by good and evil. If there is goodness then there is fortune, if there is evil then there is misfortune. This book teaches people about goodness and not about seeking good fortune. If one does not act with goodness and is seeking good fortune it is like entering the mountain looking for fish, it is like entering water and looking for firewood. Not only is it of no use, but also this disrespectful flattery will meet the punishment of ghosts and spirits.

People today often seek good fortune but instead they meet disaster, erroneously thinking that acting with goodness has no benefit; they don't understand that what they define as "goodness" is actually not goodness at all. For example, there are those people who love and respect people, but they are aloof toward their own parents. They don't carefully cherish their own parents and yet they love and respect others, can this be called "goodness"? There are those who are generous and philanthropic and yet with their own brothers they haggle over money. They artificially distinguish, "this is yours, this is mine," to an extreme they sit by and watch their brothers' difficulties without lending a hand. Can this be called "goodness"?

Know that the spirit in heaven places priority on filial piety and brotherly love. The heavenly goodness of one's love and respect for other people finds its root with father and mother. Not loving and respecting one's father and mother, then this heavenly goodness immediately vanishes. How could one then love and respect other people? The filial son must be friendly to his younger brother and respect his elder brother. One thinks of one's parent's suffering and immediately one thinks of their sons and daughters. How could there be one allowing any heartless action? Love and respect begins with filial piety and brotherly love and then this heavenly goodness is propagated outward to benevolence toward people and loving of all things clearly and without ambiguity. Only then can this be regarded as "goodness", only then can this be regarded as conforming to heaven principle.

Acting like this and yet not attaining good fortune is rare. However, the human heart acts rashly; every person has this loving and respectful heart and yet some, despite knowing it, do not act upon it, while some act upon it, but without truthfulness. It cannot be sustainable, how come? Because it is impudent and lazy. If asked how come it is lazy and impudent? People erroneously think that it does not matter if it is like this or not. They do not know that respectful and loving people have a heart containing heaven's nature goodness. If one does not respect and love one's own parents and siblings then one does not have this heaven goodness.

The illuminated spirit of heaven and earth then is not happy, so where is the benefit? Ghosts and spirits command the transformation of heaven and earth, and if heaven and earth are not happy then the wrath of ghosts and spirits descends. Therefore the nobleman must fear heaven's decree.

If there is one thought without heaven goodness one then immediately eradicates it; this is the real learning of serving heaven.

If it is not so, then it is like what Confucius calls "the little person does not know heaven's decree and so he is not fearful" and "the little person has no fear", then how could one have a proper heart? How could one have good fortune? Everyone is seeking good fortune and fleeing misfortune. Furthermore, many worship spirits and thus seek good fortune, but they don't know that ghosts and spirits don't fetch the sacrificial offerings and prayers; they especially seek out people of filial piety and goodness.

In the beginning, good fortune is not hard to seek; it only takes a proper heart. To have a proper heart, one first needs sincere intention and for sincere intention, one needs to exercise caution and be pure in one's personal life.

The *Great Learning Da Xue* and *Proper Place of Center Zhong Yong* talk about exercising caution and being pure in one's personal life: "what ten eyes see and what ten fingers point to is like a leaking roof." How could one not fear heaven and earth ghosts and spirits? Earlier Confucians were one-sided and did not conform to Confucius. It caused people to have reckless hearts and disdain principle. Some have said: "how come Confucius did not speak of spirits?" Answer: Confucius did speak of it. However, when one speaks of spirits it must be in the Dao of human to make it real and practical, thus it is said: "the physical body of ghosts and spirits has no trace to it" and "about spirits one reflects and thinks inward, one cannot calculate and think outward." This teaches people to respect ghosts and spirits and yet keep it distant; one must first serve the people with righteousness. It is not to say that ghosts and spirits are negligible and absurd. It is to say that it stops with this heaven principle.

Heaven principle gets close to my body and, opposite this, my body cultivates virtue and fears heaven's decree and so the heaven and earth ghosts and spirits react to this positively. The quotes "for this I pray long" and "know the heaven in me" have exactly this meaning. Other people with evil spirits and wild ghosts who do misdeeds have no virtue, and the upright spirit doesn't protect them.

Yaron: Our task is to understand why we live and how to make life longer. This paragraph, about spirits and ghosts, poses a challenge to modern Western readers because Liu Yuan merges the native folklore with the principle. However, if we examine the relationship between principle and circumstances – good and bad – and ask first, is there a connection and if so then how is it happening? Then this concept is not foreign anymore.

In this section Liu Yuan introduces 'heaven's heart'. "When a thought moves and it conforms to heaven's nature then it conforms to heaven's heart; if a thought goes against heaven's nature then it antagonizes heaven's heart. Like this, accumulating over time, the difference between good and evil becomes great." We find that getting close to True Nature inside the heart, removing selfish desires, becoming proper and propagating goodness is human by design; humans originally were created like this. There is not one infant that is not pure goodness.

11. **The basis of Dao is in the 'common center'. However, since the meaning of these two words was not clear to the earlier literati, people thereupon viewed the sage in a lofty manner, viewing Dao as unreachable, and so the practice of aspiring to become the sage and become like heaven was not practiced anymore**

During the Warring States period, new teachings gradually prospered and the Dao of the sage died away. Zi Si then narrated the two words of Confucius "Common Center" and developed it into a book.[29]

What does "center" mean? Not being excessive or insufficient with every single thing, instead accomplishing it with exactly the proper measure.

What does "common" mean? It is the ordinary.

Every person can accomplish this center of not being excessive or insufficient. However, without sincerity and without respect this cannot be sustainable. Zi Si was worried that people would think the Dao is difficult, that it is rare, and so he used these two words repeatedly as the standard.

How is it similar to the Confucians who talked too profoundly and who lost the heart of Confucius and Zi Si? Next I will try to superficially explain it. What we call center means conforming to principle and being appropriate. For example, with eating and

---

[29] Zhong Yong as a book title translates to *Proper Place of Center*.

drinking you should not starve, nor should you overeat until you are stuffed. This is center and it is also common. Whenever an affair conforms to principle and is done with exactly the proper measure then the human heart is at peace; one feels happy and cheerful.

It can be seen that the "common center" principle is innate for human beings. Or, for example, even the sage could not evade completely the four terms wine, sex, riches and Qi. However, when the sage drank wine it wasn't disorderly. In his own home the husband and wife relations were regulated by propriety with little desires. Naturally, he would not speak of or look at strangers' daughters, or even dare to think about it. If people know how to attain this principle then it is the common center, then it is a person of virtue.

Scholars, farmers, workers and merchants, each has his profession. If they can be diligent, cautious and frugal, not dare be absurd and lazy, with every thought not cheat or be lax, instead frequently look for the kind heart of heaven's nature, then this gradually also conforms to the common center. The Dao of the common center is heaven's nature. If it conforms to heaven's nature then heaven naturally blesses and protects it. How could one end up with hunger, cold and hardship?

A person cannot overlook this concept of Ping Chang 平常 "ordinary".[30]

---

[30] "Ordinary" has two characters: Ping Chang 平常, explained separately in the following discussion.

Ping 平 "leveled" is like a road that is leveled; it does not contain danger. Chang 常 "ordinary" is like cloth and silk, like beans and grains, there is nothing odd about it. What nurtures the person can be summed up with a few things such as dwelling, food, male-female affairs.

Cultivating oneself in order to help others or being able to rule the universe does not escape the five kinships, each person has it, it is the same for every person. How is it not the very ordinary?

Now, regarding dwelling, food and male-female relations, the simple-minded uses this to lose his head and scorn the principle and he becomes like the beasts. The nobleman uses this to cultivate himself and pacify the people, he uses it to assist nature's nurturing. Because it is such, the true or false application of principle is determined.

If one does not carefully inspect his thoughts and skips even one single thought then this cannot become sincere intention and, over time, it becomes a habit.

If one does not want to become a meager person then one must not attain this habit.

Therefore, if one, in his daily human relations and his handling of his family affairs, reaches the ordinary then the principle truly connects to heaven and earth. If one constantly restrains his body and heart, is discreet in word and deed, uses a loyal and considerate heart to act with benevolence and righteousness, then one can merge with heaven's heart.

How could it be odd? How could it be difficult? We can make it an even simpler principle and understand it as follows.

Yaron: "I crave to eat" often overshadows the simple "I am hungry". Finding heaven's nature involves distinguishing proper need from desire. This is done with everyday mundane affairs. When one performs an ordinary task without 'second thoughts' he or she reaches the common center. For example, when I wash the dishes I should wash them focused on the task without after thoughts, such as "why am I always washing the dishes?" If I have these thoughts then I have lost the common center. In practice, when these thoughts surface I recognize them, then realize they are misleading me, then having no thoughts anymore, focus again on washing the dishes. It is such a simple practice to find the common center.

12. Serving father and mother – including brothers

Since antiquity, many have talked about the principle of filial piety. Many also tried to convince people to become more dutiful.[31] However, very few were able to be truly dutiful, how so?

When parents do not teach sufficient morals, then when kids grow up their moral character is uncertain. When a child is young and can walk and talk but still knows little of odd affairs, one should teach them how to love and be respectful. For example, to not speak or act disorderly in front of parents and other respected elders, when a respected elder talks one should listen respectfully, one should take care when handling an affair, one should not criticize and make fun of others, often serve the parents, care for one's parents day and night, say good night to one's parents, look away when one tells of others. The principle one has in front of oneself should be acted upon daily. One should not be unbridled and sluggish. Over time this becomes the habit until one cannot tolerate the thought of being far away from the parents. When one grows older, one should choose an enlightened teacher, associate with good friends who guide one toward good actions, not make friends with deficient people. One should constantly be by the parents' side and, after one marries, remain like this.

The enlightened teacher and helpful friends state in detail and demonstrate how to nurture one's parents. They also state explicitly the purpose of marriage. They are worried that I will have licentious thoughts and may carry out this principle offense. Therefore, to help me avoid imagining things, they advise that I marry a wife. In addition, man and woman is the great human relation in our life, it

---

[31] Practicing filial piety.

connects above to the incense smoke raised for the ancestors, and to the support we give to our parents. When the parents get old we need to manage the foreign and domestic household affairs and not allow our parents to get tired.

Older and younger brothers are of the same flesh and bones as me, they are likewise sons and daughters. The parents love each dearly, but if one instigates the slightest disharmony then the parents' love harbors resentment, and this is largely not dutiful. The dutiful son always loves his younger brother and respects his older brother. If brothers don't get along then this is not dutiful. A person that is not dutiful and not friendly, how could he be useful?

Look, for example, at people that only look importantly at their own wives and children but look lightly at their parents and siblings, their children and grandchildren all perish. Brothers don't get along either because of money or anger, either afraid that they themselves will be poor or that their tendency is to stifle and suppress anger. This is how they create disharmony. How come one does not think that human life, clothes and salary rely on the heavenly ancestors? When I treat my brothers kindly and generously, the heaven and earth divinities, my ancestors and parents all love me.

The nobleman examines himself thrice and does not compare himself to others; so, in addition, how could he not be conciliatory with his own flesh and blood.

Being dutiful to one's parents and loving one's younger brothers is an affair stringed together that cannot be viewed separately. Therefore, when saying "dutiful", one must also mean loving the younger and respecting the older brother. When one recognizes the two affairs and one loves and respects, then it is the root for wealth and honor and long life.

One should make an effort!

Since antiquity, dutiful sons could not stand to be away from their parents just like the time they were kids. Looking up to their father as an example is the person's root. When one is a child, leaving one's parents even for a moment makes one unhappy and tearful; when one grows older one clings to external affairs and forgets about one's parents. Mencius calls it adore the young and handsome, adore the wife and children, adore the nobleman etc. Everybody knows that, so how come they do not get rid of bad habits? When one was an infant, one could not have been born without one's parents and yet when one grows older one ignores one's parents – where is there a kind heart of heaven's nature? Shun was very dutiful, he relied on his parents like a little kid, and until death he did not change. Therefore it is said: "To the end of life [he] adored his parents."

Yaron: Knowing the proper measure with parents, brothers and sisters is a grand affair; if one truly gives back to one's parents what is rightfully theirs, shares with one's brothers and sisters what is commonly shared, then the heart can find true peace and love can ripple in all directions without end. It is just like finding the source of the spring.

13. Equally respecting father and mother: One cannot distinguish father as important and mother not. Filial piety to one's father naturally means filial piety to one's mother. The forefathers mistook the *Classic of Rites*. One must discern it clearly

Father and mother are like heaven and earth, the earth is connected to heaven and therefore the mother is connected to the father.

Now, some mistook what Confucius said, but there is no error with the principle of a person's child.[32] Just like the statement that earth is inferior and heaven supreme as if there is low and high, however heaven gives birth and earth shapes a physical form, earth gives birth and heaven takes a form, birth and creation of the myriad things truly is a mutual accomplishment of both heaven and earth. How can it be divided into more and less important?

The earlier people erred with the idea that when the father died, the son then preceded the mother. Up to our generation, people value more the father and ignore the mother; being undutiful, offences are many.

I investigated the four masters and the six classics and now, redundantly, I explain it. The wife does not interact with the exterior; the common saying is "not exiting the female quarters". However, even though her proper position is inside the household, her accomplishment is similar to the one whose proper position is outside the household.

---

[32] The principle of filial piety.

Now, the wife never handles external social affairs; when the husband dies, external affairs are always handed to the son. However, the son acknowledges that his life is due to his mother and he cannot take sole possession over the decision-making. Or when the husband dies and the son is still a little kid then the mother handles external affairs.

Nonetheless, herself exiting the women's quarters, she needs to maintain the household's internal affairs and teach the children, thus she must follow the man's way of doing things. Since ancient times there were many virtuous mothers such as this.

In today's generation there are many dominant sons, the father points out no wrong action, the mother can't control it; they are onlookers on the prevailing situation in which it seems one should follow the son. They don't want to offend their son; to an extreme, the mother swallows her anger and lingers in resentment all her life. How is this not creating a legacy of fault in propriety?

Confucius said, "as for the mourning of one's father and mother, there is no more or less important!" Where could there be three years for the father and only up to the end of the current year for the mother?[33]

Now, for the ancients, mourning included wearing white hempen cloths and alterations in food and daily life. However, with time, the distinction lessened. They started omitting the practice of special clothing, first eliminating the white hempen cloths, then the white

---

[33] Speaking of the mourning period after the parent has passed.

silk hat and orange hem. Then they started eating vegetables and fruits.

If one wishes to maintain the mourning period, one should not eat rice nor wear embroidered fabrics, and should not express joy. However, if the father is still alive, all mourning practices should be refrained from, food and lifestyle should not follow the rites of mourning. Why is it so?

The father determines the length of mourning for his wife, and the young mourner should follow his father's lead. Even though the husband and wife relationship is close, like this the husband can gradually pay less attention to this hardship.

But if the son still mourns then he will invoke the father's grief. Therefore, in this case, if the young mourner's food is not sweet and his lifestyle grieving, then, to the contrary, it is not dutiful. Thus, when the ancients created the rites they intended that when the father is still alive the child will not mourn on his own, in order for him to nurture his father. He has the right to be joyous and laugh. It is not because he forgot his mother but because he wants to console his father.

Now when he is not in front of his father, he grieves his mother and does not eat sweets, when he hears joy he does not rejoice, he still mourns in his heart. Thus, when the father is alive, the period of mourning for the mother seems short because one is afraid to hurt his father's heart. Why would this indicate that the mother is less important than the father?

The sages did not stop with the feeling of the son; they also realized propriety towards the father and prohibited the father from being selfish also, with the intent of not allowing his grief to hurt his son. Therefore when the ancients' rite said that mourning the mother is until the end of the year, they also enforced the rule that a mourning son can only marry after three years, thus also considering the heart of the son. If the son were to marry during the grieving period it was feared that the son would think of his mother and drown in sorrow. In addition, when the father has married again how could the son not participate? When there is a marriage ceremony, the son needs to serve his father and stepmother; how could he mourn for three years?

Earlier Confucians did not understand this and they explained it erroneously. Their legacy is a harmful misunderstanding of the Confucian ethical code. One must know this. It should be clear that mother and father are as one. The kindness endowed by both is the same. How could the rite be not the same?

There is no need to mention the birth mother, but it is also the same for stepmothers and concubines, the child should be dutiful to all of them. The stepmother continues my own mother and nurtures me; there is no need to explain that she is like my own mother. The father's concubine is also taking the place of the mother in taking care of the father. When she serves the father she takes the mother's place and when she does not serve him she also takes the mother's actions. She worries and labors twice as much as the mother. How could the child not think this; what the parents love he should also love, what the parents respect he should also respect, what the parents think highly of and treasure he should also cherish. So why would it not be the same with the concubine?

The rites speak of eight kinds of mothers; if one upholds a dutiful heart then it is toward all the mothers. The love and respect of heaven kindness is embodied completely within the Dao, how could one preside over the people, be a parent or a teacher, not know it and lead others, how could they themselves invent a teaching?

Yaron: Today, respecting one parent and not the other often accompanies a disharmonious state between the parents themselves. Children are often drawn into the chaotic disharmony not knowing whom to respect or how to react when parents hurt each other. Parents are the teachers and teaching is done by personal example. If parents, regardless of circumstances, can conduct their daily affairs with respect towards each other and valuing harmony, then the child can learn to embody respect and harmony in the world, even through difficult situations.

14. Serving the monarch

The monarch and the parent are both important, but the monarch is greater compared to the father and mother. Because without the monarch everyone is famished and can't feed their families, and if my father and mother perish how could I come to be? Now one should not stop serving the father and mother, from childhood until old age, but when selected by the monarch to serve as an official, at times, one could retire the position, how so?

Serving the monarch, one is dispatched to a certain role; one follows neither rank nor salary. The monarch acts on behalf of heaven to serve all things, the minister acts on behalf of the monarch to govern the people, it is the bright work of heaven to calm the population, so how could it be only for the sake of fame and official's salary? If there is virtue and talent but the monarch doesn't know me, or if he knows me but doesn't trust me, even if he dispatched me to a post, how could this serve the monarch or the people?

One might as well look for another trade; why must one adhere to the position and err with the country, err with the people. The kind heart would feel ashamed. Since ancient times the sage and virtuous didn't lightly agree to take a post, or if they previously served and were not trusted by the monarch, or manners declined, or there was slight doubt, as soon as they saw the opportunity they acted on it.

For example, when Confucius did not receive enough meat to burn for sacrifice, he quit after three such occasions. How could he have made himself important and be slow with serving the monarch? The trust was inadequate and so he could not fulfill the Dao. For quite some time he deliberated on this unforeseen situation. Confucius said, "One uses the Dao to serve the monarch, if unable to follow then one must stop." Mencius said, "if a minister is executed without an offence then officials can resign their posts." Therefore if one has already taken post then one cannot be negligent or in it for the salary, and if one has not yet taken post then one needs to examine it carefully. Every post has its specific affair and every affair has the principle governing that affair. First, self-evaluate if one is qualified for the job and then bring it upon oneself; then it will not burden the monarch or mislead the people. Otherwise, it might become poor and lowly.

There are also those with talent and virtue who do not fulfil their excellent actions. They must humble themselves and continue to be virtuous and seek people to help them. Since the duke of Zhou gave up the grasp on power, Kong Ming argued that he was his earlier teacher. Otherwise, had he not done so, he would deceive himself, misleading the country and the people, and his punishment would have been worse. When examining an affair and considering words, the ancients first fixed the principle and then they took the post, they served in a post and then were ranked in nobility, each followed their strong qualities and then they took on the task. The scholar would first assess his own talent and therefore would not lose his talent or waste the affair.

Later generations were not like this, they took the post when they received an order with a seal and all their lives they did not know the correct way. As soon as they stepped onto the page of officialdom they handled affairs with many deficiencies, they commonly looked upward and used their connections to climb up; many indeed drifted along this footpath. The royal court could not receive men of good worth, the accepted scholar would not cultivate further honesty and uprightness; thus, how could there be prosperity?

When the son is not restrained by the family, it is the ruined affair of the parents; when the minister is not loyal to the monarch, how could that be the appropriate measure of heaven's majesty? The one loyal to the monarch is a person of true sincerity, only worrying about the slightest deceit; in taking the post, being scrupulous and respectful. This kind of heart begins with serving one parents with great vigor, from dutiful it thereafter becomes loyal. From the foundation to the application it becomes complete.

The great minister does not cross where the monarch's heart does not go. The small minister follows the affair and completes the task. These both can't be seen with mediocre people. It is how the accomplishment cultivates daily between the monarch and his officials. The *Great Learning* instructs every person to act like this, cultivating the self repeatedly in order to govern the people, thus there can be no shame. However, one cannot follow the neo-Confucians of the Song dynasty who have altered the root and followed a wrong path!

Yaron: Becoming an official to serve the people wholeheartedly and selflessly is a noble expression of love toward others; it means to express heaven on a grand scale. Since ancient and until modern times, serving in office often took the expression of selfish desire for fame and gain. Not only should one not engage this affair oneself, but should be willing to stand up for the principle if others are following this wrong path. Propagating selfishness on a grand scale naturally creates great misfortune. Today, more than ever before, decisions taken in one part of the world may have huge impact in far away places. Exercising proper goodness in office is even more important than before.

15. Source of political integrity, scholars and selecting talent for government service must account for this first, only then is it a real talent

The sages' teaching was to first cultivate oneself and then one may wish to help others cultivate.

How can one not aspire to save the world and instead just desire for oneself to climb high?

If one does not have a keen friend that appreciates one's talent then it is not possible to serve diligently at a post. If one thinks oneself high but trust in one is low, one certainly cannot commit to the task; how could the monarch entrust one with profit and salary?

Later generations were content with being a respectful and submissive official. This truly did not allow them to fulfil their duty to the fullest extent and this is how the trend of flattering in harmony progressed. People were simply happy to follow orders but they did not know the importance of their own thoughts. If one were to desire a pure heart it would not be possible. In addition, they were not cautious when appointing people to office; they recommended people to office with erroneous trust. Everyone seeking a post wanted to advance quickly, they were restrained by it, they galloped abruptly and were not worthy to serve the monarch.

The virtuous sages with outstanding skills retreated into the mountains. As glory engulfed the officials' forest they did not know that shallowness leads to abuse and corruption. The people at the top did not know that integrity is the root of loyalty and filial piety, and that style of being lofty comes with many thorns.

As for the educated, they compiled books in order to receive official's salary and glory.

The residence of the high official was benefiting their own family; rarely did they have true love for their monarch and country. In addition, they did not truly learn because virtue, talent and money brought together can hardly endure self-examination. Through fortuity they seek advancement and this becomes an adjunct to the principle. Not only did they have no accomplishment but they also ruined affairs. Lao Laizi said "Ones with glory, high rank and salary, one can follow these and cut with a sword."[34]

From all those who walk the path of riches and profit there are none able to be loyal to the monarch and love their country, to be sincere without compromise. There are different kinds of high officials, some aspire to be aloof from politics and material pursuits and they don't delight in their official career, some desire a reputation of being aloof from politics and material pursuit, with the idea of deceiving and concealing it. They both do not follow the Dao of 'common center'.

Only those who truly have Dao and virtue like Confucius, Mencius, Yi and Lu could really self-cultivate and become sincere under heaven. They ultimately instigated the monarch to emulate the

---

[34] They are all corrupt and can be done away with.

rulers Yao and Shun, they caused the people to emulate the people of Yao and Shun.

When these people do not meet such an opportunity, they are still happy with the Dao, not becoming crooked and giving in to other people, they see ten thousand cash as if a pair of worn out sandals. If the monarch is not virtuous, they certainly rely on themselves and are self-assured, they do not deliberate about sincerity, loyalty and devotion, their compassion and pity is a hundred fold more than that of common people, like Confucius and Mencius who did not gallop in official posts, they were sure to cherish the generation in their bosom.

When one has the Dao of a sage, naturally one cannot leave behind one's parents, cannot turn one's back on the monarch. How could the superior one not look beyond the standard and worry about what is esteemed? When people know this then they heed the Dao of cultivating talent. When the generation knows this then they have fewer careless and despicable actions. I wanted to bring this to light with my explanation.

Yaron: What is in the heart cannot be assessed by the appearance alone. One self-reflects and then he can see.

16. If the three cardinal relationships of social order are not proper then the five kinships are not proper. Therefore the superior one cultivates himself

Dao is embedded in the five kinships and the five kinships emphasize the three cardinal relationships of social order.

The one who emphasizes this does not emphasize one's own status, but rather one's responsibility.

Only the son of heaven holds simultaneously the tasks of being a monarch, parent and a teacher. He should be respected like heaven; for the people he is like the father and mother. Being loving and nurturing, cultivating to the people, in his midst he also holds the Dao of a teacher.

Heaven above loves the people but it cannot itself nurture and teach, and so it creates an heir to deliver this accomplishment on its behalf. Could a monarch make himself extravagant and self-reliant without incorporating the heaven's heart?

Confucius used heaven to describe Yao. He praised that the brilliant monarch Yao not only must have had heaven's heart, but also that as his Dao is heavenly, all can become upright. Underneath the son of heaven, the hundred officials divide the monarch's tasks; they also embody the three tasks of monarch, parent and teacher. If they only aspire to fame and money, they betray the monarch and they offend heaven.

Therefore when the bright and kind become peaceful like Tai hexagram[35] then they become auspicious and harmonious. The fathers and mothers of the world know the secondary responsibility for their kids but they do not know about accumulating virtue to leave for their descendants, and to teach them goodness, which is the Dao of father and mother.

Confucius said, "The son is the descendent of the parent, how can a parent not respect it?" Only when the forefathers accumulate benevolence can the children bear grandchildren. When one does not think of the kindness of one's parents and only thinks that one can become a parent, then it is possible to endow one's offspring with negative fortune. One's small words, deeds and intention cannot constitute the proper measure. This substantial momentum results in laziness; many commit this offense. They exaggerate and tangle, blame their kids; who would know that it is actually the parents' offense.

Therefore Confucius said, "one should first know how to be a son, then one will know how to be a father." Being without kindness is the same as being not dutiful. Seldom are there people who know this. Mencius said, "The one with center nurtures the one with no center, the one with talent nurtures the one with no talent, therefore people are happy that there are virtuous people, fathers and older brothers. If the one with center gives up on the one with no center, the talented gives up on the one with no talent, then the

---

[35] Earth trigram on top of the heaven trigram, image of heaven and earth in harmony.

virtuous and the unworthy cancel each other, not amounting to anything" and "if one does not act with Dao then one cannot act with Dao toward one's wife and children; if one causes others to act with no Dao one then cannot bring Dao to one's wife and children." Should father and mother not think of this? Husband and wife is the first amongst human kinships. Confucius said, "first there is husband and wife and then there is father and son, monarch and minister, above and below.

Male and female assuming proper position is the grand meaning of heaven and earth. In human Dao, marriage is very important, therefore the rite is to crown and the parent goes to meet the bride. Zi Si said, "The nobleman's Dao begins with husband and wife." Since antiquity there was no sage who was not paired with a virtuous wife. When Confucius arranged the *Book of Poetry* he deleted the poem of the concubines from the south that had five verses; it talked about the excess of concubines, and so the idea of what he wanted to teach us is clear.

Later Confucians mistook the classic's idea, saying that the *Yi Jing Book of Changes* states "suppress Yin and support Yang" and that women talk only about food and drink. They did not know that Yin and Yang merge together and only then there is creation. Creation doesn't go beyond the five phases, and so the heaven gives birth and the earth forms, the earth gives birth and the heaven forms, they have this accomplishment together. In the statement "earth Dao does not form and it has an end to it", "does not form" means that, at times, it is being granted movement by heaven, it is not that "earth's origin constant abundance" is different from "heaven's origin is the beginning".[36]

The poem of Si Gan talks about the completion of building a house, congratulating the tenants for the distant peaceful taro fields. There arises a male and a female, the male is the king and the female is gentle and agreeable, she marries the husband to get the man, it is appropriate to have a house and family, there is no irreproachable affair, also no expecting impressive and dignified ornaments, however at times food and drink delight them, Ah! These are words of praise and prayer. So how could the perception of women only being concerned with food, while drink and family internal affairs not be included.

One should know that the sages established what is proper inside and what is proper outside, the meaning of Yin teaching and of Yang teaching and how they are connected. Later Confucians misunderstood this poem. They caused future generations to erroneously think that the husband is important and the wife is inferior. Some would not cultivate themselves and explode at their wives with violence, or with others their wives had little virtue but the husbands had not the moral character to influence them positively. If above they did not serve their parents and in the middle they did not respect their siblings, how could they then create a family, teaching their children and grandchildren?

---

[36] Two lines describing heaven and earth from the *Yi Jing*.

Among them there are also those who emphasize marriage, while following the path of sexual desire to bring each other closer; they don't distinguish right from wrong within the principle, they follow the animals' trend until morning, which is a hundred-fold error, their damage cannot be calculated.

The woman grows up within the female quarters not listening to external affairs. The sages' methods relied on the husband to be the head rope of a fishing net. One needs to put this principle in good order and teach it, the virtuous respects it, the non-virtuous needs to be taught with goodness.

It must be done through all my own words and actions, they all become my own method; gradually this transforms the other person. If I am fierce and without a method, then it will be rejected and denounced, which will not lead to a wife dealing solely with domestic affairs. Some then will look for a more virtuous concubine, some will send the wife back to her mother's home; if they cannot return to their mother's home they will still bring them to another place. However, if it is nurtured like the old way then until the end of their years one will not have to separate. Encouraging the other to become virtuous is achievable by most people. It depends entirely on the person exerting himself and that is it. As for the teacher instructing the five kinships, he preserves the customary teaching.

Affairs like loyalty, filial piety, benevolence and righteousness must be guided by a knowledgeable teacher. Therefore it is said, "the father gives birth to it, the teacher completes it. The people are born with three but the affair is as one. If there is no principle of heart,

True Nature and human relations, then without a virtuous teacher how could one guess this?" Since antiquity every sage had a teacher, but later Confucians started saying that the sage had learnt it from heaven and had not received transmission from an earlier teacher.

The students accepted it and could then use the sage's innate endowment as an excuse. They then looked lightly on the teacher's Dao. They thought that the teacher practicing virtue and acting his art of Dao did not need to be congruent, believing it could be extravagant and self-serving.

They thought that one did not even have to practice human relations daily with vigor. They only thought that one has to read texts and not care about the hundred tasks involved in this art. They did not train body and heart, instead simply learning about it in a conventional school. How could this generation have talent?

So when we talk about the minister, son, wife and younger brother, if the monarch, parent, teacher and husband are not virtuous then there is not one iota they can censure. And regarding the monarch, parent, teacher and husband, they must feel no qualms about self-examination. It is only after this that human relations attain their advocate and human talent develops.

This is the key to the Confucian ethical code.

This is the root for the world to be prosperous or corrupt.

One must investigate this; one must be diligent with it!

Yaron: Every person has talent. Talent thrives when one's heart is passionate about it. Human relations between husband and wife, parent and child, brothers, friends and strangers is such a talent that every person has. Having passion in proper relationships is easily done. It only requires removing one's selfish desires and willing to be kind.

17. Monarch and minister must act as the sage

At the beginning of civilization, people lived with the animals. They had no dwellings, clothes nor prepared foods; they lived no differently from the beasts.

Then heaven gave birth to sages who became monarchs and ministers and they allowed the people to differentiate themselves from the beasts.

Before Tang and Yu,[37] the monarchs resembled today's chiefs of tribes. Each one lived in his native land and each led his own people; ones who had virtue like Yao and Shun stimulated others to follow them. Nonetheless, they simply yoked together an interconnected system and that is it. Therefore it is said: when everything goes back to that one it is called the king,[38] the truly clever makes the primary sovereign, the primary sovereign is the people's father and mother, only heaven bestows kindness on the people, only the monarch presents to heaven.

If it does not embody heaven's virtue and only speculated as virtue, and if it does not embody heaven's heart and only speculated as heart, how could that represent heaven granting principle to phenomena? How could that transform the people and become a customary practice?

Therefore Confucius described Yao as following heaven, the model for the entire world. Now, when Yao and Shun embodied heaven to

---

[37] Legendary dynasties formed by Yao and Shun.
[38] Go back Gui Wang 归往 is King Wang 王.

bring about times of prosperity and peace, in order to remove selfishness in the world they had to select as heir a supremely virtuous person, not a false one. They knew that there could not be another sage equal to the monarch. Looking back, one realizes that sages do not come about often and the country cannot be one day without a monarch and therefore the Charges were created, their father is the sage, and so with them it became possible to teach the sage's Dao to his children and grandchildren.

When, after a long time, these were not followed then came virtuous ministers to assist. They too corrected and supported and governed in peace, like Yu who had Qi and Tang and Wu who had Yi and Zhou.[39] When they started their undertakings they had no motive to profit from the heart of heaven; as a result, heaven followed and protected them.

When following generations could not follow in their footsteps then Jie and Zhou came about.[40] Yao and Shun cultivation of virtue was vast; their education had a foundation. These three dynasties enjoyed lengthy years.[41]

Later generations sought profit in the world. Virtuous leaders that people followed were rather few. They already did not know how to embody heaven in loving the people nor how to select a virtuous person to govern. They followed their desire to consolidate power over rivers and mountains. They protected their ancestral gods but

---

[39] Kings Tang and Wu who had Yi Yin and duke of Zhou to assist them.
[40] The last corrupt rulers of Xia and Shang dynasties who, with their bad behavior, brought the collapse of their dynasties.
[41] Xia, Shang and Zhou.

their virtue was faint. The ministers too were not kind, so why would it not turn into a disaster, within the brief moment that it takes one to turn on his heels?

Alas, heaven gives birth and selects out of the people their leader; if it ends in collapse, it is not without reason. Now, the smart one who serves as original ruler must succeed by means of good instruction. Since antiquity, the king sage himself served as the model, which allowed following generations to prosper. When they wanted to teach the generation's children they had to select a person with great virtue, like Kings Wen and Wu of Zhou who used a sage's support as a fatherly figure; they did not think to diminish the family teaching, offering themselves as role models. They used Yu Xiong and Tai Gong as teachers, they counseled the predictions of Fang Guo, convened together with Bi Rong; in the king's court were many virtuous talented people. How could their descendants and heirs not likewise consult the virtuous and knowledgeable?

Therefore the initiating monarch diligently accumulated accomplishment and benevolence; in addition, he sought wisdom from able people. Following monarchs had to self-examine and remove excesses, make themselves humble and seek the virtuous. Heaven thus cares for the son of heaven, the son of heaven cares for all under heaven, serving upon heaven as serving upon his parents, he loves the people like he loves his son. How would heaven and human then not respond to each other in an amiable and compliant way?

When it comes to people serving as officials, taking assignments from the monarch, it brightens the heaven's workings and fosters the primary origin. It shares in a similar way the monarch's undertaking.

If one did not follow yet the Dao of the *Great Learning* by making one's intention sincere and heart proper then, even if talented, one naturally misses many things; in addition, one cannot see the monarch with a heavenly view, cannot use benevolence and righteousness to govern the people. One secretly becomes negligent, still holding a salary and, to an extreme evil, deceitful with both hands. How can one climb high in the world with low morals? Will heaven not bring down this great crime?

Yaron: Liu Yuan repeatedly speaks of heaven's wrath when the heart is not proper. Losing the proper measure makes one lose the principle in the heart; the punishment of heaven is already there.

18. Cultivate talent, treat the wise courteously and cultivate the scholarly, it is the urgent task of the country and of the family

Every monarch hopes to have good ministers and every father hopes to have virtuous sons, but if they fail to explain the Dao of cultivating this trait then this is unskillful. What does this Dao of cultivation rely on?

Self-cultivation and that is it.

Dao of self-cultivation is not limited to one thing, but rather relates to heart that is loyal and compassionate, actions that are benevolent and proper, not one single thought going astray, all are with sincerity and respect and that is it!

The kind heart of heaven principle is benevolence; acting upon it and creating goodness is properness. Benevolence and properness begins with filial piety and respecting your sibling and from there it expands to the hundred actions. When everything is done with care then virtue is luxuriant.

If one is unable to do it in such a manner but often examines one's heart's typical movements, if one is afraid that the heart will not be at peace or that one won't conform to principle, then with perseverance this will also become virtue that can be transmitted to children and grandchildren.

That the monarch has the authority under heaven and that, for him, cultivating talent is easy, this need not be explained. That a father nurtures and teaches his children and grandchildren is self-evident like a tree root that is nurtured on water.

For one's own body to have virtue, one must seek a heart free from shame. Vigorously practicing benevolence and properness, loving and respecting until it reaches sincerity, the humble heart gathers benefit and self-reflection becomes without faults; this suffices to become a model for future generations.

Also, when one makes friends they should all possess goodness, children and siblings see and hear it with their eyes and ears as if entering a room full of irises and orchids,[42] witnessing it for a long time then they transform themselves. Thus how could they suffer "jumping over the river bank to the other side?"

From antiquity all the way through to today, only very few people have been born unworthy. In such cases, if it is not apparent to the monarch or the father then the family does not become family the way it should and the country does not become a country the way it should. It is with no choice that the words must expose this.

The Zhou clan worshipped the God of grains and taught the people how to sow; its accomplishment was endowed by heaven. From Gong Liu onward they were all sages, their benevolence vast like the great king who shifted the roads. When King Wen undertook affairs, his great compilation included preliminary discussions about the auspicious and harmonious, its root being to cultivate oneself first and then help others cultivate. If it weren't due to King Wen's

---

[42] Symbolic of noble character and true friendship.

enduring contemplation of how to become a proper person then how would King Wu, Duke of Zhou utilize the eight hundred people in Feng Tian, most of whom were virtuous. Meng Xizi told Confucius "I heard that the sage had brilliant virtue and so his future generation must have reached the state of a proper person, now this has reached to the master himself." These two measures[43] are the origin that propagates, successfully creating family and country. Otherwise, without it, if one hopes to be filial and loyal, virtuous and sagely, surely it is impossible.

Yaron: The practice of becoming proper is simple. One becomes aware of the heart dichotomy that increases desires and calms it, one recognizes True Nature inside the heart and embodies it.

---

[43] Cultivate oneself first and then help others cultivate.

19. Dao takes place with daily practice of human relations, and yet fulfilling this Dao is rare. It is because the path is separated into heart and True Nature, customary and sagely not conforming. One must differentiate it clearly and practice it vigorously

What does "using it daily" mean?

Every word, action and affair.

People rely only on four things for their life: dwelling, clothing, food and drink and man and woman. Due to these four things, the common person scorns propriety and hurts their heart.

The sage, because of these four, serves heaven to establish life – how so? Using propriety to regulate emotions, neither departing from the customary nor giving in to the customary. It is ingenious. With dwelling, one avoids rain and wind; with food and drink, one avoids hunger and cold;[44] with male and female, one continues the previous generation into the next.

Making proper his heart design and cultivating his undertaking, he uses the kind heart of heaven nature as the core.

The four are under his control and he uses them as he sees fit, thus not coming by hardship. The fixed principle of heaven retribution to human is when one follows one's desires without restraint, seeks

---

[44] The text omits clothes here, a probable typo.

dwelling without principle, then to the contrary one comes by calamity, some even get toppled over,[45] one can only sigh!

The five kinships come about with daily application; however, the Dao is not the same for each one of them. Monarch and friendship use properness to be complete. Confucius said "Use Dao to serve the monarch, one cannot break this form. Sincere advice in the Dao of goodness, one cannot break this form." It is best for one to pursue these two kinships with one's heart until the end. In a difficult time these will surely complement each other. No matter father and mother, older and younger brothers, husband and wife – they all possess these; one cannot live outside the scope of these two. One cannot be exempt from these and still possess Dao. Confucius in the *Yi Jing* said, "the father as the father and son as the son, older brother as older brother and younger brother as younger brother, the husband as husband and the wife as a wife, and then the family order is proper and everything under heaven is stable."

So how is everything under heaven stable if family order is proper? If there are no other people other than these three kinships, then if one can fulfil their Dao and put his family in order then what other things can happen under heaven? Since antiquity the king sage put his family in order for the purpose of putting the country in order.

Other than using human relations daily, what other Dao can there be?

---

[45] Mencius saying that if a tree is slanting then heaven topples it over, yet if it is upright then heaven cultivates it.

Father, son, older and younger brothers, husband and wife are all close kinships. They often interact in harmony and at times with disharmony, in which case emotions and affairs become disorderly. If one wishes to fulfil this Dao then one must understand the division of proper roles for each one. One must fulfil the natural course of the assigned heaven's True Nature for each role; one should not simply follow his mood in this process.

When goodness drives the course of events then there is no shame.

Father and mother are heaven, one performs with utmost sincerity, waiting upon and supporting them until the end of one's life, this needs no further explanation. One especially needs to come clear with making oneself good and sincere and then instruct one's family with this Dao. If the son wants his parents to have happiness and longevity, then he should want his parents to cultivate, because if there is something in their words, actions and heart design that is not proper then this will exhaust them.

Therefore when one hopes to be a good family member, one should follow one's family members and one must fulfil the Dao of that kinship.

The older and younger brothers are like the arms and legs of the body, comparable to the root of father and mother. When they think of their parents who love each and every one of them, then there cannot be siblings who do not love each other. Therefore filial piety and friendship, filial piety and brotherly love are talked about together as one construct. If one is not a good friend and not a good brother then one cannot be dutiful. If one thinks that other affairs are more important then one will always lose; the spirit in heaven and the ancestors will not guard him. Guard against it!

Guard against it!

If one is an older brother he should be like Shun, if he is younger brother he should be like the king who sees a thing and comes by the proper method to address it. Whenever brothers are not harmonious it is either because of money, anger or slanderous talk – it is these three. If heaven wants me to be poor, how can I eat full and be warm? If heaven wants me to be rich, how could I be hungry and cold? So why would heaven like me? I must guard to the death the kind heart of heaven's nature, then I will conform to heaven's will and, with that, I'll attain good fortune.

Money in its nature is a public instrument; when friends get along they may gift each other a thousand gold coins, so how is it not with brothers? I have tender affection for my brother; I am only worried that he may suffer cold and hunger. Heaven and earth, the divine spirit, ancestors, father and mother – they are all delighted by my action, so where could there be a principle of poverty and hunger? Look under heaven – people who are generous are all prosperous, stingy with their brothers they all perish early. How can one not urgently reflect back on his actions?

When it comes to finding out what is right and what is wrong, one clearly differentiates it in order to cultivate oneself. However, brothers often can't talk reason amongst themselves. In the family relationship there should be mainly love and harmony, but when it falls out of harmony, then one should slowly try to talk sense into the other, one should not discharge it abruptly. One cannot grasp the other firmly. For example, when there is interaction in an ordinary day, with an issue of who is right and who is wrong, and an argument breaks out, either the older or younger brother's words and actions are not proper. One should receive it as if one were silly and deaf, but slowly try to talk sense into the other. If one cannot talk sense into the other then one should oneself be lenient and allow the other to win over and not hold a grudge in one's bosom. If one makes one's duty like this and benevolently gives way to the other, then the wife and concubine and outsiders' slander naturally does not pierce one's ears.

Making one's guiding principle proper, one teaches goodness to one's wife and children, eradicates greed and lust, always cultivating oneself, not cruel to one's wife and not ashamed of any single word and action that one has taken. At this point one can be a proper husband, a proper father, nothing is wasteful and it is all self-sustaining. One does not become someone who themself is improper and yet tries to teach their wife and children. In this fashion, a father is a father and son a son, older brother an older brother and younger brother a younger brother, husband is a husband and wife is a wife.

Cultivating the Dao of human relations, using it daily with every single affair then naturally the heaven principle is fulfilled.

The common custom is not to carry out the Dao of human relations. Instead, people cave to their desires to nurture themselves, they like riches and fame in the world around them; without a doubt it is not proper!

Confucians talk high about True Nature and life decree, and they don't engage the customary affairs that allow pursuit of intimate relationships. Sincerity and respect inspire confidence in them, they fulfil the talk about principle but they enter an imaginary realm.

When one talks about Dao and, at the same time, scorns worldly customs, how could one possibly know that heart, True Nature and human relations, their internal and external aspects are of one origin? One must merge and cultivate the root and the branches and, when an occasion demands it, one points to the proper center.

Since antiquity the sages' virtue is the same, but the affairs they engaged in were different. They followed their times' customs and, accordingly, formulated their business. Trying to escape the world's customs and still talk of Dao, discussing True Nature and life and yet having no practical accomplishment, how can this conform to Dao?

What benefit is this teaching giving to the world?

Guard against it!

Avoid it!

Yaron: One lives in the society of today, with its customs and designs. Acting properly means acting in accord with current customs. Liu Yuan explains that human relations include an action beyond the customary, a permanent situation, where a father is a father and a son a son, a husband is a husband and a wife a wife. These relationships, when performed correctly, are heaven's nature; the intended expression of life.

20. In order to teach, one must first nurture. Later generations found it most difficult to dwell in nurturing. One must act according to circumstances, the authority should lie with the monarch, parent and teacher

For the sage who governs the world it really comes down to two words: abundance and teaching.

If every person could avoid cold and hunger, if every person could act with goodness and expel evil, what other affair would there be under heaven?

It is a pity that the human heart is hard to govern. A common saying goes: "Eating fully and being warmly clothed gives birth to licentious desire; being hungry and cold awakens the thief heart; poverty makes one improper and secluded, becoming rich makes one arrogant and excessive; the human heart is hard to control, there is no avail!"

In the Zhou dynasty, they worked out that if every worker had a field, and every scholar was learning Dao, this could be called thorough and proper. However, generations of officials, serving in order to get salaries, became arrogant and imperious over time, as well as cruel. As above, so became the situation with lesser officials. Every farmer still had a field so they did not suffer hunger, hardships and other such worries, and over time the farmers started having it their own way.

Coming down to the Spring and Autumn period, many affairs transpired that could not continue; fields were deserted, the system of fiefdom was abandoned and people followed the shackles of commerce in their actions. Did this not deviate from heaven's intention?

The human heart goes easily astray; if it does not go through some hardship, rarely does one become spontaneously gentle and kind. If the heart did go through a bit of hardship then in a single day it can turn prosperous again. If still there is a lot of extravagance in one's life and one lets oneself lose control, then how could one grow to have wealth and rank?

The monarch has to sternly establish the proper method, and with goodness decide his actions. He must take care of the people's dwelling, clothes and food, command the people to be unequal to the literati and officialdom. The literati and officialdom must, in turn, have virtue in order to advance prosperity and therefore they are educated with the Dao of the *Great Learning*. They must have six virtues and six actions[46] to become truly virtuous.

When the people have excess wealth and have no use for it, they should gather under heaven as one, advocating benevolence and appropriateness. Being literati, farmer, worker, merchant or trader, each should diligently perform their profession. However, if they can perfect their heart design and cultivate their conduct, be

---

[46] 六德 six virtues: knowledge 知、benevolence 仁、sagehood 聖, righteousness 義、loyalty 忠、harmony 和. 六行 six actions: filial piety 孝、friendship 友、amicability 睦、serving 任、caring 恤、marrying 姻.

hardworking and thrifty to support their families, then how could anyone suffer cold and hunger? It is only when and if, despite the good monarch, the parent and teacher's nurturing and teaching, they still unexpectedly, carelessly and eagerly pursue riches and rank. They do not follow heaven's nature; if they win they are happy, if they lose they dwell in sorrow.

I never saw someone that could endure this for long.

In the imperial court there are no important and virtue-less people, in the wilderness there are no improper and rich scholars, this is the norm for the multitudes.

Yaron: With a bit of hardship the desirous heart is stunned. Luxury that was once thought necessary is no longer needed. The heart that was lost finds center again. My heart needs only a little to be happy so why dwell in excess?

21. If responsibilities are heavy for monarch and parent, then the task should go first to the teacher. If one does not practice the Dao of the *Great Learning* then certainly it is difficult to seek the teacher

The *Book of Rites* says, "if the teacher is not proper with the five dresses,[47] then all kinships are not attained." The Dao of the *Great Learning* instructs the son of heaven to never face north. What is the purpose of this?

The father and mother cannot fulfill the task of virtuous sage. First, there is a sagely teacher and then one knows Dao. Then, one acts in accordance with Dao to fulfill the principle of being human. Being human successfully means that when serving one's parent, one must be filial and when serving the monarch, one must be loyal.

This enterprise – of first cultivating oneself and then helping others cultivate – can be performed by everyone.

The monarch and the parent must also have a teacher and then they can have virtue, it is important for both. Since antiquity all the sages have had a teacher. The Yellow Emperor's teacher was Guang Cheng, Yao's teacher was Wu Guang, King Wen's teacher was Yu Xiong, King Wu's teacher was Shang Fu, Confucius's teacher was Lao Dan. Lao Dan being Confucius's teacher is not acknowledged by the later Confucians, I will discuss this redundant aspect later, but not here. For example, Wang Ji and King Wen both were sages, and

---

[47] 五服 Five different mourning garments worn by relatives of different levels of closeness to the deceased.

yet they had a teacher to instruct their sons. How come they were so modest?

The principle of body and heart, True Nature and life, and the Dao of using human relations in daily applications, it is ordinary and common, it is refined and pure.

When the parent develops with the sagely teacher, from morning until evening they pursue it, hurrying along with every step, then isn't it easy to be refined, detailed and entirely continuous?

This idea, that the sage got his instruction directly from heaven and not from a teacher, comprises words that do not reflect the Dao.

Ones promoting such idea did follow the notion that heaven and mankind's True Nature and life are connected as one, however they resolutely did not step-by-step attain a high level via physical practice. Therefore, they attained one aspect of knowledge and they ended there. They caused future generations to look loftily at the sage and look lightly at the personal teacher. They say that any local tuition cannot capture the essence; they say one can rely on one's heart, and that Dao can be guessed.

The harm they inflicted is beyond words.

Confucius said: "I heard that Lao Dan researched thoroughly the ancient times but also knew the present, therefore he is my teacher. I will go in his direction and learn." When he followed Lao Dan and assisted in a sacrificial ceremony, Lao Dan whispered his name and just before departing he also named him You Long. Zi Xia told the marquise Wen of the state of Wei: "Zhong Ni's[48] teacher is Lao Dan. Secretly he is associated with Lao Peng." This speaks of Lao Zi. Master Zhu Zi[49] when writing his commentary also initially pointed to Lao Zi, but because others forced him, he later changed his opinion saying that this person was actually the senior official Shang Xian.[50] Yet the official Shang Xian is actually Lao Zi. In the Shang he was the guardian of the historical records, named Qian Keng. In the Zhou he was the keeper of the histories Zhu Xia Shi, but because it was over so many years one was worried that this will puzzle people, so they changed his name frequently.

The art of the hundred occupations all come from a teacher, so how would the sage's teaching differ from this? To have life, one serves heaven, carrying forward the cause and forging ahead into the future; it is the filial son. The well-versed minister assists and consults the emperor, he teaches with favor and his Dao is vast, the various applications are grand and his many gongfu cannot be attained within one day. How is it possible to attain all these without a teacher, how could one take all the necessary actions?

Now, a teacher has the virtue of a sage propagating it to the world, despite difficulties. His students' character must become proper by making their heart upright, by practicing human relations without deceit, and by not being casual about it. Then it becomes possible. Next to that, he teaches them to excel with learning and know about various products and skills, otherwise the talent is hard to develop.

---

[48] Confucius.
[49] Zhu Xi from the Song dynasty.
[50] Virtuous Grand Official of the Shang.

However, if students are negligent and do not cultivate the root, then their talent will not come about; in the family it is a filial son and in the country a loyal minister. Alas, only when one is warmly familiar with the old but also knows the new that one can be a teacher. Very few people know this.

For the time being let us settle on this. The "old" means heaven's nature. There is no place where heaven's nature is absent. From human relations in daily applications to heaven and earth and the myriad things, there is no too small or too big, it includes everything. Now, its origin finds itself within heart and True Nature, a principle received from heaven. It comes with birth and so it is called the "old".

The sage taught people exclusively to preserve this heaven's nature and, with that, recover the beginning of life coming from heaven. Through that, the heart becomes pure with benevolence. Actions become proper, fulfilling the human True Nature, and the True Nature of all things; everything propagates via its own True Nature.

"Warm" means like a fire that warms things, by analogy it demonstrates the accomplishment of perseverance. Inside, one makes one's divine spirit resilient; outside, one does not slack with one's will.

Talking about nurturing Qi, Mencius describes a process of seeking it in every part of myself, which then replenishes by the grand Qi of the universe. The clear eyes see the arched back, and without words the four limbs are there expressed.

Confucius mentioned the explosiveness of Qiu Yang. Zi Si said that his body completely changed. One should be warm towards the other person. On the outside, take care of the body and external spirit circling in the air in harmony; on the inside, preserve actions with virtue. The *Proper Place of Center* describes this as the gongfu of wringing the Dao. It specifically narrates Confucius's words – if this is not understood as the vast Qi of the universe that then replenishes one and makes one more vibrant, then one really does not know the meaning of "warmly know the old". How could one only know the new and be a teacher?

In Daoism there is a common phrase: "warmly nurture", which resonates this same meaning. It is a pity that later generations got confused. They said by analogy that spirit is fire and that Qi is medicine and herbs. The spirit nurturing the Qi is like fire cooking the herbs, they continued this line of thinking and said that with vigorous fire one should not forget and not assist, whereas letting things take their natural course was called mild fire warming and nurturing. Indeed, this is only another name for the same preserving spirit and nurturing Qi.

The spirit and Qi of a person is connected to heaven and earth. The sage merged his virtue with heaven, and basically his heart was pure with heaven's nature. However, the common person's heart often goes astray, and so they don't attain heaven's True Nature. The sage fulfills True Nature, heart pure with heaven; it merges with heaven. If one tries to investigate what lies behind it then one finds that the will, just like the spirit, is vast and replete between heaven and earth.

The heart is spirit; it is the master of Qi. Qi is what animates the body alive. Speaking of principle and not speaking of spirit and Qi is empty talk about heart and True Nature. Heart and True Nature…where do they belong? True Nature is heaven principle, it is called the origin spirit and the vast Qi of the universe, it is the Qi of heaven's origin.

The heart that recognizes situations and circumstantial reality is not True Nature. Some say that the Qi that we breathe from the mouth and nose is Qi, and this already circumvents Buddha and Lao Zi. One does not know the ancestors anymore. It was the philosopher Gao Zi who had already lost the truth of the sage.

What cannot be expressed with words cannot be sought after with the heart. If one knows that it is wrong then one cannot take it to heart. If one does not seek it with Qi, one cannot know it at all. The True Nature of heaven's life principle is Qi. When principle and Qi rule, it is called spirit. How could it contain something seen on the outside? If one does not understand the Dao of Confucius and Mencius and still wants to be a teacher, then Confucius and Mencius must be sighing!

Yaron: Gao Zi lost the truth of the sage by advocating that the heart has no fixed principle to it. If people influence it to become bad, it becomes bad, and if they influence it to become good, then it becomes good. This contrasted the sage's understanding that with diligence and sincerity, and entirely independent of external influence, every person can rediscover the goodness that already exists within. A teacher must convey this to their student.

This situation is relevant to modern times, with political correctness and post-modern relativism, everything is artificially on a level playing field, you are allowed your truth and I am allowed mine. It is unfashionable to say there is an enduring immutable truth and in this climate people miss the chance to penetrate this teaching of heaven's nature kind heart, not knowing there is something trustworthy within that is innate and effortlessly good that already belongs to them.

22. Where there is a sagely teacher, there are his sagely disciples. Becoming sagely is not extremely difficult. The ancient literati mistook it for something far and removed, creating obstacles and waste for future generations. Be sure not to err due to their mistake

Confucius said "At birth, at peace, Study, Benefit, Despite difficulty, exerting oneself;" only the one that despite hardship does not learn is the low amongst the people. In order to learn, one asks, thinks, differentiates, acts sincerely, then even if someone is dull minded they will still become clever.[51]

Mencius said, "Every person can be like Yao and Shun."

Since Dao basically means "heaven's nature," and since every person has heaven's nature inside them, every person can become a sage.

What is heaven's nature? The kind heart, True Nature and bright virtue.

It is like fruit that contains a seed, and therefore it is called benevolence.[52] True Nature is the benevolence, righteousness, propriety, wisdom and trust[53] of the entire body, collectively acting

---

[51] The quote is abbreviated, assuming the reader knows the full quote, where Confucius describes the different levels of knowledge; intuitively at birth, learning it until it becomes one's nature, learning and knowing it as external knowledge, learning hard until reaching it, and the lowest level is one who learns hard and extensively and still does not get it.

[52] Ren 仁 means seed, and also means benevolence, the pun being it is like a tree fruit that has a seed Ren, this is why it is called benevolence Ren.

[53] The five virtues of Confucianism 仁，义、礼、智、信.

as benevolence. Confucius honestly viewed people with benevolence, saying "if one aspires for benevolence, carries no evil, then one can act vigorously with benevolence, one experiences no lack of vigor. People then easily know and act upon the kind heart of heaven principle. To cultivate the body they use Dao, to cultivate Dao they use benevolence. Benevolence means a human being."[54]

Mencius said, "Benevolence is a human being. The two words together mean Dao." The virtuous and sages omitted the four words "cultivate self [then] cultivate others", "without Dao no harmony"; these four words became odd teachings. Since the Han dynasty, Confucians mistook characters and were scarce with words and articles about benevolence, the Song dynasty Confucians therefore said that the Dao of human is great. Confucius was scarce with words, therefore in the *Analects*, when students were asking about benevolence they said that Confucius's explanations were numerous. What is the meaning of this? Confucius used propriety to teach people and so he said "If a person is not benevolent how can they have propriety?" and "ceremonies, how can they only mean jade objects and silk fabrics?"

So what was the idea contained in these words? The harm was done by people mistaking the word "propriety" as "ceremony". They said that Confucius used ancient ceremonies without altering a single step, so that it became a fixed method. They did not know that Confucius used the ceremonies to socialize and interact with other

---

[54] Benevolence and human being are phonologically the same in Chinese, both pronounced Ren 仁者人也.

people. Like this, benevolence could mature and righteousness could become pure. Following one's heart would not surpass the established rules, every word and every action, every movement and stillness,[55] they all naturally possessed heaven's nature, they all took the natural course as they should. It was not subjected to the constraints of Kings Wen and Wu and the duke of Zhou. Therefore it was said "it is not possible and it is not impossible", and "the heart movement of the generation is the Dao under heaven, the words of the generation are the method under heaven, and the actions of the generation are the rule under heaven."

So how could it be that one wrongfully guarded rules of previous generations and stuck to their ceremonies? Later Confucians mistook the book *Ceremonies* for a sagely work and, in turn, restricted all the ceremony books of the Han dynasty claiming that they cannot truly reflect Confucius and Mencius. The disease of obstruction by clinging to the ancients was on the rise. Looking at Zi Lu and his going back to ancient ceremonies, Confucius saw it and said "Whomever says that they need to be obeyed does not understand ceremonies."

One can clearly see the middle at midnight. In addition, all the constraints that came after the three dynasties are not from the ancients, people used the ancient ceremonies to teach people how to sculpt themselves like wood carvings. How is that not an error? Therefore, ceremonies are the tradition regulating and supplementing heaven's nature, its root is with the kind heart of

---

[55] The heart movement and stillness.

heaven's nature regulating excessiveness and supplementing its deficiency. This is a ceremony.

Preserving the king's restrictions means learning the simple and thrift aspects of the sages and the virtuous, aspects one can follow. However, the aspect of worshipping should not be followed. There is not just one thing that determines it, but also not many things that determine it. When benevolence matures then righteousness naturally refines. Without any special wisdom, any simple-minded person can do it. Thus, every single person can cultivate themselves and then teach others. How could the Dao of the teacher not be formed?

The greatness of Dao is within the five kinships. Its principle is with the heart and True Nature. If one follows the Dao of the *Great Learning*, removes selfishness and reaches the root of becoming clear, firstly making intentions sincere, guarding against evil, promoting goodness, and then stopping only at ultimate goodness, then in this way one quietly nurtures heaven's True Nature, nurturing both the inside and outside. Even if we cannot be one hundred percent pure, we still can avoid becoming like the beasts and animals.

Confucius therefore said, "if one fixes ones will on benevolence, has no evil, is vigorously able to act on behalf of benevolence, then one always has strength."

Since earlier Confucians have altered the ancient *Great Learning* text and those that came afterwards, the sage's gongfu became vague. This negative influence lasted more than a thousand years. Where could one find an enlightened teacher anymore?

Confucius said, "If there is proper teaching without manipulation, even if one is dull minded one certainly understands it clearly." Today, people say the sage received the teachings from heaven and that people who read the books and learn Dao can hardly aspire to be a sage. After Confucius and Mencius, very few people knew Dao. Sigh! Every person has heaven kindness, the sage did not exceed embodying the full human principle. And so when people claim that ordinary people cannot be like the sage and the virtuous, and that they must imitate some Confucian model, how is this not a loss! That heaven and earth give birth to human, that the sage teaches people, that people are different from the animals and beasts, try to contemplate it with a peaceful heart, see if this is not possible!

Yaron: A sage teaches people the method of becoming good. He does not teach rules and regulations or models to copy. To become good is to investigate inward, to find it within. When center is reached within, rules from distant lands naturally appear similar and actions of different people appear related.

23. Dao is not beyond human emotions and the innate law of things. Therefore each person can do it. However, one must use heaven principle in order to assess it and it must conform to the times

Extending from ancient times is the benevolent person, is this heart principle, therefore the sage king did not look lightly upon the people while ruling.

Human emotions are associated with different desires, yet for nurturing life they do not exceed these four: dwelling, clothes, food and man-woman.[56] If these are deficient then one actively pursues them, however, if these are ample then one often develops an insatiable desire for excess. When one disdains the principle and loses one's heart, this creates all sorts of miseries.

When the sage king ruled the world, desires were to come together, evil was not to be carried out, and all things were done to nurture life. For affairs concerning desire and evil, he created ceremonies to restrain them. Human emotions were joyful and so attracted to it, culminating a habit over time that became the norm. Therefore, other than human emotions and the innate nature of things, human life had no other principle and the sage king had no other affair to deal with.

However, human emotions and the innate nature of things should not only conform to center and appropriateness, but they must have heaven principle as their core. If the heart is severed and the aim is

---

[56] Includes sexual desire and wish for offspring.

discarded then one will not conform to the ceremony and absolutely stop acting upon it.

Ceremony is an affair concerning human emotions and the innate nature of things; it prevents excess or deficiency.

It is not necessary to act exactly in the same way as the ancients. Earlier Confucians did not understand that the four words "heaven's nature kind heart" are the great Dao, and instead they taught how to exactly copy the ancient ceremonies. It ended up with a secular trend of great opposition, where people publicly resisted the king's articles until it became an idealist Confucian philosophy of the Song and Ming. People clung to outworn rules and ideas; fearing it and making it distant, they finally stopped understanding the Dao of the *Proper Place of Center*.

Wang Anshi repeatedly called on Lian Xi, vehemently saying, "How is it that only I cannot go back and seek the six classics?" The revered Si Ma died and Cheng Yichuan arranged the funeral, covering his entire body with bamboo basket. Dong Po said "one less affair yet". Yichuan asked "what affair?" He answered "it is written in the official document that the king of hell and the great king broke apart." Master Zhu Zi was rude to a guest; the guest said, "in the mountain's midst there is no wine measuring spoon for the chicken."

To satisfy the prohibition of fake doctrines, the Confucians of the Ming dynasty stuck to the ceremonies. They ordered that men should not die at the hands of their women, and so they obstructed the wives and daughters; when the person died, his family members did not know when he died. They were not connected to the human emotions and to the innate nature of things; they claimed the Dao as being far and unreachable. Without impediment they acted like this, obstructing people from learning the sage. One, therefore, must clearly analyze this and act upon it.

Yaron: Copying old customs is unproductive, but learning from the old brings accomplishment. Seeking goodness, a timeless practice, creates life and yet people change this method with liberty. Liu Yuan explains that when customs change, at times, the simple and natural way is lost. However, to recover it is easy, one seeks a kind heart and that's it!

24. Human emotions and the innate law of things cannot be separated from common customs. One should not praise the past and condemn the present, nor look lightly at customs of the ordinary people

At the time of the five supreme monarchs, they did not follow ceremonies and during the different times of the three kings, they did not seem to follow music. As times change, human emotions and customs change. When one is born in a certain era one follows the customs of that era and then, at one's discretion, conforms his emotions to the innate nature of things, center and properness. The sages were all like this.

Confucius said "The people, they walk the Dao of the three dynasties," and "If I do not follow in the footsteps of others, who else can I follow?"

What is pure, thrifty and practical one can follow, whereas that which is worshipped one cannot follow, as it is just the outer dressing. How can one claim Dao to be outside the customs of the current generation? Yet, one should remove the wrongs and maintain the correct. Therefore, following the customs while maintaining center is something that can be done by everyone.

For example, in the summer it is hot but when it rains one must add a layer of clothing. In the dead of winter it is very cold but when the warm sun comes out then one removes a layer. One acts according to the circumstance and all affairs are like this. Nobody can escape the fact that when one reaches center, the proper measure is evident.

Later generations became distant from the important role of human emotions. Disciples of earlier Confucians often read the ancient books, spoke highly of the ancient ceremonies, but they did not know how to adapt to the changing times. Thus, there was not one person who could cultivate themselves to help others. The words of Confucius and Mencius became like a picture of a pie in the sky.

Cultivating, organizing, ruling and making peace became rare.[57] The Dao of the *Great Learning* simply teaches people to follow their heart and cultivate human relations. Everyone is capable of doing this.

There is no difference between ancient and modern times.

If one understands this principle, while following the times, one remains centered. Unlike the earlier Confucians – who altered and ruined the ancient texts – without knowing it one follows the meaning behind the ancient words successfully.

Yaron: Sometimes excess desires are the reason behind certain customs. One should not always follow the modern conventions but, rather, find the proper measure. If, for example, the convention today is to view elderly parents as a burden on their children then this notion should be examined and corrected. To know the times, customs and to live in society implies to know about one's desires and comforts and even more so about one's self.

---

[57] Cultivating oneself, organizing the family, ruling the country, making peace under heaven.

25. Sorting and Reaching is the skill of nurturing both inside and outside. If this is understood as meaning to reflect outward, it teaches people to probe into the root of external things, which results in knowledge without moral scruples. It is to pursue the trivial and forget the essential

The sage's teaching is entirely within preserving stillness and inspecting movement.

In itself it is not a difficult undertaking.

Social intercourse presents as a myriad of transformations, but they all rely on this one heart. Now, if the heart is not of pure goodness, then it often embodies selfishness. Why would the human heart embody selfishness so often? Since material needs exist, then the ears, eyes and mouth have to have desires. This necessary desire allows the person to live; it is the human heart.

A person cannot escape desiring material for their life.

How could one possibly get rid of the human heart and become a sage? Is a sage different from regular people? Answer: A human being takes orders from the Dao heart. What is a Dao heart? Answer: True Nature. How could True Nature possibly be outside of the human heart? Answer: It is not. So how can one heart have two names?[58] Answer: The divine aspect of the heart is Qi, all Qi at the beginning of life is pure, and therefore it is said: the True Nature of

---

[58] Dao heart and human heart.

the human being is always inherently good. When it attains the principle Qi of heaven and earth this goodness manifests itself as a human being. When it then sorts clearly the proper Qi of heaven and earth then this is True Nature.[59]

True Nature exists in the center of the grand void.[60] The person attains its reflected light. Father and mother then merge their physical bodies. Then the principle Qi within the void merges together within this new body, and as a result it has a heart. This aspect one can inspect further.

True Nature, however, is connected to heaven and earth in the grand void; it is where the principle Qi is pure. Where could there be words to describe this?

The teaching of the *Great Learning* allows a person to preserve and nurture, purifying their origin, examining the harmony of the movement when it is regulated by center. Their applications become those of goodness.

If there is no stillness, how could one know of movement? If there is no basis in the vast energy of the universe, how could one use physical force to support movement? Therefore, when one removes things then the will and Qi become pure and clear. When knowledge, based on center, arrives then one is not confused by right and wrong.

---

[59] The two sentence referencing 'it' talk about a divine principle allowing the heart and the human being to come about. It shows a world view where center is the beginning point and the human heart and body its result.

[60] In the universe, in a place entirely independent from human dichotomous perception, where "center" is dimensionless.

Talking about removing things means removing human desire and protecting clarity.

"Reaching knowledge" means learning and differentiating right from wrong. It is a strengthening and not restraining process, and is one aspect of inspecting movement. Now, it is very difficult to completely avoid straying with selfishness of the human heart. If one does not nurture upon the vast Qi of heaven's origin, then one cannot eradicate the exhaustion created by material desire. Mencius's "nurturing Qi by not moving the heart" was the true accomplishment of the ancient sages. As the generations have declined, they could not bring this to light anymore.

How could anyone understand the meaning of remove, reach, sincere, and proper by not knowing this principle?[61] The earlier Confucians could not detangle the origin of the human heart and Dao heart. They also did not know how to nurture Qi by not moving the heart. The Dao of the *Proper Place of Center* turned from healthy branches to thorns and thistles. When reading books and learning Dao and aspiring to the sage and the virtuous, how is it not like the human heart? How could one see the sage and the virtuous as heavenly people? Worldly customs have been followed and worshiped while the principle has been buried in oblivion.

---

[61] Remove selfishness, reach to knowledge, make intention sincere, and train the heart to be proper.

Yaron: Our words and thoughts commonly express and desire worldly affairs. Using ideas and words to describe True Nature can only be what Confucius describes as "it gets close to it." However, if one develops awareness of desires and a skill to make these smaller and fewer, then in between there is a sense of evenness, one is neither happy nor sad, satisfied nor disappointed. It reaches to the place where thoughts do not induce movement. Liu Yuan describes it as preserving stillness. It is the foundation for finding a proper movement. The application is of goodness and the knowledge is of correctly differentiating right from wrong, helping from hurting. Simply put, one cannot use a desirous heart to assess what is proper and what is not.

26. To nurture Qi and not move the heart is the core teaching of the *Great Learning*. If one does not understand this principle then one argues against Buddha and Lao Zi. One's false argument is one's crime against the truth, extinguishing "understand the heart and observe True Nature" along with "cultivate truth and nurture True Nature". The correlation of heart and Qi, the wide difference of propriety and sincerity, all remain a mystery

Before the Three Dynasties there was no heterodoxy. The ruler was acting above while the teacher was instructing below.

The Zhou created the grand minister who instructed the people and brought forth the six virtues, six actions and six arts.[62] From the son of heaven to the common people everyone knew these arts, everyone knew benevolence, righteousness, center and harmony.

What later generations named "all the difficulties," earlier generations learned diligently. The principle is possessed within each person and therefore there was nobody who could not learn it.

When Zhou declined, the teaching of ceremony was gradually burnt in oblivion. Confucius therefore attacked the heterodoxy and sighed, because at that time heterodoxy did not respect people following the six virtues and six actions. Truly, what the master despised the

---

[62] 六藝 six arts： ceremonies 禮、music 樂、archery 射、charioteering 御、literature and calligraphy 書、mathematics 數。

most was that above there were vulgar people and below were hypocrites.

That Buddha came before Confucius and that Lao Zi and Confucius were of the same time, and followed him to study ceremonies, this cannot be named heterodoxy. That the emperor Qin Shihuang had no Dao, breaking the bronze images and seeking the Buddha from the west, and then Lao Zi rode his ox to hide in the west. Since Zhong Xia people favored Buddha and Laozi, while Confucians cultivated improper ways, daily their chaotic ways increased.[63]

People detested this state of confusion, avoided it and hurried toward the Buddhist path. As Han dynasty prospered, people suffered under tyranny, being plain and simple brought peace, therefore when Xiao and Cao served as ministers they drew a painting with a poem about clear purity. They said that what sufficed to become of the Huang Lao Daoist sect, was that the Yellow Emperor wore beautiful garments and his virtue was like Yao and Shun, that Lao Zi knew the ceremonies and was praised as You Long, how could this be called heterodoxy?

Buddhism started in the Qin dynasty, the Eastern and Western Han dynasties had very few Buddhist monks. Starting from the Wei and Jin dynasties, when chaos was usurping the land, Confucianism declined, and Buddhism surged when Da Mo Buddha came to the east to reveal the true essence.

---

[63] This convoluted paragraph explains the many erroneous notions people had throughout history.

I am afraid that this was also a fake story transmitted excessively. They created errors for the generation to come, blaming Buddha. To one's surprise after numerous transmissions, the ancestral transmission was lost, even high acclaimed scholars started commenting and expanding on these stories. These brought about an increased number of Buddhist monks and people studying Lao Zi.

In Buddhism, "make heart clear and see True Nature" is called "fulfil the heart and know its True Nature", and, while studying the void they assumed the heart is True Nature. With Lao Zi's "cultivate truth and nurture True Nature" is what they call "guard the evil and preserve sincerity", and so they assumed that there is some additional mysterious art. They did not know that there is no sage outside the scope of heart and True Nature, so where is there Buddha and Lao Zi outside of this?

And so they painfully rejected others and discarded the gongfu of human relations. Now the Buddha had a wife and son. Discarding human relations is the old custom of the four descendants; it is not the Buddha instructing it. China's Buddhist temples support the poor people; they cannot avoid supporting the wives and children. Lao Zi's articles were of not neglecting human relations, but since Zhao Song, Daoist priests were prohibited from marrying. So the offence of discarding human relations cannot be performed.

The false and stray actions of Buddhist and Daoist monks are all to mislead the people, answering their perceived need for something new. Yet they all suffer the net of justice. Prohibiting the false and preserving the truth should be used to nurture the poor people in the Buddhist convents, Daoist and Buddhist temples. This must be the principle. They think they demote Buddha and Lao Zi if they limit Dao within daily human relations. The sages were all like this, so how are only Buddha and Lao Zi walking a different path? Buddha says, "all within the Buddha field are part of the heart." Lao Zi says, "many words until the end are not equal to guarding center"; these are the same as inwardly preserving the heart and nurturing True Nature.

Ferrying the lives of the masses and then one can become a Buddha. In the hall the parents worship the great Buddha, three thousand hidden good deeds, eight hundred virtuous actions, the human Dao is fulfilled and then the immortal Dao begins, on the outside this shows as the practical experience of daily human relations.

Going astray with the monk's feather, how can one offend his root like this? Today the still heart belongs to Zen, nurture Qi belongs to the mysterious group. If one avoids Zen and the mysterious then one does not put effort either in following the heart and True Nature. If one wants to practice human relations, often one cannot, and instead only talks superfluous words. If one avoids the grand void and mysterious emptiness[64] then one nurtures Qi but one's heart flickers; one does not understand the meaning of supporting the will.

---

[64] This paragraph talks about Confucians, who avoided practicing anything related to Buddhism and Daoism. "Void" is an aspect in which Buddhists place their ultimate meditation, whereas Daoists place it in mysterious emptiness.

Yaron: Searching for spirituality often results in sectarian bias; one gravitates toward a certain group or theory. The sages looked for the truth, but their followers always claimed that only their sage knew it. Liu Yuan explains that every person should look for the truth and not for the sectarian heart. Confucians who claim that Buddhists do not have it, Buddhists who claim that Daoists do not have it, Daoists who argue that Confucians do not have it, neither understands the purpose of the sage. In a word, one cannot possess a sectarian heart and seek the principle.

27. The myriad affairs all begin in the heart. The myriad principles converge in True Nature. Preserving the heart and nurturing True Nature, only then can human relations be controlled and practiced. The truth of Buddha and Lao Zi is nothing other than heart and True Nature. If one refutes this and loses the truth of preserving and nurturing, then one is not on the real path

Heaven has only one principle, and humankind attains it as True Nature.

The sage did nothing other than fulfilling True Nature.

Daoists call it "cultivate truth and nurture True Nature." To understand what they mean by the terms "void" and "mysterious," it is only that at the time of nurturing True Nature there is no shred of selfish thought; reaching center, suddenly there is nothing. It is called empty. When the entire heart is happy and heaven brings clarity, it is called mysterious. In what way do these words imply that one discards the gongfu of daily human relations?

Today the trend of the Zen sect is to call it "Zen Fix," the altar of the six ancestors. They nurture the conscious heart, mistaking it for True Nature. Wise and enlightened are many, however, this is not the true accomplishment of the Buddha.

Zhou Lianxi attained his teachings at Shou Ya, Cheng and Zhu continued it, and then it became a sagely doctrine. They also said that Buddha and Lao Zi are adjunct to Confucius and Mencius, the natural endowment of the superior. In their heart, desires were few. Sitting in meditation for long periods, they became wise and enlightened. They also managed to establish themselves as a famous sect. People are not dull minded and simply follow them after they died. However, they were not like many other Buddhist and Daoist monks who guard their rules fervently.

Therefore they did not understand that "empty void" and "pure clarity" are methods of nurturing the heart. If these four words are gone, and if one lets go of the heart, one is lost. One cannot understand reaching ultimate goodness, becoming fixed in calmness and peace. The gongfu and Dao of the *Great Learning*, and the necessity to practice it are unattainable.

What is the purpose of rejecting it by followers of Buddha and Lao Zi?

Alas, the post-heaven heart does not resonate with True Nature. The heart of preserving emptiness generates the Qi of heaven's origin. Qi then fills up and the inside and outside merge and cultivate. It becomes great and transforms into spirit, only thereafter does the heart not move from center.

Yaron: Desires belong to the post heaven heart. They are the heart's normal action after birth and throughout life. True nature is within the heart beyond desires, it is similar to the fetal heart inside the womb. Liu Yuan explains that human behavior in different relationships is often not fixed. When one eradicates selfish thoughts one's behavior changes towards others; one turns kinder, more patient, more helpful.

28. **The accomplishment of heart and True Nature is the root of daily human interactions. If one erroneously explains the Sorting, Reaching, Sincerity and Proper of the *Great Learning*, and one does not know the truth of Buddha and Lao Zi being the same as that of Confucius, one separates into many different paths, each with their own heterodoxy. Then the scripture does not describe the proper truth, so how can the common people follow it excitedly?**

Dao is not greater than the five kinships.

The five kinships are the basis of heaven's nature in society. Every person has heaven's nature.

So how come people with loyalty, filial piety, benevolence and righteousness are so rare? Only because there is a selfish fallacy buried in the human heart that is difficult to weed out.

The desires of the ears, eyes, nose, mouth and four extremities are set in motion upon contact, so we pursue material things and change accordingly.

Even though a thousand oxen are hard to pull, this habit lasts for so long that it becomes reality.

Following this path, humans and beasts then have no difference. Ceremonies restrain them, and laws prohibit them.[65] One cannot tolerate the excuse that the improper affairs of ancient times are

---

[65] From behaving like beasts.

unlike those of today. Error was always, and remains today, due to the improper human heart. If one does not urgently practice the Dao of the *Great Learning* with vigor, then how could one tranquilize the human heart and act honestly within the five kinships?

The earlier Confucians knew only how to refute Buddhism and Daoism and how to revere their own sage. Yet in reality they could not practice the true teaching of the sage, so their teachings to others did not surpass the level of calming the heart. They often inspected and restrained themselves and they did not act upon the desire for material things, so why then did their original intent not attain benevolence?

They wanted to be clear about each and every affair. Now, why was the sage seeking one principle penetrating all, and not about the vast myriad ways of knowing? They did not know that the sage's accomplishment with heart and True Nature had a proper sequence, from superficial to deep. So they said that following Confucius and Mencius preserves the great Dao, yes to their heart, yes to their person, but not to their specific teaching. As soon as they altered the ancient text of the *Great Learning,* the way to approach the accomplishment of heart and True Nature was lost.[66]

---

[66] The explanation here is of earlier Confucians who agreed to follow the persona of Confucius and Mencius, they believed that the sages' intentions were correct, but they altered the *Great Learning* text, they contradicted the teachings of the sages. This specifically refers to the concept of Ge Wu sorting ones heart. Later Confucians explained this concept as sorting phenomena in nature in order to reach knowledge instead of sorting one's own heart.

Since antiquity until today, even without self-cultivation and training a proper heart, there are ministers and officials who are loyal, filial and righteous. But, generally speaking, this is their high-level naturally-occurring talent, their character is not the same and each follows his customs. They liberally stimulate excitement and often meet an untimely death. By no means is this an isolated case.

When Confucius speaks of a benevolent person and a person of ideals and integrity, and when Mencius speaks of scholars of exceptional ability whose honor is like the sun and the moon, they are referring to the maintenance of proper human relations, which is an entire lifetime wishing to not let the proper die. There were only very few who, from learning this teaching, reached the objective and made virtue complete.

When the father and teacher set an example, demonstrate how to calmly nurture their own center, how to carry harmony within their movements, then those who excelled entered the realm of the sages and spirits. Those next to them were all benevolent, all embodied propriety. There were none who deceived the monarch or their parents, or caused hardship upon the people. Therefore the sage said: the teaching does not create categories,[67] the knowledge is one; the accomplishment is one.

Since the time when earlier Confucians believed that the heart was the same as True Nature, being aware of the principle could not thread together the myriad affairs. They altered the *Great Learning*,

---

[67] Differentiate between people.

they claimed that you have to investigate the myriad things to attain accomplishment. They caused people to exhaust their ears and eyes, becoming the servants of their minds, trying to exhaust the myriad things under heaven. This has no benefit to the body and heart.

Very few knew that they should not leave their parents behind, and not to second guess their monarch. They said "it is not easy to understand the Dao, it is not easy to make the heart proper" but they did not realize that they had no foundation of how to preserve and nurture the heart and True Nature.

After Confucius and Mencius, there was still true transmission by educated literati who were self-assured that the myriad affairs and myriad principles had no root in the heart, and they only understood the need to maintain daily human relations.

How are daily human relations not rooted in the heart?

If the heart is not proper, the intention not sincere, one seeks fame and gain, desires are diverse and confused. They say: "this is daily human relations," but they do not know the task of the heart within actions. The petty heart follows desire and turns its back on heaven's nature; fame and gain become the new Dao. Thus it can never truly be loyal and filial. Disciples who scold Buddhism and Daoism for discarding human relations do so on empty claims. The fake ones amongst Buddhists and Daoists truly created chaos with the people, but the proper ones truly are aloof from politics and sever themselves from customs. From ancient times until the present day these cannot be falsely accused.

How come the Confucians cannot tell black from white and mix them all together, then despise and discard all of them? Buddhists and Daoists have wives and children, homes and families, they do not discard human relations. Their teaching instructs: all the fields of the Buddha do not depart from the realm of the heart. Many words are not as good as guarding center with its core of heart and True Nature. They also say: If one helps the masses ferry across then he becomes a Buddha. Three thousand hidden good deeds, eight hundred virtuous actions, this simply means that cultivating Dao is practiced through benevolence and righteousness. This is not outside the scope of human relations and self-cultivation.

Throughout the world people are bearing it patiently and not saying a word. If still there is no one to point this mistake then the great error is transmitted through the generations. This is why humble me goes against the masses with too much talk.

Yaron: Human relations involve heart emotions and desires interacting with each other; when one person desires then another person reacts. With less desires, heaven's nature creates a shared experience of goodness on the outside. This fulfils life. It generates proper relationships between parents and children, siblings and friends.

29. Loyalty and filial piety come from practicing virtue. Yet from antiquity until today the mistakes have been many. One must follow the original meaning of Confucius and Mencius, then one becomes a survivor and not a dead follower, loyal and dutiful are then present with distinction

All affairs look to the sage as a teacher, so how would human relations be greater than this? One should be loyal and dutiful with the monarch and parents; everybody knows this. If one is not loyal and not dutiful then one's Dao is insufficient. However, if one knows loyalty and knows filial piety but does not attain one's center, then one cannot merge with the sage.

Even though there is no harm with loyalty and filial piety, people will still dispute its effect. This misleads those coming after. Dressing up with loyalty or expressing the existence of filial piety, they attain the outer aspect, missing that which is important.

Now, the many who are refuting it did not do so on their own, but rather the nobleman damaged it with dressing it up. Why can't one be like Taibo of Wu?[68] That the fox dashes forward early meant that the crown prince convinced him, the situation was extremely difficult to redeem. That the monarch and parent wished him death also requires careful examination according to principle, moreover the wicked people made false accusations against him, thus the monarch and parent were deceived momentarily. The ancestors

---

[68] Taibo 泰伯 legendary founder of the state of Wu 吴.

merged with Gods of the land, deciding that killing him would injure the ancestral virtue. How could one not be cautious?

Confucius said, "the Dao serves the monarch, one cannot stop it." Zeng Zi saying melon is being cut open, Mencius saying to be an official without crooked Dao, when talking about filial piety they said attending parents and following the parents both be fulfilled. When talking about loyalty they said sort the heart and create goodness. Therefore to die in the name of virtue means that one's ability is extreme.

If the monarch and father have died, righteousness does not generate on its own. Some are dispatched to a very important task, and if they do not complete their task, then they must die. If, however, one says that the ultimate in loyalty and filial piety is that one will sacrifice one's life for it, then this is false.

Wei, Ji and Bi Gan[69] were all valued officials in the past, having the same joys and sorrows as the country. Master Wei escaped to a distant place, Master Ji pretended to be crazy, and their action was unlike the death of Bi Gan. Confucius thought that they all were benevolent. The person criticizing Bi Gan did not wish him death, but it was a matter of misfortune. For burning the granary and abandoning his rank, Shun could have been put to death, but he was not. He served until the end with great filial piety; dying would have carried no benefit. How could someone serving their monarch

---

[69] Weizi 微子 Jizi 箕子 and Bi Gan 比干 were revered by Confucius as the three sages of the Shang dynasty. Bi Gan recommended the evil ruler Di Xin to change his ways, and so the ruler ordered his execution by 'extracting of the heart' to see if the sage's heart had seven orifices.

and parents be put to death? In addition, when the monarch and parent got angry, at one point they knew their unrepentant heart, letting him stay to have a second chance. When the monarch and parent came to see the truth, that until the end he is loyal and filial, how could that not have been reassuring?

But had he been denounced and chased away when the monarch and parent would be in danger, how could he go save them? If he could not save them then he would not be able to live his life; at this point, dying for the cause, how is this not superior? The grace of monarch and parent is the same but their source is not. If one is not eating from the monarch's salary then one should not perform a task until death.

When a son is adept with Dao he should offer his parent instruction about Dao, but if the parent does not comply and he gets in danger then the son should submit himself until the end; however, there are also cases in which he should not submit himself:[70] If submitting himself means that no offspring remain to serve the ancestral alter, or in order to prevent family disgrace. Therefore, to submit one's life for loyalty and filial piety has great political integrity; however, submitting to death for pure goodness is extremely difficult. If one does not master the Dao of the *Great Learning* with one's benevolence matured and righteousness refined, then how could one distinguish clearly if it is right or wrong? When an adherent dies for a noble cause, sometimes it is not proper toward the parent, or has no real benefit to the parent and monarch.

---

[70] Sacrifice his life.

In addition, the monarch and parent may regret it dearly, and their hatred will become extreme. How is this not a regretful event at the nine origins? Therefore the actions of the sage and the meaning of Confucius and Mencius should be discussed daily.

Yaron: Goodness creates life-benefit for the person themselves and for everyone else. In advancing goodness there is no "sacrifice" involved, only a question of being proper or not. Liu Yuan explains that sacrificing one's life for the monarch is in most cases improper. One knows the properness of an action when the heart is calm and sincere.

30. In order to find a loyal official, one must look amongst dutiful children. One must carefully study cases in the history annals describing loyalty with no filial piety or filial piety without loyalty in order to prevent people from suspecting that loyalty and filial piety contradict each other

The connection between filial piety and loyalty lies clearly with them both being reflections of heaven goodness; one does not deceive one's parents and naturally does not deceive one's monarch.

However, father and mother give birth to me and raise me; since childhood to old age, throughout my entire life, I am close to my father and mother. This is unlike serving the monarch when one is selected for service. There are those who feed on salaries, those who support everyone, those who receive official gifts, and those who receive exceptional recognition, and so their roles in service can be distinguished as small and big. Mencius says that there are three kinds of accomplishments and three kinds of rejection. Some exit,[71] some remain, some stop and some progress quickly, along with many considerations, this does not take place casually.

Therefore, if one wants to observe an official, one must observe his relationship with his father and mother. If he is sincere and cautious and not deceptive or lax, then naturally he will not deceive the monarch and not be lax in his office. Therefore to find a loyal official, one must look amongst dutiful children.

---

[71] Exit means to leave home to serve as an official.

Now, because the monarch has impressive strength, he causes people fear, and because the monarch offers salaries, he causes people greed. Therefore, there are many who are respectful while serving the monarch, but there are very few who sincerely respect their parents.

When the heart of loving the parents and loving the monarch is there, then being respectful and serving derives naturally from heaven's True Nature. In addition, serving the parent must be instructed by the Dao of serving a parent, then this is a great filial piety. Serving the monarch should follow the Dao of serving a monarch, and then one is an outstanding minister. Being filial and loyal at the same time has not even the slightest blemish. Without superior wisdom, one is unable to perform it.

Serving one's parents is always at their feet, while serving one's monarch depends on one's talents, and therefrom appropriately one receives a task. When one is a corrupt official, one keeps oneself inside and locks the door in order to avoid hunger and cold, or for seeking a salary. When one has talent and virtue, even if one is amongst rivers and lakes, one does not forget the monarch, and never submits people to a crooked Dao. How could one view the monarch lightly?

The official should be loyal to the monarch, with his body willing to die. Even though he cannot take care of his parents at the same time, loyalty to the monarch is like filial piety to the parents. Therefore if one keeps the monarch's salary then one must be trusted by the monarch. If one benefits the monarch and the people, then it is adequate. This is the trend of Yi and Ge, which is hardly ever seen amongst the ordinary generations. After the Three Dynasties, officials and eunuchs largely tied themselves up with official ranks, they did not plan to attend to the monarch and benefit the people. Even though they threw up words and raised actions in the manner appropriate for officials, those full of words were many, and those with actions were few.

Articles flourished in the land and mandarins became teachers. At the upper echelon, nobody knew the way of cultivating their family. They did not know what their heart toward the monarch should look like, and therefore their loyalty and filial piety assumed different paths. Exiting and remaining became estranged and the loyal did not have to be dutiful, and the dutiful did not have to be loyal. That they both stem from the same origin turned obscure.

In ancient times, the dutiful son only knew that he has parents he needed to make happy, even with only worn-out sandals to his feet. How could he desire to leave his parents for glory? Yet the monarch believed in him and used him, because he could see that he did not have an iota of deceit. Therefore the loyal minister was one who first was unwilling to leave his parents behind, one who could not tolerate turning his back on his parents. Only then he could excel in becoming a loyal minister. How could one deceive his monarch while being so earnest with filial piety?

However, the world is changing rapidly, and the Dao of the *Great Learning* is largely misunderstood. Hardly anyone understands the complete ways of loyalty and filial piety. Therefore the cases of being either loyal or dutiful in the history annals narrate people who missed heaven's True Nature. One can know their hardship of abandoning life.

Now, from ancient times until today there are those who have reached absolute sincerity in loyalty and filial piety, walking their path with compassion. But those who forgot their monarch or their parents did not understand the great Dao. Their human relations were improper, and so they received the punishment of being either a minister or a son.

Yaron: Guarding the water coming into my tap and the lake from which water is drawn to reach my tap are both important. Taking care of one and not the other will impair the proper Dao.

31. From ancient times until today, for the country to be in chaos and to perish was always due to being unclear about the correct Dao, which sprouts many hypocrites. One should urgently correct this

The Master said, "human life is upright; when crooked is born it is best to prevent it" and "these people, during the Three Dynasties, their Dao was upright and therefrom they acted."

Gao Yao[72] had nine virtues and the first one was being upright. Mencius nurtured the upright with doing it no harm as the root of nurturing Qi. People often neglect this one word.[73]

The flipping upside down what is right and what is wrong, confusing which is which, is the great malady of the nation. Well-governed days are few while chaotic days are many; one cannot but sigh! Upright does not mean slanting-upright, outspoken-upright, solitary-upright nor stern-upright. All these misrepresent the principle. Rather, when one serves True Nature, only then it is possible. Upright means that it receives heaven's nature and then the action takes place.

What is right and what is wrong is not even the slightest bit crooked, nor is it achieved by following one's temperament or acting in solitude, disregarding harmony with worldly customs. Confucius, when explaining attainment, said, "when the substance is upright its meaning is good, calculating words and looking at things is

---

[72] Minister of Law for the legendary emperor Shun.
[73] Upright.

considered a lower person." Upright is upright like the trunk of a tree. Heaven's nature is distinguished clearly between what is right and what is wrong; the one who guards it is stable. However, one does not dare to be self-assured and therefore one endlessly gathers the proper heaven's nature, follows its goodness and maintains a selfless heart. Like this, the principle is upright, one's social intercourse is constantly warm, kind, respectful and frugal and one gives way to others. Virtue is then surging and fills every action.

People who customarily use the word "upright" largely do not understand the principle embodying it, angrily clinging to their concept of upright. Or there are those who glimpse it but then easily dismiss the multitude of people. Some who exit or remain instigate affairs or bring misfortune; these are certainly not isolated cases. Some view the upright Dao as taboo, saying: to respect and to give way is the foundation of one's body, it is like mixing light with dust, it is the monarch's Dao. While this sounds correct, it is actually false. The hypocrites follow their own heels filling under heaven. By failing to distinguish right from wrong clearly within the principle, by not inquiring into affairs being small or big, light or serious, acting upon them all with indifference, this, I am afraid, brings an offense against the parents and monarch.

Ah Yi followed the crooked[74] and so his inherent loyal and loving heart declined daily, he was afraid to offend officials, so his behavior leaned toward external things. If we transpose this story

---

[74] This idiom means that one wants to be filial and so when his parents or superiors have errors he follows along. True filial son, when he sees an error, he corrects his parents and superiors.

into today's world, regarding those living with their family or acting as officials, they are often afraid of reaching calamity, so the minister follows things that he should not, selling the upright for scrap. How could there be upright Qi under heaven?

The book of poetry says: the good is honest and upright; this peace is heard by the spirits and surely brings good fortune. How is this not heaven principle filling up the vessel of the people.

Honesty and uprightness cannot be even the tiniest bit crooked. Upright must be proper, if it is not proper it cannot be upright. If proper and upright are not acted upon then loyalty and filial piety are merely superficial. Power goes to the wicked, who shapes a social model; this fraud cannot be described with words. Mencius said that Confucius was thinking of the crazy and timid, but he hated the hypocrite.

Those who were against the scriptures had no evil in them, yet those who researched them had evil thoughts, like the philosophers Yang and Mo. Without knowing it, Mencius was pointing out the hypocrites. The fraud of Yang and Mo is not adopted by the knowledgeable ones. The hypocrites are those who on the outside seem modest and courteous and on the inside seem soft and pliable. They follow the modern customs and conform to the world, the crowds are all happy about them. The monarch and father do not investigate them, thinking them loyal and dutiful. The masses do not investigate them, thinking them virtuous and kind. They cannot see that right and wrong have been flipped upside down; the upright Dao has entirely vanished.

Mang of the Xin Dynasty worshipped Yi of Zhou. Cao, of the kingdom of Wei, abdicated and gave the crown to another, how was that not conforming to an upright person? How was this calculated as a usurping of power? Confucius said, "elevate the upright and eliminate all crooked, then the people obey." Get rid of people who deceive life, view the hypocrites as thieves, let people know that if they are not upright they deserve to die. There is nothing worse than stealing and hurting the human heart. It is a pity that people are fond of flattery and hate uprightness, they would rather not understand right from wrong. Those unwilling to commit an offense are only few.

Yaron: Political correctness, spirituality, dressing up an appearance of virtue and politeness do not help the upright or finding proper measure. For Liu Yuan, repealing selfish thoughts is the method.

32. The Dao of *Great Learning* encompasses everything, swipes clean everything, it is easy to know and easy to follow. If above it becomes a teaching and below everybody practices it, then there are no worries under heaven

Since the time of the sage, true teachers have been rare.

Confucians learn the shallow but they want to talk with high words. One after the other speaks absurdly. They tell the people that it is hard to learn the Dao, that the sage was born in heaven, and that the healthy flowers are thistles and thorns. They do not realise that since antiquity until today the myriad different affairs play out, but their essence was, and is always, within the human heart.

When the human heart is upright, then it matters not what kind of situation it encounters, the kind heart of heaven never becomes corrupt. Therefore, all of the ceremonies, ritual music, laws and prohibitions are all easy to know and do; they are all a practical method. If the human heart is not upright, then even if one assumes a post with a hundred and one talents, one must apply it without being proper. So how does the heart become upright? One must put into practice the Dao of the *Great Learning*. And that is it!

To "sort things" means sort out our selfish desire for material things. To "reach knowledge" means to reach to the knowledge of principle. When desires are removed then the clear heart and principle are easily understood. In addition, one learns and differentiates, then reaches knowledge. The daily practice of human relations, observing movement and stillness, these are the path to the silent principle.

When one meticulously clarifies what is right and what is wrong, this understanding is practiced diligently. This is called "sincere intention". Sincere intention means to examine what is right and what is wrong carefully in every small place of movement. The wrong needs to be carved out and expelled, the right needs to be acted upon with a complete heart.

Intolerance means no benevolence, and no courage means no righteousness; not cheating, not being lax or slack, ridding wanton desire first in one thought, and then in every single thought, first in one affair and then in all affairs. Goodness can then accumulate and evil vanishes daily, and then the root becomes pure.

From this grace one makes poetry and books and lets everyone know about it. The father and mother can be helped by it; competent teachers and friends can use it. If they practice the truth within their hearts for a long time, they can aspire to the sage and heaven, and next to that to the monarch and the virtuous.

Even at the lowest level, people will not agree to concealing matters of a good heart. Therefore the Dao of the *Great Learning* is the great application supplemented by the sage. In addition, no matter if one is wise or dull minded, all what one wants is to eat until full, be warm and safe, and that is it!

To make oneself full, warm, and safe is a power grasped by heaven. Being rewarded for goodness and punished for evil, abundant celebration or excess calamity is all within heaven principle, and that has never changed. If one can practice the accomplishment of sorting, reaching and sincerity, then one must abide by heaven's decree. Guarding heaven principle, one then merges with heaven's intention.

In addition, if one does not follow one's emotions and subject oneself to desire, then the art of preserving one's body and nurturing one's life is easily practiced. What Mencius says about guarding the body is critical. The Dao of the *Great Learning* is simultaneously to guard the body and to make it sincere. I, the humble one, have already explained it.

Every person is able to know it. Every person can practice it.

Extending life and benefiting the people is this Dao. So how come the root is so close, and yet they seek that which is distant; the root is so easy and yet they seek that which is difficult? They cause people to lose what they already possess, making them run down the wrong road!

Yaron: To practice Dao is truly unassuming. It involves daily trivial affairs; there is no glory or recognition, a thankless job! But when the simple things become grand, every trivial affair becomes important, then every moment is significant, every moment is alive. No matter the affair being small or grand, the heart is always in it. For example, if one cuts vegetables to make soup and at the same time one thinks of other things occupying his mind, then this makes cutting the vegetables trivial. But if one cuts the vegetables and thinks about what goodness will come out of this soup and how much health it will bring to everyone eating it, then this becomes a grand affair. One's heart is in it.

33. **Only if Dao is centered for the current times can everyone manifest it. If it is looked at as lofty then it leaves a legacy of trouble within the family and the country. From ancient times until today, it was always like this. What a pity!**

Mencius said that Confucius was the sage of the time. This was interpreted later as "centered for the current time," as if the sage could only ever be Confucius. What a big mistake!

From Fu Xi and Shen Nong to Confucius and Mencius, they were all sages. But their affairs were different, how so? The Five Supreme rulers lived in a different time, they did not follow the prescribed ceremonies. The Three Kings were in a different generation; they did not follow ceremonial music. Confucius said: Yao taught Shun, Tang got rid of Jie, King Wu attacked Zhou; different times, different measures. Each monarch was centered in his own time. If every monarch is centered in his own time, how come only the time of Confucius counts?

That other sages did not assume any position since the time of Confucius; people rarely understand this. Therefore, Mencius celebrated Confucius with great vigor. That which Confucius took to heart: clothing, words and actions, is hardly different from other people. This truly sums up the earlier sages, they were centered in their own times.

Mencius expressed it as: being the sage of the time meant to allow people to learn about Confucius. How could one say that Confucius was the only notable person of the time? Were the Five Supremes and Three Kings not notable?

In addition, being time-centered is not difficult to know or to understand. It is like in the summer if it is suddenly cool one adds a layer, or in winter if it is suddenly warm one removes a layer. Lifestyle and food follow the times, increasing or decreasing appropriately. This happens many times. Every simple man and woman knows this. So why is it only when it comes to people who learn the sage's teaching that they look loftily at these two words: "time centered"?

Even worse, when it comes to ruling the country and putting the family in order, how come they do not realize that these also must change according to the times? If father and son promote evil, following the sage will leave behind disaster. Even victory ends in a deep sigh. Alas, within a family, a father ploughs the mulberry field and the son inserts hairpins in his hair, the son is an ignoramus and the father serves as a minister of high office.[75]

What they experience is their times, however, ones who can cultivate themselves and have virtue reach to varying degrees. Everyone can make pretty statements. Since Wang Anshi enacted political reform and brought calamity to the Song Dynasty, the following generations saw political reform as taboo. They did not understand the assertion that if there are three years without

---

[75] It appears that there is no continuum from father to son.

change, action is needed. They did not contemplate the meaning of the word "Dao".

In situations where the father had goodness but the son had none, Confucius specifically formulated the statement "not to alter the father's Dao". However, when the father does not conform to Dao then the son must change rapidly in order to become dutiful. He becomes the pleasing one to the parent; he starts observing great filial piety. How is it like Ah Yi following the crooked and superficial version of filial piety?

Although the sage's principle method does not age or wear out, it does rely on following the current times to be rectified and corrected. Using Dao to preserve it, it allows us to return to the proper measure. That the ancient sages and the virtuous dealt with venomous snakes[76] did not enter the discourse, just like Kings Wen and Wu who possessed the same virtue. They did not have the same policy of revolution, and yet Confucius named Wu as the continuing goodness of the Zhou dynasty.[77]

Whenever the earlier people spoke and acted with goodness, it is proper to not forget and not overlook them; however, the times are changing and the current situations are different, so it is also proper to adapt with the changing times. In addition, it is not that the practice of pure goodness is without any blemish. More so, when people stubbornly guard the old then it comes to a trend of evident

---

[76] Meaning corrupt rulers that needed to be brought down from power, like Jie and Zhou, the last rulers of Xia and Shang Dynasties.
[77] King Wu was the one using violence to bring down the Shang dynasty.

fraud on the verge of destruction, the principle cannot stretch anymore. This harm is clearly seen in the annals of history. However, if one does not cultivate oneself and establish virtue by following famous virtuous people and their deliberation, then one cannot reach complete goodness.

The Tai Zu emperor of the Ming Dynasty did not allow the eunuchs to intervene, and Yan Wen designed beautiful clothes to protect his children and grandchildren from disaster. He dispatched his family members into vassal states to usurp the throne, while ordering his relative kings not to be in charge of the military, but at the end his children suffered the misfortune of riches and wine. What was not supposed to change changed, and what was supposed to change did not. Both are inappropriate. When there is a country and a family, one should cultivate deep loyalty and educate talent, and then it is long lasting. Yao and Shun did not selfishly select their sons from all those under heaven, rather, they chose the virtuous.

Yaron: Changing with the times involves changing and adapting from one day to the other, from one situation to another. It is finding the proper measure at any time and at every place. Therefore, finding the proper measure must have a method. This method, for Liu Yuan, is inspecting movement and preserving stillness; observing and becoming familiar with one's heart desires and thoughts as well as keeping and prolonging the times when desires and thoughts are absent. Like this, one reaches a proper measure.

34. Words convey the Dao. Yet, Dao's meaning is worn out by words. One must first practice it in person and then, from within, compose words, sayings and books. Then the garden of the Dao is not overgrown with weeds

Since the engraving of books prospered and refined elucidation came about, affairs regarding human relations and numerous other things became dependent on the written word. Confucius also stated, "the refined aspect is within these words, so how could the Kuang people be like me?" Thus, one acknowledges the importance of the written script.

However, talented and knowledgeable literati who fail to learn deeply and yet follow their own opinions, their actions go astray. Inadvertently, their deeds and words harm the Dao.

Confucius has already sighed about this, "not knowing and yet acting." Those with no true virtue discuss the principle; taking fixed rhyming patterns and decorating them with their flashy opinions. This situation has been ingrained for a long time.

Mencius talked about dealing with the literati's perverse opinions, and if it were not due to the fire of Qin torching books and the lost manuscripts of Zhu Si, how could there be so many perverse arguments against heterodoxy? Burning books, prohibiting books, not allowing people to read books... this is odd and, since antiquity, a previously unheard-of story. But assessing the situation after it happened, written scripts were often mixed and confused, and heaven's heart disliked it. People blamed everything on the Qin emperor. The classics were set ablaze by the cruel and fierce fire, while the stringed bamboo book found hidden in the wall became precious.

Refined elucidation on its content prospered, connecting the world's Dao and human heart. Truly, it was due to the fire of Qin that the teachings of Confucius and Mencius flourished. From the Han Dynasty onwards, the number of books became vast; however, amongst them, books that puzzle the world and confuse people are there in multitudes.

Different schools started based on the Confucian Principle School, such as the Confucian Forest school, the Script and Art school, and so on, each carrying their own banner. Thus script and Dao became independent of each other; one did not have to reach both "knowing" and "doing". The learning of heaven and human, True Nature and life, declined daily into a vast obscurity. Daily application of the human relations became superfluous and complex. Manuscripts increased daily, while the Dao sank into gradual obscurity.

Master Zhu Zi claimed that it is good to read and learn from books, but how could one read them all? How did it come to a situation where the sage's disciples memorize his books and, based on this, claim glory?

The great Dao is nothing more than human relations. The wise and the foolish, they both can know it and act upon it.

At infancy they know to love, when a bit older they know to respect. The virtuous father and mother are good with nurturing and teaching; they do not allow a loss of heaven kindness. The enlightened teacher and the beneficial friend help each other by exchanging knowledge.

Like this, one cannot bear to harden one's heart toward one's parents, and this is further expanded toward one's siblings and ancestors, and one eradicates the attitude of turning one's back on the monarch. One's earnest and respectful heart toward one's elders increases daily, and one expands it to the wilderness and the wild tribes at the periphery, making them all respectful. Where could there be one who is slow with respect for the monarch?

Mencius said, "treating parents like parents is benevolence, respecting the elders is righteousness, there is nothing else! This extends to everything under heaven."

Alas, people all have things they cannot tolerate. But if they bring it to a place of tolerance, then this is benevolence. People all have things they don't want to do. But if they can bring themselves to a place of action, this is called righteousness. How is this difficult? When one reads books to understand the principle, one basically needs to understand this one point, and that's it! When a text describes the Dao it basically needs to describe this one thing, and that's it!

When a scholar learns the books of sages and the virtuous, but he fails to speak of the kind heart of heaven's nature, then he wanders the path of fame and profit. Forgetting about his own self, he gives into such things, seeking that which he should not tolerate. Thus, benevolence is lost. He dares not do the proper thing, silently making the heart not righteous. Then when he compiles his books, inadvertently this impropriety becomes the rule. As if fulfilling the sage's understanding of human relations and inspecting things, it morphs into rules and regulations; it has turned into a dead letter. People who became famous like this were many. The written text then, to the contrary, becomes an insect biting into the great Dao. How is this not damaging?

There are also those who want to keep the customs and set up their own personal banner, they do not set a pattern in their artistic style, but their practical experience is not deep. They call themselves protectors of the Dao, but in reality they make the Dao obscure. Like Wang Tong and his opinion of "classics overstepping their authority," and that Confucius drafted the *Book of Changes*. People know that this is not the case, so it left Confucius's books as open-ended questions, arbitrarily he changed the meanings, and then people could not resolve the text anymore.

In reality, the sage's words all speak of heaven's nature, therefore fearing the sage's words means fearing heaven's nature.

If one speaks outside of heaven's nature, making explanations outside of the sage's scope, thinking that one alone has arrived at something great, then it only appears like one arrived, while actually one is lost. The ones who do not understand the Dao of the sage, how is it not the case that their writings are all divergent from the truth?

Alas, any article written glorifying the Dao and virtue should include human relations and then the numerous things, and only then does it have a benefit for the life of the people. These words[78] should not be sparse; otherwise, a frog that cries like a bird hurts one's ears.

It will cause people to gradually follow the customs' superficial fallacies. They will practice the daily Dao of human relations less diligently, forgetting their body, True Nature, heart and life. In addition, if they do not nurture inside and out, the root and branches, and instead they follow the wrong road, this adversely affects learning. Where, then, is the value of written texts?

Yaron: Words describe one's heart movements; desires, thoughts and ideas. Heart movement is the impetus that creates the outward reality and customs, and these are continually changing. For Liu Yuan, using texts to conform to the times often leads to errors with finding a proper measure. It makes one believe that finding it is with the customary. Human relations is an unchanging heaven's nature principle and so Liu Yuan recommends to write and read more about it.

---

[78] About human relations.

35. The words "having emotion in the world"[79] everybody knows. However, they do not know how to differentiate them clearly and act upon them energetically. Instead, people act contrary to the Dao

Every human spirit between heaven and earth has True Nature and emotions, and this cannot be ignored. Emotions are connected to True Nature, while True Nature means heaven's nature.

Heaven's nature has no sound or smell, one cannot peep through and look at it, yet it creates images and physical forms. It brings about the myriad phenomena and, through them, one is able to fathom the emotions of heaven and earth.

The Master maintaining the human heart is likewise invisible; however, happiness, anger, sadness and joy discharge as words and actions and, therefore, whether emotions are evil or proper can be gauged. Therefore, the word "emotion" should not be looked at lightly.

Nonetheless, emotions are the application of True Nature, but they can also be the thief of True Nature. Its focal point lies within being proper or not proper.

So how do human emotions fulfil the requirements of being proper? If there is no pure nurturing of True Nature, a stable center, and the seven emotions connected to the one True Nature, then how can properness be without deviation?

---

[79] These words represent a Buddhist concept of "knowing about life and death".

When an ordinary person wishes to make their emotions proper, they must learn, inquire, contemplate and differentiate in order to understand the principle. They must earnestly take actions in order to make their own self sincere and then they know how to stop only at ultimate goodness.

When preserving stillness takes effect, then every single thought is without deceit. It is not lax. Every word and every action must be sincere and respectful and as soon as it starts, it is managed with effort.

One perseveres like this for a long time until it becomes habit, and thereafter, going astray with evil decreases while the emotions of likes and dislikes become proper. How could one then act arbitrarily, make themselves happy and joyous and believe that, with this, they have proper emotion in the world?

Within human life, the many things that people seek comfort with are all included within the categories of clothing, food, and the affairs of a man and woman. The sage too was not outside this scope. Thus the principle of the many affairs, and the myriad written words about them, points to having proper emotions and then True Nature stands fast. If one loses the proper measure then one's emotions sweep away from center and then True Nature cannot stay put. Therefore, even if the sage speaks absurdities and makes himself crazy, he still requires of himself to take charge of his center.

There are seven emotions and there is one True Nature. True Nature is the one regulating the emotions. One cannot let one's emotions go and put True Nature in chaos. Mencius said if one puts oneself under shackles during the day then one becomes closer to the birds and beasts. How is this not going astray due to the seven emotions?

The monarch should act like the monarch, minister like a minister, father like a father, and son like a son. Of the five kinships each has its own Dao, leading one to act with sincerity. The crooked[80] is able to complete its Dao.

Thus, reaching to the place where emotions accumulate is the same as reaching to the place where True Nature stands.

If one then expands it to benevolence toward all people and all things, then at its root the one heart connects to the millions of people far and near, reaching to the true meaning of having an emotion in the world.

Since it became rare that people practice the great Dao, and instead commonly submit to selfish desires, believing that it is the proper state of True Nature and emotions, they mistakenly believe that life is about making themselves happy. So heaven's True Nature gradually becomes shallow and moral conduct gradually becomes warped.

To an extreme, it becomes such that with the *Book of Poetry* and *Book of Historical Documents* people swipe away self-restraint and instead dwell in a carefree style. Not knowing what fault they have and, to the contrary, creating poetry and articles and all sorts of wayward stories, they brag about themselves as being distinguished and admirable.

---

[80] Even the one who follows the kinship in a superficial way like Ah Yi, mentioned earlier.

Therefore, while they fool a few, the people get bored with these books and discard them hastily, and instead they seek peace and tranquility. They go to learn with Buddhist monks how to leave their home to become a monk, and be puzzled by the odd teachings of Gods and spirits.[81] In order to allow people to enter into a place of center, instead of reading the *Book of Poetry* and the *Book of Historical Documents*, they need to learn and practice the Dao of *Proper Place of Center*.

On the inside, they need to make their heart proper, while on the outside, they need to put in order their discipline. They should not enter the realm of the carefree and unrestrained style of action.

In such a manner, everyone under heaven may be successful. How could anyone suffer under the malady of bringing heterodoxy into chaos? Thus, if the one word "emotion" is proper, then there is no heart that can be improper. Where could there be people who trample the Dao of sorting, reaching, sincerity, and properness?

Yaron: For Liu Yuan, "Proper emotions are the application of True Nature" describes a mechanism for delivering heaven's nature from center to the world via human relations. A human being is a conduit of heaven's nature. If emotions go astray then this nature is easily obscured, whereas with proper emotions heaven's nature is revealed.

---

[81] Because the articles they write about the books of poetry and history don't have real virtue, people then rather become Buddhist monks or follow mysterious theories of the Daoists.

36. The numerous words of the sage all sum up to one principle. The principle is what heaven and human share in common

Heaven, earth, human and spirit connect as one Qi, with their root threaded together by the single principle. Human is the focal point of the three treasures. To fulfil the "human merging with heaven" doctrine, one needs only to complete the principle of being a human being: being worthy of heaven and earth. Then how could one shame one's father and mother?

Thus, discriminating against heaven, earth, human and spirit, and reaching to such a degree where the Dao of the *Proper Place of Center* is seen as something outside of one's own body, how could one not sigh? What a pity!

The sage himself was a person. Why did Confucius say, "know the heaven in me"?

How was King Wen solemn, similar to heaven? Confucius said, "Human is the heart of heaven and earth." Mencius said, "The myriad things are all embodied in me." Heaven and earth is like the father and mother. When human's Dao is complete, it is heaven's Dao. When one fulfills human's Dao and merges with heaven's Dao then one merges one's virtue with heaven, like a child who learns from their father and mother, who acts with their father and mother just like they would with the sages and the virtuous. This is not an odd affair.

When in heaven it is heaven's nature and when in human it is the kind heart. Every person has the "kind heart [of] heaven's nature." Every single thought does not depart from these four words. The great application of this may reach to the sage and to heaven, while the small application makes one completely loyal and completely filial. Therefore, when one learns the sage's books, when one learns the sage's actions, when one is afraid of the sage's words, the entire meaning of this is within these four words, then one is worthy of being a human being.

To no avail, the early Confucians jumbled their explanations, positioned themselves on a high place and said that the Dao is something the common person cannot reach to. They caused the sage's Dao to become like mist and fog.

Heaven, earth and human being linked as one, as well as the proper state of the living spirit, are collectively the divinity of heaven and earth's proper Qi. It is what leads the transformations of heaven and earth to benefit the people. It is what decides the life of the people.

The Confucians, without exception, denounced it as fallacy and deceit. Thus, whatever Confucius physically did not leave behind was all categorized as false. For a long time, everyday Confucians claimed that ghosts and gods are absurd and vague. Yet, when holding a memorial ceremony, it is as though the departed exist, and holding sacrificial ceremonies for the spirits as if they exist. So is it possible that Confucius was a fool?

They did not know that heaven and earth are without words, that they instead reveal themselves in the fine details.

Sincerity spreads and pours down; divine spirits follow this momentum with brilliance. Like a great wind that uproots a tree, like a startling thunderbolt that soars through the sky. How could it be assumed to be void and absurd for lack of seeing or hearing it? Even when the thunderbolts and wind are still and silent, the astonishment and shock preceding them, where do these belong? Is it not due to the finest of details still concealed within? And so the meaning of the two words "void" and "emptiness" is revealed. Not only to speak highly of the principle extracted from things seen and heard, but also knowing the virtue of the invisible. Although concealed, it can also be revealed, which is similar to the actions of heaven with no sound and no smell, the so-called solemn.

Invisible virtue was the pure virtue of King Wen. Heaven's Dao is like this, and human's Dao is also like this. As a result, heaven and human merge together. If one does not understand this meaning then the properness of Buddhism and Daoism is seen crookedly. The ones learning Buddhism and Daoism turn their back on Buddha and Lao Zi in order to seek the mysterious. Heterodoxy and evil arts are tangled together, while Confucians are busy rejecting and excluding it. Yet, from beginning to end, they cannot prevent it. How does this not represent Confucians cultivating reality while never reaching the truth? The cultivation already rules their body, and yet they cannot understand it.

Yaron: Buddhists and Daoists who pursue mysteriousness, as well as Confucians who reject mysteriousness and yet cannot prevent the people from believing in it, according to Liu Yuan, are missing the true meaning of the classics.

Heaven's virtue is invisible but it is not elusive; it spontaneously reveals itself in the fine details. When human emotions do not go astray and properness leads to rediscovering True Nature inside, then the mysterious is not a mystery and the physical is no longer dead material. The fine details of heaven's virtue can be experienced within human relations, at the moment when one person cares for another, each relationship with its proper measure. These fine details cannot be felt if one assumes a posture of caring for everyone all the time in an artificial manner, but rather it can be felt when the proper measure has arrived. Loving, respecting, being loyal and friendly, sincere and earnest, here the principle exists!

The Long Arduous Way of Learning the Simple Things

Liu Yuan

劉沅

Translated by
Yaron Seidman
and Vita Revelli

©2016 Hunyuan Research Institute
www.hunyuaninstitute.com

"The Long Arduous Way of Learning the Simple Things"[82] Preface

Dao[83] is just like a path, it contains only this one meaning. Heaven, Earth, human beings and spirits all have it and therefore it is called Dao.

The difference between human beings and other creatures is minute, it is 'Heaven's Nature'.[84] Nothing else! When one embodies this fully then one is a human being, but if not then one is something else. Those who preserve this minute difference are sages. Thus, sages are those who embody this thing that make people humans and that is it!

Confucius says: "A human being is the heart of Heaven and Earth, accomplishment derived through difficulties or perseverance is one and the same."

Mencius says: "All people can become like Yao or Shun[85]. There was never a time when Dao meant selecting individuals". Thus, Virtue of

---

[82] 梯航 Ti Hang is short for 梯山航海 Ti Shan Hang Hai, Scale Mountains and cross seas, meaning a long and arduous path.

下学 Xia Xue comes from the analects chapter 14 論語・憲問第十四: 子曰：不怨天，不尤人。下學而上達，知我者其天乎！ *The master said: resent heaven not and fault man not. Learn the simple things close to you and [like this] reach the higher realm, [like this] know in thyself how it resembles heaven!*

[83] The word Dao means a road and here road and path are synonyms.

[84] 天理 Tian Li also translates as Heaven's Principle, however the English word 'principle' loses some of the meaning here of 'the true quality behind heaven'.

[85] Yao (c. 2200 BC), one of Five legendary Emperors, second son of Di Ku.
Shun (c. 22nd century BC), mythical sage and leader.

sages is also the constant affair of any living person. For example, the old fisherman of the Pan stream or the brick-worker building a wall, even though they are simpletons, how are they not sages and saints? Earlier people mistook the instruction of great virtue, it caused people to not dare to become sages, they only felt content when they made themselves as fools.

Now, a sage is a person who has reached far with human relations. All people, during their life, cannot escape the five kinships. How could it be that a sage will learn to strengthen the human ties without a teacher?[86]

Today, to be sagely is high and lofty, in every measure it is modernized, it is viewed as esteemed under heaven, it is ultimately portrayed not like a regular person. Because of this, one is afraid to self-cultivate and is content with having no progress, like this many of these who speak of a "sage" miss the mark by thinking that it is too far and lofty.

They do not know that there is no difference between a sage and an ordinary person, except that the former steadily acts in accord with the Dao of "The Doctrine of the Mean."[87]

The Dao of "The Doctrine of the Mean" is very ordinary, but it is also extraordinary, and since its extraordinary aspect reveals itself within the ordinary, its title is "The Common Center".

---

86 Criticism to those who believe that a sage received his transmission from heaven and not from a human teacher.

87 中庸 *Doctrine of the Mean* is the title of a Confucian work but it also means the common center, the proper measure for every simple affair happening daily.

I am already an old man and it is difficult for me to answer to all the people who, indeed, come to the house asking for guidance. I have no other alternative, but to instruct my sons Song Wen, Yi Wen, etc. to jot down my humble viewpoint and pass it on to those who come asking for instructions.

The explanations transmitted are in one family and the viewpoint of a man declining in years. I am reluctant to somehow replace the words of the Master with those of a grass and firewood gatherer. Knowing the intention and forgiving the mistakes then it is very fortunate indeed.

Written by Liu Yuan, aged 83, in Shuangliu County, on the 9th day of the 9th lunar month of the Geng Xu year, the 30th year of Dao Guang reign.

The Long Arduous Way of Learning the Simple Things: Heaven Nature Heart Goodness

Heaven has a certain nature and when human beings attain it, it becomes heart Goodness. It is also called the directive of heaven is 'true nature'.

The term '[human] true nature' xing 性 comprises the particles '忄 xin, heart' and '生 sheng, life', and it indicates that human beings attain the proper Heart of Heaven. Heaven's Nature is Heaven's Heart, it is Tai Ji and sincerity. When a person attains this nature it is then 'true nature'.

Although all the myriad things come from Heaven, amongst them, only humans are endowed with the fairness and honesty that pertain to Heaven Nature, which is for this reason called Virtue. Before birth,[88] and since one attains all aspects of heaven, it is called bright virtue.

However, after coming into the world, the seven emotions create disturbances and sensual desires bring confusion that it becomes increasingly impossible to recover the natural state of attaining center. Recovering true nature and fulfilling what one has been given, likewise, is called virtue.[89] The root of heaven and earth endless creation, when applied to human beings, is the source of the

---

[88] Pre-Heaven, xian tian 先天.

[89] Bright virtue is the pure state before birth, the complete embodiment of heaven. After birth, recovering the pure state is called virtue.

myriad principles, just like a fruit that has a kernel and therefore it is called 'ren 仁 benevolence'.[90]

A sincere person has this Principle and then truly is a human being. Dao is like a wide path common to all people, thus all people are endowed with Heaven Nature Heart Goodness.

The sage ultimately fulfills these four words and successfully connects to Heaven and, by upholding these four words as foundation for all actions, merges with Heaven Nature.

At the same time, being worried about excesses and lacks, he creates rules and rituals called 'rites'. With no excesses or lacks, actions reach their proper measure and it is then called 'righteousness'. Wisdom means to know the truth and trust means to always act with sincerity. This is why the five Confucian virtues[91] are simply about these four words: Heaven's Nature Heart Goodness.

Everybody knows Heaven's Nature Heart Goodness, but none can put it into practice. Does it mean that they do not have Goodness?

When the father's and teacher's instruction is not proper then the eyes and ears acquire bad habits that trick them.

Below, I will talk briefly about the meaning of the life-giving Heaven Nature.

---

[90] rén 仁 has double meaning Kernel and Benevolence.

[91] Benevolence (rén 仁), righteousness (yì 义), rite (lǐ 礼), knowledge (zhì 智), trust (xìn 信)

Preserving Stillness

When the heart floats to the surface, help it sink and, when it shows at the exterior, help it submerge. These two words 'sink' and 'submerge' are the two methods for withdrawing the heart. *The Doctrine of the Mean* says: "Even though [the fish] submerges and hides at the bottom, it is still seen clearly".[92]

The place where the nobleman cannot be paralleled is a place that others cannot see. How can people be casual with this secret they are unable to see? When one purifies whatever is concealed in the most secret recesses of the heart, then true knowledge arrives and thereafter there is stability.[93]

Confucius called it 'benevolence' and Mencius called it 'nurturing Qi'. [The practice of] 'preserving heart and nurturing true nature' embodies the meanings of *The Great Learning's* 'reaching ultimate goodness' and the *Doctrine of the Mean's* 'attaining center'.

Stillness is the seed of movement and, indeed, to be still is the prerequisite for knowing the movement [of the heart] and like this 'attaining center' can reach harmony. Otherwise, [the heart's]

---

[92] The Doctrine of the Mean cites the book of poetry 潛雖伏矣, 亦孔之昭！故君子內省不疚, 無惡於志,君子所不可及者, 其唯人之所不見乎！ 'Even though [the fish] submerges and hides at the bottom, it is still seen clearly!' The nobleman tirelessly self-inspects and therefore has no repulsiveness in his mind. The place where the nobleman cannot be paralleled is a place that others cannot see.

[93] The Great Learning says: true knowledge arrives and thereafter there is stability 知止而后有定. True knowledge means to know heaven inside one's heart whereas stability means to be able to recognize and maintain heaven in the heart in the midst of heart movements and thoughts.

coming and going is unanticipated and unable to know its heimat. Like this when one lets go of the heart[94] one does not know, and when trying to control it, one is unable to restrain it.

The Book of Changes says: "Pass to and fro with hesitation, the thoughts coming are many". Without exception, the 'post-Heaven heart' of everybody is like this. In order to preserve the mindful heart, one must nurture the 'true nature', which resides in stillness. It is unlike only nurturing the thinking heart. I humbly repeat myself.

---

94 Calm the desires.

Observing Movement

The heart cannot be seen, [however,] when it moves it appears through one's words and actions, and then right and wrong exist. What is proper is beautiful, but what is not proper is called 'repulsive'. When the 'repulsive' appears on the outside then its repulsiveness is easy to recognize, but when the 'repulsive' remains hidden within one's heart, then its repulsiveness is more severe.

Therefore, if one cherishes Virtue, one must first correct evil thoughts. One should enhance and promote proper thoughts, but restrain repulsive ones right at their onset. If one recognizes its onset and can restrain it right at this time and prohibit it from causing one's own demise then in *The Great Learning* it is called *Sincere Intention*.

Naturally, if one, right at the onset, does not know what is right and what is wrong, how could one then have sincere intention? Master Zhu Xi supplemented [and amended] the idea behind Sorting Things, and especially emphasized the [external] things as vast and limitless.

This was not the sage's original intent. Confucius said: "Those who do not understand goodness cannot make their Self sincere." Indeed, those who wish to make their intention sincere, should, first of all, know how to obtain this knowledge.

Below I shall explain the Dao to obtain knowledge.

Teacher's Instruction

The two paragraphs above, speaking of preserving stillness and inspecting movement, were likewise mentioned and practiced by earlier Confucians. It is a pity that the stillness they talked about only referred to the conscious heart. They did not realize that the sages purified the heart and indulged in its inner refined truth.

When the earlier Confucians observed movement they researched the material world's nature, ignoring that the knowledge of [heaven's] nature is gained only through the heart's 'True Nature' and 'Five Kinships'. As material things under Heaven are immeasurable, how can one come to the point of knowing all the affairs?

The sage uses a single unity that pervades all things. Inside he nurtures the heart to complete ripeness where every single thought embodies Heaven Nature. This is called 'benevolence'. Outside, his observation conforms to [Heaven] Nature so much so that every affair becomes proper and then it is called 'righteousness'.

Benevolence matures first and then righteousness becomes refined. 'Refined righteousness' must come from 'matured benevolence'. To 'nurture the vast Qi' comes from correcting one's Self until this gradually transforms into spirit. Without the teachings of an enlightened teacher and without eternal sincerity, this does not come about.

A person of wisdom knows [heaven's] nature and then he practices this accomplishment. A person who is clear about goodness is basically clear about this one point. This is all there is to it.

It is important to understand that even a single improper thought could lead to one hundred wrongs. Thus, one should eradicate every single evil and distracting thought; one must also realize that a single improper action may lead to a disharmonious moral character, and therefore, benevolence, respect, filial piety and parental compassion must be practiced daily.

Every single person is endowed with Heavenly Goodness. However, when it comes to a person being 'evil' at present, it has started with a single faulty thought and a single lost affair.

Now, if one did not have a virtuous parent or teacher, who could provide them with a positive example, impart instruction, and give them training, they then got used to it and made it their life habit.

For this reason, the art of preserving stillness and observing movement reaches real accomplishment when there is an enlightened teacher who imparts instruction. Then right and wrong, achievements and failures, impressions and positive influences are easily understood.

Moreover, the 'Four Books'[95] and the 'Six Classics'[96] have already illuminated the human realm. The sages' scope imparted bright instruction and so one appreciates it until it ripens, practices it with vigor. How could one not enter Virtue?

In order to widen one's horizons and prudently make a good circle of relationships, it is imperative to expand one's knowledge and, most importantly, make a fine distinction between the two words

---

[95] 'Great Learning' (Dàxué, 大學), 'Doctrine of the Mean' (Zhōngyōng, 中庸), 'Analects of Confucius' (Lúnyǔ, 論語), Mencius (Mèngzǐ, 孟子).

[96] "Book of Songs (Shījīng, 詩經), 'Book of History' (Shàngshū, 尚書), 'Book of Rites' (Yílǐ, 儀禮), the lost 'Book of Music' (Yuèjīng, 樂經), 'Book of Changes' (Yìjīng, 易經), 'Spring and Autumn Annals' (Chūnqiū, 春秋)

'good' and 'evil'. "To see goodness and emulate it, to see evilness, and examine one's own inner world," and "three men walking, my teacher must be amongst them" are two guidelines by Confucius that, if practiced, make attaining [true] knowledge easy.

Other than that, in regards to all ancient teachings of the 'Hundred Schools', one should adopt what is beneficial to heart, true nature and the Five Human kinships, and discard the rest.

Confucius, therefore, discussed learning, investigating, pondering and differentiating,[97] he talked about those who have or do not have these four. Attaining [true] knowledge is limited to these four and it does not revolve around teaching people about every single thing that exists under heaven.

For what reason, then, should one choose the complicated over the easy?

---

[97] 中庸 Doctrine of the Mean "Study extensively, investigate cautiously, ponder carefully, differentiate clearly, act earnestly 博学之，审问之，慎思之，明辨之，笃行之"

On Correcting Errors

Is there a person with no errors? [No!] Nonetheless, when one is at ease and accommodates it or feels ashamed and hides it, then the [initial] error thereupon becomes evil.

If an error was caused unintentionally and one corrects it, then this does not count as an error. This concept does not require any discussion. In addition, even when there is an intention to do evil, but suddenly the person awakens to reality, abruptly and quickly faults oneself and resolutely does not repeat this offense and, more so, over an extended period of time accumulates goodness, then, in turn, this clears up all murkiness.

The average person is afraid that their error may be discovered by others and therefore they dread correcting it. They do not understand that a sage becomes a sage simply by correcting oneself daily.

Even Confucius started avoiding errors only after age fifty when he studied the "Yi Jing", so why not ordinary people?

Cheng Tang[98] "the faults of the people are my fault" and king Wu of Zhou[99] "the masses mistake is my mistake" took upon themselves the blame for the faults of the people living in their kingdom. Can one then avoid taking fault with their own error? If one does not correct their own errors then in no way can they learn the foundations of the sage.

Beware! Beware!

---

[98] Also named Shang Tang (1646-1588 BC), was the legendary founder of the Shang Dynasty

[99] King Wu of Zhou (-1043) was the first king of the Western Zhou dynasty, 1046-1043BC.

On Earnest Behavior

Confucius had suggested that through the 'three aspects of moral conduct'[100] one reaches Virtue and that by practicing the Five Human Relationships[101] one can attain Dao. The way of erudition should be that of learning, enquiring, contemplating, differentiating, and carrying it out earnestly. In order to reach knowledge one learns, enquires, contemplates and differentiates, whereas 'carrying it out earnestly' means its earnest practice. Confucius also added that there are some things that cannot be researched owing to the fact they are many and one cannot grasp their original root; the only obligation is that one practices the Five Relationships daily. Eagerness with regards to the Five Human Relationships is a non-optional effort.

The word 'earnest' includes the meaning of 'resoluteness' and 'firmness'. Zengzi[102] said: "A scholar cannot be anything else, but resolute and firm." A scholar's duty is substantial and their Dao is far. Substantial means [that they must adhere to] righteousness whereas Dao being far means [they must pursue it till] death. Laymen look at it as impractical. They do not understand that benevolence means Heaven Nature, and that without Heaven Nature a person is not a human. Could it be that those who reject benevolence do not wish to be humans? Nonetheless, the skill of benevolence cannot be accomplished in a short period of time, and it cannot be let go even for a brief moment and therefore one must

---

[100] Knowledge (zhī 知), benevolence (rén, 仁), and courage (yǒng 勇)

[101] King-subject, father-son, husband-wife, elder brother-younger brother, friends

[102] Zengzi (505-435 BC) was a student of Confucius. He is the presumed author of the Confucian classic 'The Great Learning' (Dàxué, 大學).

be resolute and firm. Resolute and firm is the definition of being earnest.

For any person the enjoyment of life is being satisfied by dwelling, clothes, food and men and women[103]. The sage, likewise, is not excluded from these needs. However, he uses Heaven Nature to regulate emotions, curb his desires and refuses to give himself in to lust. Over time, this then becomes the regulatory force of his life, which leads him to take care of what is above him by looking after the temple of the ancestors and of what is below him by teaching the next generation of children and grand-children. He does not betray the notion that heaven and earth, monarch and parents give and create our lives. Inside, he preserves [heart] and nurtures [true nature] while discarding the common view of heaven being distant. Outwardly, he observes his own actions, corrects the errors and advances goodness, until the day of his death. This is when Virtue comes about and one's name becomes known.

Reaching this [virtue] were Yi and Zhou,[104] where exhausting this principle were Confucius and Mencius, personas indispensable for this world. If, however, one does not treasure his own self and instead gives in to desires and only on the outside seems to behave with propriety and dignity, then the powerful and rich can only feed their physical skeleton, the poor even more so become like vegetation.

Mencius said: "How sorrowful it is to abandon the proper path and have nowhere to follow, to let go of the heart and not seek it back". Indeed, one must know the cause of this sorrow!

---

[103] Sexual relations.
[104] Yi Yin 伊尹 and Duke of Zhou 周公.

Life needs are not more than dwelling, food and man and woman. Benevolent sages and virtuous men, heaven must bring blessing upon them. How could anyone die from hunger, cold and suffering? The filial piety that made Boyi and Shuqi[105] die of hunger, by sacrificing their lives[106], implies both benevolence and righteousness.

Completed and received it, completed and returned to it.[107] They had the same good fortune as heaven and earth, sun and moon, it was not a terrible misfortune. However, such an unfortunate

---

[105] Boyi and Shuqi were the sons of Yawei, the lord of the state of Guzhu, a vassal state of the Shang Dynasty.

[106] When the ruler of the Shang, father of the two young men died, the succession to the throne was given to Shuqi, the youngest son, rather than to Boyi, the eldest one, as tradition dictated. Rather than entering into conflict with each other, the two brothers left the state, moving to the Zhou territories. However when, after king Wen, the ruler of the Zhou - who had become their protector - died, his son, Wu immediately took up arms against the Shang. The two brothers tried to dissuade him from carrying on these actions, appealing to the duty of filial piety. According to it, in fact, Wu should have waited for the customary mourning time to elapse before engaging in warfare. Although Wu was offended by their remarks, they were spared from sure death thanks to the fact that their criticism was rooted in high moral standards. However, the war continued and the Shang were defeated. In sign of protest, Boyi and Shuqi started a hunger strike and then moved to the woods of Shouyang Mountain (now, Xianxi province), where they lived for sometime. After being told that whatever they ate in the mountains also belonged to the Zhou, they died of starvation. They are an example of faithfulness to filial piety, even if this meant losing their life.

[107] *Book of rites: When father and mother are complete they give birth to [the son], when the son is complete he returns to [his parents], this can be called filial piety. When one does not lack in his body or humiliate himself then this can be called complete.* 禮記祭義：父母全而生之，子全而歸之，可謂孝矣。不虧其體，不辱其身，可謂全矣。 This line speaks of Bo Yi and Shu Qi being filial sons, sacrificing their lives in order to not humiliate their parents.

encounter, how could it be the fate of benevolent sages? If one does not understand the meaning here and instead chaotically causes gossip, then he might say that goodness has no benefit.

Differentiate it! Be careful!

In the five sections above, I have emphasized exhaustively the most crucial points and yet it is still quite difficult to explain this one issue of 'attaining knowledge'.

In the "Four Books" and "Six Classics" the meaning is refined and the texts are many. Transmitted through history are numerous books, complex and hard to differentiate.

Finally, I jot down annotation known to all. One should not regard it as shallow; 'follow what is true and resist what is false and like this enter Virtue!'

The four-fold discourse of Confucius

If Not Proper Do Not Look at It

The heart's spirit is completed by the eyes. What the eyes see makes the heart discharge. If [what the eyes see] is proper then [the heart's spirit] becomes Heaven Nature and if not proper then [heart's spirit becomes] like a beast. Sexual lust easily leads young people to evil. What is beautiful one should look at as their own younger and older sister. What is evil one should look at as jackals and tigers. This is the first achievement in seeking the lost heart.

If Not Proper Do Not Listen to It

The ears connect to the ocean of true nature. [Words] entering the ear can bring chaos in the heart and then evil and stray thoughts come about. This requires no further explanation. From the son of heaven to the common people, there are many who misunderstand this principle and therefore listen to false words, slander and evil conduct and therefrom bring upon misfortune. Therefore sever it! Forbid it!

If Not Proper Do Not Say It

Words express the depth of one's heart. The Five Relationships, that extend everywhere, must come from a place of kindness, friendship, and thoughtfulness. When vigorously practicing uprightness and benevolence, how is it possible not to rely on words to facilitate flow and harmony? Be it explaining Dao and Virtue, narrating the sage's teachings, or when settling a dispute, one needs a great number of words. However, day to day, one ought to self-cultivate first in order to illuminate the meaning of Heaven Nature, as only then it becomes possible to speak of the true underlying meaning of things.

An ordinary person speaks at random not knowing how to look within and restrain themselves. Not only those who speak lies and make vicious remarks, or harm moral behavior, are not worth looking at, but also those who craftily assume responsibility, if they too do not pay careful attention to their words and actions, may end up shaming themselves.

This is why Confucius taught over and over again to be prudent with speech. Generally speaking, fewer words are better than many, and silence is better than chat. Speaking with the wrong person, speaking not proper words and speaking without self-restraint are all errors.

If Not Proper Do Not Do It

Movement is both internal and external.[108] External movement alternates between movement and stillness and it must conform to [Heaven] Nature. Internal movement speaks of wrongful thoughts that must be eradicated at the root. That is it!

---

[108] External movement means actions that one takes, internal movement speaks of thoughts surfacing in one's heart.

About the four-fold discourse of Confucius

Preserve heart full of goodness, take actions full of goodness, speak only good words and make only good friends.

What is in one's heart can be seen in one's actions and words. And so one must first preserve their heart and be cautious about it and at the same time apply the skill of movement and stillness mentioned above. To have good words one must follow the sage's words as a teacher, to make good friends one selects in a discerning way, one completes [the rules of kinship] and selects. This [principle of being taught by] parent and teacher and selecting friends are within the [Analects] chapter [7] *Three men walking*.[109]

---

[109] In this chapter Confucius explains that when three people are together some think, say and act good things and one should learn from them, while others think, say and act evil things and one should also learn from them, what not to do. In Conclusion, Confucius says, *when three men are walking/acting my teacher must be amongst them.*

Yu Cheng Tang[110] Family Precepts

Liu Yuan

劉沅

Translated by
Yaron Seidman

©2016 Hunyuan Research Institute
www.hunyuaninstitute.com

乃為誠意養心養氣小效無可述年戒己成人功夫
全在大學道須深造功在返求在上不正其趨人十
從何而出倫常本於心性故曰一以貫之學業鶩於
浮華所以萬事墮矣戒之勉之庶乎不替祖訓

戊午歲穀雨後五日
華陽顏楷敬書

---

[110] Yu Cheng Tang 豫誠堂 Joy and Sincerity Residence is the name Liu Yuan adopted for his residence.

Heaven Nature Heart Goodness is what makes a person human. Being generous and kind is the reason heaven and earth last for eternity. Obscuring goodness and going against [heaven] nature then one is not human.

How can one conform to heaven while being impatient and ungenerous?

When one attains heaven nature he then becomes human, therefore heaven and earth are like one's father and mother. My father and mother gave me my body, therefore my father and mother are like heaven and earth.

Deceiving one's physical parents is easy; however, deceiving the parent's above one's head is difficult.

Even a single thought deceiving heaven makes one not filial. Even a single thought deceiving one's parents becomes an offense against heaven.

To cultivate Dao is an imperial decree toward one's parents; respecting one's father and mother like heaven and earth, fulfilling one's true nature like an envoy and serving heaven and earth just like serving one's father and mother.

Filial piety comes from cultivating virtue, while virtue comes from cultivating one's heart. Transforming [a child's] filial piety into a faithful [official] reaches the objective of not deceiving and not being reckless.

Preserving stillness, one can begin [properly] inspecting movement. One must not be lazy or forget about this practice. When one offends with licentiousness he becomes like a beast and when he desires power and profit he changes into a mean and despicable person.

To take good care of one's health and perform good deeds is the meaning of keeping oneself flawless and sincere.

To know what is wrong and constantly correct one's own errors is the path for aspiring to the sage and virtuous.

Life is [short], like a dream, where cultivating goodness and doing good deeds receives blessings [and is the only meaningful thing].

This Dao [of learning how to become human] is hard to learn and therefore one must follow his parent's and teacher's instruction.

When one carries shame in his heart how can he set an example at home as a husband or a father? When one takes an action being insincere how can he be a [loyal] minister or a [filial] son?

To govern the country there is no need for many methods other than thoroughly nurturing and teaching. Where could there be difficulty in learning the sages' [teachings]? One only needs the Dao of forgiveness. When one is diligent with his profession and cultivates his heart how could he suffer hunger and cold? [In contrast,] when one has greed and lust it will harm his heart and life.

Between brothers, the principle should be giving way to each other, while bringing the household in order, [harmony between] husband and wife comes first.

Having enough to eat, clothes to wear and avoiding disasters is the definition of a carefree life.

When one is gentle and kindhearted, respectful and modest then everyone and everything he deals with [prospers like the] spring wind.

With regards to reading, one must read virtuous books and with affairs one must act [according to] Confucius and Mencius; to be human one must become a good person, and must revere the spirit in heaven [restraining himself from doing any evil].

[Hoping] to accomplish good for one's children and grandchildren, accumulating virtue [and leading by example] by far surpasses accumulating money. When one often cheats and swindles, this only hurts himself, how could it hurt others?

Prior generations had many aphorisms but the crux lies with us putting it into practice.

Where does such sagely [outstanding] achievement come from? One must first make his heart proper [and remove selfish desires]. After removing selfish desires one then truly becomes smart. Thus reaching knowledge is preceded by sorting one's heart. When thoughts are good then right and wrong are distinguished clearly, one's [daily] practice is that of a sincere intention [and pure conscience].

To nurture's one's heart and make one's energy proper, at a minimum, can prolong one's longevity.

The skill of making oneself proper and then helping others to become proper is entirely within the lines of The Great Learning. This Dao must be pursued endlessly, while its skill comes from constantly reflecting on oneself. If above one does not properly lead by example then wherefrom would [future generation's] talent come?

[Various] human relations stem from one's heart and true nature and therefore they are [collectively] described as 'one principle penetrates all'.

When the study [of this skill] is flashy and without substance then all the affairs deteriorate!

[The bad things] avoid it!

[The good things] make an effort to do it!

In sum, do not substitute the ancestors' teaching!

Learning the Sages' Capacity for Forgiveness

Liu Yuan

劉沅

Translated by
Yaron Seidman

©2016 Hunyuan Research Institute
www.hunyuaninstitute.com

1. A Great Compassionate Heart

Feeling compassion for others is benevolence; benevolence is the human heart. It is Heaven Nature Heart Goodness.

People must first have benevolence and only then can they think [proper] thoughts and handle affairs [with properness]. Only then are they worried about not knowing a person's good and evil and, with each of their words and actions, they are concerned about forgoing others.

As for the human relations, which naturally include loyalty, filial piety, friendship and brotherly love and exclude deception, laziness and recklessness, there is no extra explanation needed!

The benevolent one, who is then called compassionate, begins initially with one thought and then with all his thoughts, begins with one affair and then with all his affairs. [This progression] should be incorporated in the intolerant heart, resulting with inflicting no harm upon insects and vegetation. Fulfilling one's true nature in order to fulfil human nature and the nature of all things assists the creation of life. This is the root for everything.

2. A Great Vast Heart

Vast refers to selflessness. The ancients said: "when one is selfless he is having good fortune." But, when selfish, one's heart harbors narrow mindedness; he sees true principle and yet he cannot understand it. One's temperament is agitated and his knowledge is limited to [what benefits] himself. One does not know that there are others, he thinks only about profiting himself without worrying about harming others. One is self-assured and does not utilize goodness, self-centered and does not forgive people, selfish and is not tolerant of others.

For one to be selfless, he must all day reflect back and criticize himself. With every word and action he is worried about departing from [Heaven] Nature, worried about hurting others. One examines himself every single moment.

Even though other people may be angry with me, scold me and treat me unfairly, I will not pay attention. I will rest at home reflecting and asking myself, asking my heart: was shame introduced? Did I add an unjust action?

All those [wrong actions done toward me] I completely ignore. With those other important human relation of monarch and father [and mother] to brothers and friends, submitting to an insult without retaliation, this requires no further explanation!

3. A Great Heart at Ease

What does 'at ease' mean? It means being flexible with [handling] affairs and courageous with acting properly.

Humans get along with each other and co-habit this world, they mutually interact and welcome each other and this falls under the five kinships.

Within the five kinships there are variations [such as] great and small [compassion], superior and inferior [position], intimate and remote [relations] and [the capacity to be] virtuous or not.

For example, one serves the monarch and father and mother with only utmost and wholehearted respect. When monarch and parents are virtuous, one can mirror their virtue. When monarch and parents are not virtuous, one remonstrates and is able to correct the wrong. One carries it out in a thoughtful and thorough fashion causing the monarch and parents to become sagely. This is the undertaking of being loyal and filial. There is no difference between ancient and modern times. It is the duty of the minister and the son. When one lacks this skill and then serves the monarch and parents in a thorough way it cannot be described as 'at ease'.

Other than that, siblings and friends, amongst which kinship may be close or far, some being virtuous and some not, one cannot view them indifferently as equals.

Serving an older brother, loving a younger or trusting a friend, one first cultivates his own Dao and then loves the other, respects him and does not deceive him. Being like this for a long time without compromise, ignoring if he says that I am right or wrong, I rest only when I fulfil his heart and his Dao.

I seek a shame-free heart. If person A has an affair, as long as it is not contrary to [Heaven] Nature, my true heart will do the labor for him. Using my whole heart I will help his winding road turn a good affair. This is the Dao of 'at ease'.

However, affairs have difficult and easy, circumstances have good and bad, situations change constantly and, even though we say 'at ease', one should deliberate the reason and common sense of [handling] the phenomena. One cannot act upon all situations indifferently. For example, for saving a person who has fallen into a well, one should not jeopardize his own life or humiliate his own parents. Therefore the ancients said: "If one is able to do it one should exhaust his ability. If one's ability cannot do it, then one should still use his heart thoroughly [and help the best one can]." These words describe a relationship between affairs and [Heaven] Nature.

When one cultivates virtue in a modest self all day, in each word and action, each step and pace and despite difficult affairs being many, his self feels at ease; his accomplishment is genuine and easy to practice.

As long as one pays attention, not being lazy or reckless, then he can feel at ease in all situations. For example, when he walks on the street and sees a rock or tree obstructing the road, he will remove it [effortlessly] as he is worried it will obstruct others. Other hardships like hunger, cold etc. he is concerned that others will suffer them.

Having enough to eat, being warm, safe and other such positive realities, he is concerned that others will have enough of these necessities. At any time and in every place he feels at ease. This word 'at ease' encompasses the two words 'benevolence and righteousness'.

4. A Great Purified [of illusion] Heart

What does 'purified' mean?

One sees money and desires it not, sees sexuality and loves it not. In thoughts or affairs one does not follow his desires or contradict [Heaven] Nature. He is law abiding and diligent in his profession, cultivates his heart, contemplates human life in every step [and understands] that it is all part of his destiny. 'Heaven loves man' is reflected in [the concept] Heaven Nature Heart Goodness. With each of my thoughts I never depart from Heaven Nature Heart Goodness.

Regardless if it is for morality reasons or simply being proper, I elect one [course of action] that conforms to Heaven Nature with every affair. For example, if I work as a merchant, I focus on learning this art, being diligent without slacking, industrious but not excessive, honest and not greedy. I focus without scattering and carefully examine each thought, not losing even a tiny bit of heaven goodness.

Like this, no matter what the situation is, I can make a living and pass my days [with dignity]. It becomes a habit to rely on heaven for my actions.

The human heart goes astray endlessly, one cannot conduct himself unrestrained and unchecked. As long as one does not suffer hunger or cold and he is able to provide for his family, as long as he more or less has enough, then it is a beautiful realm.

As for wealthy and famous people, who also accumulate goodness and virtue, those that heaven has blessed with riches and good fortunes, I do not possess their accumulations, how can my thoughts go astray as if I were them? Sure enough, intentionally I retreat my interest from wealth and glory. I constantly eradicate stray thoughts, and so over time it becomes the rule. Then no matter if I am poor or in difficulty, with a calm heart I keep on going. Only like this can an ordinary person curb selfishness. This is how one makes oneself study the method of purification.

When an educated and enlightened person is able to preserve his heart and nurture his true nature, step with benevolence and pace with properness, be kind to everyone under all circumstances, then after a while whatever vulgarity he had naturally disappears, external [heart] movements [naturally] follow propriety, and, after some time, the feeling of good and bad completely vanish.

Therefore, one must preserve stillness and inspect movement. From beginning to end and from root to branches, this is the needed skill.

The sage is not [acting or thinking] for Dao or righteousness. Instead, he does not think of taking a penny for himself unrightfully so. He does not look at high salary or [an offer] of a thousand chariots [and bend his ways]. This is his Dao. The two words 'pure heart' represent, at the highest level, aspiration to the sage and virtuous men, next to that – it represents guarding one's actions and conducting oneself with restraint, next to that – it speaks of heart emotions being like water, they adapt naturally to any circumstance. In humans, [heart] could be like this naturally, but it becomes like this only with effort.

5. The Great Gentle Harmonious Heart

Harmonious speaks of a kind friendship extending everywhere. Its noble aspect is the cultivation of joy, anger, sorrow and happiness all being regulated by center; it is reaching Dao of all under heaven. Acting equally upon all generations and all people is the profoundness of heaven and earth. Only a sage reaches the ultimate of this 'harmony'.

Next to that, one speaks of the five kinships, each with its Dao and proper place. Kindness is present and friendship prevalent, ties of friendship are not deviated from and this is harmony's vital importance that one cannot do without. It is what a person should explore to the fullest extent.

Next to that, having no tolerance means no benevolence and having no courage means no righteousness. One is careful and cautious; he evens his heart and calms his Qi and only worries about not hurting others, spoiling an affair or causing a disaster.

One is modest and compromising, and when there is an affair of great unfairness or something that he cannot tolerate, someone who is really hated or offensive, then he passes by in silence. If at home there is great competitiveness or anxiety, with great vigor he softens it and calms it down, and therefore it is called gentle and harmonious. It is said [in the Doctrine of the Mean] "generous and soft is used for teaching, not seeking repercussion for non-Dao, the nobleman resides in this realm."

If not this meaning then the word gentle has negative connotations such as being lacking in goodness, being weak etc. How could this be the real meaning? Whenever a person cannot endure humiliation or tolerate rejection it is because his blood and Qi are stiff and unyielding and his emotions are agitated and explosive.

Therefore he must soften his Qi in order to follow true principle, make his emotions harmonious in order to become compatible to others, only then can kinship and friendship extend everywhere, the actions then may be without disaster.

Liu Yuan's Life Story

Translated by
Yaron Seidman

©2016 Hunyuan Research Institute
www.hunyuaninstitute.com

Main compiler: Lü Xiaolong 吕笑龙

Arrangement: Shuang Liu County Social Sciences Federation 双流县社会科学界联合会

Shuang Liu Traditional Culture Association 双流传统文化研习会

Translation: Yaron Seidman 孟亚伦

Liu Yuan's Life Story is extracted from *Huai Xuan Summary: The Master from Western Sichuan Liu Yuan and the Huai Xuan Doctrine* 槐轩概述：川西夫子刘沅与槐轩学说

Part 1: The move to Sichuan at the end of Ming and living in Shuangliu for generations

Liu Yuan (1768-1855 C.E.), courtesy name Zhi Tang, another courtesy name Ne Ru, art name the Scholar of Qing Yang and the scholar of Bi Xia was born at the 33rd year of Qing dynasty Qian Long era (1768), a person of Sichuan province, Shuangliu township village of Yun Xi Li (today belongs to Peng Zhen township, Yang Ping village). His ancestors lived in Hubei's Ma Cheng district village of Xiao Gan. As the end of Ming dynasty fell into chaos, the ancestor Liu Chaobi (courtesy name Feichen) during the eras of Zheng De and Jia Jing, moved his entire family to Sichuan in order to escape the chaos. He settled down at the southern bank of the Min River in Sichuan's Mei Zhou. The sixth generation ancestor Liu Yuzhou (courtesy name Jiaoyun) was a military officer of the Ming and was elevated to the rank of a general. When Ming perished he kept his allegiance and retired from public life to live in seclusion. The great-great-grandfather Liu Kun (courtesy name Houyan) lived in Ma Yi mountain around Ba Zhang Zhou of Sichuan's Mei Zhou, he was a professional teacher teaching the five classics. At the end of Ming, and because of the war chaos, he first found shelter at E Mei and then sojourned in Wen Jiang county Dong Guan township Dong village. Sometime thereafter, since his family grew in numbers, he moved to Shuangliu county Yun Xi Li village and until today a part of the Liu Family clan still lives there.

Liu Yuan's great-grandfather Liu Jiazhen (courtesy name Yuhan) was weak and sickly at his earlier years. He indulged in classical literature, loved to read the two Han dynasty histories and was adept in calligraphy.

His grandfather Liu Handing (courtesy name Junmo) had outstanding moral integrity and was keen on learning the book of changes. He authored a book titled *Expounding on the content of the book of changes Yi Yun Fa Ming*. He often taught his family "be frugal with oneself and help the accomplishment of others, conceal your own talent and be diligent with virtue."

His father Liu Ruqin (courtesy name Jingwu) followed his family's teaching since a young age and penetrated deep the principle behind human true nature and heaven principle. He was proficient in the book of changes and at his prime joined the army to follow Yue Zhongqi through the Min River and Bo Mountain and participated in the great battle of Jin Quan specifically dealing with army rations. Thereafter he returned to his hometown and lived a secluded life. He instructed students and then set up a school in order to teach kids. Liu Ruqin loved to learn books and was charitable; an eminent person in his township. Still extant from his writings are one poem and commentary on the *Revered Classic of the Jade Emperor Yu Huang Zun Jing*, 3 scrolls and commentary on the *Treasure of Repenting of the Jade Emperor Yu Huang Bao Chan* 1 scroll.

The great scholar and writer of the Qing dynasty Ji Yun (courtesy name Xiao Lan, a successful candidate of the highest imperial examination during the Qian Long era, served simultaneously as the minister of rites and minister of state) himself wrote *Epitaph on the Memorial Tablet of the Honorable Jingwu*[111], here extracted: "Assistant of heaven in the highest illustrious virtue, an auspicious legendary bird spreading its wings, loyal and filial maintained his family, unparalleled in his generation, strongly fragrant distinguished and sincere, was able to predict the myriad things, with clarity repaid with kindness, an eternal virtuous person, it is my testimony here on the stone tablet."

The teacher of the Qing dynasty Jia Qing emperor Zhu Gui himself wrote in *Eulogy of the Honorable Jingwu*: "What easily decays is the physical body, what is not worn out is the spirit. More so, if one is not only reliant on the body to live then his body and spirit both will enjoy longevity. As for the life of Jingwu, his filial piety was the like of an auspicious sight, his righteousness was like the kingdom of Lu during the Zhou dynasty, he relinquished old grievances with the Wangs and clarified miscarriage of justice with the Jiangs, was completely respectful to the institution of marriage and set ablaze title deeds worth a thousand gold. He performed this and other such deeds that men normally cannot do. He lived an ordinary life and earnestly kept harmonious relations with people around him. Himself modest and yet saving others on such grand occasions that are simply too many to enumerate. He was such a sincere hero, what a good fortune to inherit from the virtue of one's parent? The Eulogy states: Grace and favor have turned upside down, the ways of the world are hasty, scarcely taking care of one's parents and

---

[111] Liu Yuan's father Liu Ruqin.

discarding of the old ways, the not crazy are taken for crazy, and yet only this honorable gentleman had an excellent virtue, a generous heart with a high generous spirit he contributed money like water. His scholarly achievement had lingering fragrance and was much blessed by heaven with talent. As for the country's glory, he was stationed in a distant land and shined like green jasper at the front gate of the palace. He had no short comings and only good qualities with his image affecting other people. Your letters in a bamboo case are concealed in this hall till the end.

In a grand manner Zhu Gui kowtow here and writes this worship."

Liu Yuan's older brother Liu Shu (courtesy name Fanggao) at an early age entered the county school, and in the 59th year of Qian Long era (1794) passed the county level exam. At the first year of Jia Qing era, he was a successful candidate at the highest imperial examination. At the capital eventually a title was conferred upon at the Hanlin academy and dispatched by the emperor to take charge of Ministry of Punishments. He served as an official in Zhizhou in Guangxi Yu Lin prefecture. The honorable Fanggao relating to the Maitreya Buddha once said: "opens his mouth and there is laughter, laugh about the ancient and laugh about the modern, he laughs off everything. His big belly can contain a lot, it contains heaven and it contains earth, what can it not contain regarding man?" While reading it one may open his heart and mind.

Part 2: Climbing the imperial examination system, resigning from office to become a teacher

In his younger years Liu Yuan was physically weak but brilliant with learning and intelligent beyond the average. At the age of seven he was already able in literature and praised as a child prodigy. At the years when his hair was hanging down in a coil he attended a private school with his older brother Liu Shu at the Yuan monastery in Yun Xi Li. There was Mr. Gu Chun, courtesy name He Feng,[112] who after resigning from office returned to his hometown at Muma mountain, in Banqiaozi at the Wen Chang [deity of literature] palace where he opened a library and educated children. Liu Yuan and his brother heard of Mr. He Feng's morality and literature and both left home to study with him and humbly assumed a place as his students. Later on they became Gu Chun's highly regarded disciples. Years later, Liu Yuan and his brother, even though early on had already ascended to scholarly circles, did not forget their hometown mountains and rivers. Confessing their memory of the times seeking education in Banqiao they left behind poems. One of these poems can be universally appreciated. The poem goes:

"The voice of the returning goose shows the distant path, the undertaking of attending school is floating majestic in memory. From eight thousand miles many know me, from thirty years ago the old Banqiao.

---

[112] A literary celebrity in the county, in the Qian Long era during the annual tribute of the protectorate he once took up post as an official instructor of the entire prefecture, he worked with painting and calligraphy and indulged in chanting verses. He wrote *Poetry Collection by He Feng* and his portrait today is stored at the British museum.

Once the chicken flock left foot prints in the snow, furthermore there was no phoenix companion to share the sky.

Since those times it has aroused the smile of the rivers and mountains, the former little boys' hair is now already old and withered."

Before liberation in Shuangliu's Huangshui Banqiaozi at the Wen Chang palace western wall there was still a 10-foot tall stone tablet erected and on it was engraved "The place of study of the Confucian scholars, the brothers Liu Zhitang"[113] in gold plated big characters, so magnificent to dazzle the eyes, unfortunately it was destroyed during the decade of turbulence.[114]

At the age of eighteen Liu Yuan left Wen Chang Palace to enter the county school, at the 50th year of Qian Long reign (1785) he entered as a champion student in Shuangliu county school. In Qian Long 52nd year (1787) he was a scholar living on a government grant. In Qian Long 53rd year (1788) he was selected and promoted as a person specially versed in the Chinese classics and in Qian Long 54th year (1789) because of his outstanding scholarly achievement he was selected by the local government as an outstanding scholar. In Qian Long 57th year (1792) he was selected again as an outstanding scholar for civil service and to participate in the provincial examination, which he accomplished. In Qian Long 58th year (1793) 60th year (1795), Jia Qing first year (1796) he participated three times in the doctoral exam preceding the imperial exam but didn't succeed. At that time Liu Yuan was

---

[113] From a book by Mr. Wu Zhaoling of the Qing dynasty Hanlin academy.
[114] Means 1966-1976 including the Cultural Revolution.

thinking of his parents, his mother was the only one left and was old and weak, his family was poor and so he didn't have the heart to continue a pursuit for an official career. After being selected by the local government as an outstanding scholar he remained in his hometown of Yun Xi Li at the small Zhao Yang Buddhist convent where he wrote books and taught students. Whatever gifts he received from students filially he gave to his mother in support or helped financially his family expenses. After his brother Liu Shu has passed the highest imperial examination Liu Yuan once said "The grand affair the older brother is already doing, I need in person to attend to feeding of the dogs and horses." He thereupon stayed behind to take care of his family's affairs and attend to his mother.

Zi Bo Shan Mountain Liu Hou temple

Part 3: Running into the recluse and starting to see the source of the Dao

At the first year of Jia Qing reign (1796) when Liu Shu successfully passed the highest imperial examination and after being conferred upon at the Hanlin academy an official position, Liu Yuan followed his older brother in their travel north to the capital. The two brothers while traveling via Shaanxi's Zi Bo Shan Mountain Liu Hou temple, Liu Yuan met one who will become the most extraordinary person in his life; the Daoist recluse Jingyi (Stillness Unity). The recluse Jingyi and Liu Yuan conversed deeply and the Daoist explained to him the Dao of self-cultivation. Upon their parting he also presented him with a copy of Lu Chunyang annotations of the Dao De Jing. Liu Yuan was "amazed that it is just like my own Confucianism." He discovered that the Daoist life cultivation and the Confucian self-cultivation have much in common. At this point he began to pry into the countless ties between the two. This chance encounter undoubtedly was a transformational point for Liu Yuan. One can say that it was the point in time when Liu Yuan established the fundamental core of his teachings. In years to come Liu Yuan paid attention to researching Daoism and himself established the motto for his teaching "Confucianism is the main principle and additionally consider Buddhism and Daoism."

Part 4: Becoming a disciple of Ye Yun, cultivating body and nurturing True Nature

While Liu Yuan stayed at the capital two events took place causing him sorrow and grief. First, his older brother Liu Fanggao's second son has passed away and immediately after that the family graveyard was invaded and occupied by a bullying neighbor, which due to the aggravation caused his mother to fall ill. Liu Yuan ignored the journey's difficulties and hurriedly returned home. Due to rushing to resolve these difficult circumstances while studying hard, his health deteriorated, which brought about exhaustion of his body and mind. He fell ill and was bed ridden and even though he was young his appearance became like a seventy or eighty year old man. He worried that his life will not continue much longer, in which case he could not serve his mother till her last day. With this thought in mind he became even more pessimistic.

In the second year of Jia Qing reign (1797) Liu Yuan met, just by a chance, at the local market of Peng family an old person selling medicinal herbs. "His physical appearance was unusual and with a loving heart respectfully, Liu asked him for instruction on the method of lengthening life." This was the old Ye Yun Mr. Li Guoyuan. Old Ye Yun gave Liu Yuan a prescription of herbs to help with his ailment and he further explained that "the benevolent one enjoys longevity, whereas having great virtue one certainly will enjoy longevity" and "the human body possesses within itself the elixir for prolonging life indefinitely" and other such sagely words. He pointed out "probe to the very root of the principle and fulfil the true nature, it is the accomplishment of inside and outside from the foundation to the manifestation", he convinced him to "preserve the heart and nurture true nature" and "go back to seek out the entire body and heart and this will do." Liu Yuan realized that this old man was not of the ordinary having his unique enlightenment and thereupon he became his disciple. From then on under the tutelage of the old man, taking his medicine and following his instructions, cultivating his body and nurturing his true nature, within two years the weak and sickly Liu Yuan fully recovered and grew stronger as days went by. The old Ye Yun transmission of "preserving spirit and nurturing Qi actually meant preserving heart and nurturing true nature." Its essence is the combination of both Confucianism and Daoism nurturing life and cultivating true nature. Liu Yuan's practice had a significant effect on his health and on his enlightenment, however due to scarce means of livelihood and handling everyday matters he still wasn't able to summarize a theorization of his practice.

In early summer of the 9th year of Jia Qing reign (1804) old Ye Yun, who was intimately close to Liu Yuan, resigned this realm. He instructed Liu Yuan nearly eight years. Henceforth with ever greater determination Liu Yuan continued with the practice of self-cultivation and nurturing true nature. His body and heart increasingly became healthy and vigorous. From the age of sixty to the age of eighty he had eight sons and he passed away close to the age of ninety. Later on in his life while reflecting back he sighed: "When I reflect back on my life it was full of tasting bitterness, but as if I was born twice, if I had not met the old Ye Yun then, early on, I would have passed to the other realm." Old Ye Yun was decisively Liu Yuan's greatest influence. He initiated the great cultural doctrine of "Lao Zi indeed was Confucius's teacher" and "Confucianism and Daoism are one school of thought." This became one fundamental concept originating the Huai Xuan doctrine and one of its special characteristics. Within the Huai Xuan teaching this point occupies an extremely significant position.

Part 5: Opening a school, accepting students and gaining importance in academic circles

From the 51st year of Qian Long (1786) when Liu Yuan started teaching in Shuangliu county Ganzi township at the village of San Sheng (the old name was Yun Xi Li) and until the 12th year of Jia Qing (1807) when Liu Yuan paid final respects to his mother and moved his residence to Chengdu southern gate Chunhua Jie street (also called San Gang Zi, in 1959 during the construction of the Jin Jiang Auditorium this street was completely demolished) Liu Yuan always built his own dwelling and established his school. In Yun Xi Li at the old residence in the middle courtyard was a 200 year old locust Huai tree, and when he moved to the provincial capital in Chunhua Jie street at the new residence courtyard were also three old locust Huai trees, providing dense shade and mingling of light and shadow, creating harmonious and tranquil atmosphere. Liu Yuan therefore named his home the locust tree canopy Huai Xuan (Appeared in the book by Mr. Wu Zhaoling of the Qing dynasty Hanlin academy 'Residence of the Confucian scholar Liu Zhitang'). From that point on Liu Yuan continuously held a school and taught students at Chunhua Jie street in Chengdu, concentrating his effort and devoting himself to academic studies, research and teaching of the younger generation. Disciples could be found in provinces all across the south western regions and it was named by that generation as the 'Huai Xuan school of thought'.

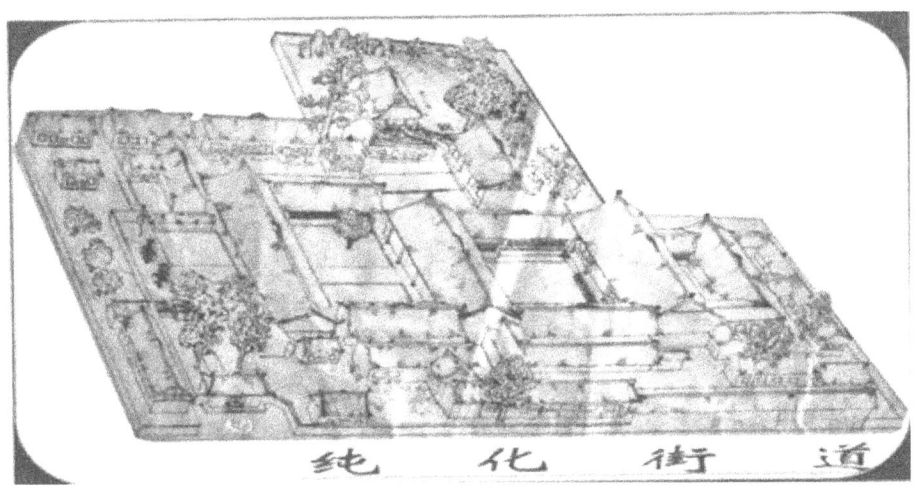

The old home of the Liu family at Chunhua Jie street in Chengdu

In the 6th year of Dao Guang reign, the ministry of rites issued a letter, choosing Liu Yuan to become the county magistrate of Tianmen county in Hubei province. Despite accepting this call for duty Liu Yuan's interest in official life declined, he urged his superiors to take leave and not attend this position using as an excuse his family's great hardship. In Beijing he spent several months, the imperial court dared not disregard his request and based on common sense considered his filial piety and sincerity. The initial civilian post he received was of the second rank; high counselor to a head of state and this was amended to a Dian Bu[115] of the seventh rank and thereupon he returned home. In the *Qing's Official History the Story of Confucian Scholars – Biography of Liu Yuan* it states: "He was happy to lead a simple virtuous life, was reluctant to serve as an official in a distant location, his official

---

[115] Dian Bu during the Qing was a low rank official position of the seventh rank. These officials main task was to draft, review, or annotate official documents and would normally serve their post at the imperial academy Dian Bu hall. With the fall of the Qing in 1910 this official rank was abolished.

status was corrected to a Dian Bu, he asked for a leave of absence and thereupon returned, he succeeded in living in seclusion and teaching others" this describes the aforementioned affair.

Since bidding his hometown farewell and moving to Chengdu, Liu Yuan gave lectures and pursued scholarly research for 48 years in his school on Chunhua Jie street until his passing at the age of 88. He provided education to all without discrimination. He didn't give any consideration to tuition payments. Students from poor families could learn for free just the same as paying students. In addition to Confucian classics and histories the teaching also revolved methods for stillness cultivation in order to allow a strong and healthy body. Year in and year out the average number of students at any giving time was over 300. Altogether, throughout this time, many thousands of students followed him. Because of this Liu Yuan was often called the 'hero amongst teachers'. According to *Qing's Official History the Story of Confucian Scholars – Biography of Liu Yuan*: "*Successful candidates at the highest imperial examinations and recorded in the book of virtuous men were more than a hundred, winners of imperial examinations were more than three hundreds, fragrant and kind hearted accomplished with filial piety and the proper virtue of kinship, holding virtuous names in their local townships were too many to count.*" Amongst his students were peasants, workers and merchants as well as scholars, officials and noted public figures. Without exception and regardless of public status none of the Huai Xuan students ever bragged.

While Liu Yuan was still alive his teachings have already spread far and wide to other provinces. He was respectfully named 'the master from Western Sichuan' and since his disciples were found in and out of Sichuan province people often called them collectively 'Huai

Xuan school of thought' as well as the 'Liu School' (in the same way people designate a 'Confucius school' and 'Master Cheng school' to these academic groups). After Liu Yuan's passing, his children and close disciples took his lifelong numerous compilations, arranged, examined, corrected and published them, giving them a summarizing title 'The Complete Compilation of Huai Xuan'.

Mr. Liu Yuan was married to Mrs. Peng, his concubine was Mrs. Chen, his second wife was Mrs. Yuan. "He followed all the virtuous etiquette, with goodness and principle managed his household and therefore the master didn't have domestic problems, he scrutinized intensively and instructed diligently and tirelessly till old age." (Liu Fen's *Epitaph on the Memorial tablet of Mr. Zhitang*) Amongst his offspring were officials residing in the capital, some at the Hanlin academy some serving as clerks in office, while others led a tranquil life in their hometown, some as successful candidates of the provincial imperial examination, some as known local virtuous scholars, happily and peacefully maintaining the achievements of their forefather, concentrating on scholarly research, composing prose and literature, all demonstrating outstanding talent.

On the 5th year of Xian Feng reign (1855) twelfth lunar month the 19th day at the hour of Zi[116] Liu Yuan passed away at the age of 88. The following year at the 2nd day of the 10th lunar month he was buried in Shuangliu 10 Li west of Peng family field at Yu Xi Li ancestral tomb. On the gravestone was engraved "Qing dynasty imperial college with official rank of Dian Bu, Liu Yuan the scholar from Qing Yang". The master's close disciple Liu Fen wrote an epitaph titled 'An epitaph on a stone tablet of the Qing dynasty

---

[116] Midnight.

reclusive scholar Liu Zhitang.' After the master's grave was moved to another site his great-great-grandson Liu Hengbi (courtesy name Dongfu) wrote once more on the tombstone "The tomb of the Qing dynasty reclusive scholar Liu Zhitang." The self-title 'reclusive scholar' was used by Liu Yuan himself during his life.

In the 31st year of Guang Xu reign (1905), the official compiler of the Hanlin academy and Chengdu's Zunjing academy of classical studies director from Qiong Zhou, Mr. Wu Zhaoling (courtesy Songsheng), Mr. Yan Kai from Hua Yang, Mr. Hu Jun and others, applied through Sichuan's governor-general, Mr. Xi Liang, to the emperor seeking his reaction, earnestly requesting to introduce Liu Yuan's life story and achievement to the official historiographer office so as to write his biography. In the memorandum to the emperor it stated "Because of the gentleman's scholarship and moral conduct being so exemplary we beg a favor to appropriately turn it over to the imperial historiographer's office to compile his biography as a reward for cultivating himself in quiet privacy." In the same year the 12th day of the 10th lunar month, the Qing government sent the comments made by the emperor: "Affected in accord with your request. The responsible government office was notified. Qin Ci!"[117] Therefrom his name was listed in the *Qing's Official History the Story of Confucian Scholars – Biography of Liu Yuan.*

---

[117] Qin Ci is a written expression marking the end of the imperial order. The history of a dynasty was always compiled after the dynasty has collapsed. Here the request to be included in the official history and the government's reply demonstrates everybody's acknowledgement of the last years of the Qing.

Qing dynasty Sichuan governor-general Mr. Xi Liang

(1853-1917) courtesy name Qing Bi, native name Baiyuete, a Manchu from Xiang Lan in Mongolia, passed successfully the highest imperial examination in the 13th year of Tong Zhi reign (1874). In 1903 Xi Liang was transferred to serve as governor-general of Sichuan and in 1907 was transferred to serve as governor-general of Yun Gui. He served as an official for 37-years was honest and upright, assiduous in government affairs, pragmatic and widely known. A person having a prosperous official career at the end of the Qing, an historical personality with great contribution.

Wu Zhaoling

(1826-1915) courtesy name Songsheng, passed the highest imperial examination and scored the second place.[118] In late Qing he served as a scholar in the Hanlin academy and was a known educator. A person of Sichuan's Qiong Zhou (today's Qionglai). After returning home he was a teacher at Chengdu's Jin Jiang academy of classical learnings for many years. He was a calligrapher and excelled in classical Chinese prose.

From Chengdu's Jin Jiang academy of classical studies there are relevant sayings: "What is useful for heaven and earth is called accomplishment, what is beneficial in teaching the people around is called fame. What has a glorious spirit is called rich, what has humility is called precious. Studying the beginning is called Dao, when one attains it in himself it is named virtue. Disdaining superficiality is culture, while not engaging arrogance is the rule." (Excerpts from Yixun Cun Lue- first scroll)

---

[118] During the Qing, the imperial civil-service examination was done in 3 levels. Here the title conferred shows the second place in the second rank of examinations.

Yan Kai

(1877-1909) courtesy name Yongqi a scholar and calligrapher, a person of Sichuan Hua Yang. In 1905 was dispatched by the Qing government to Japan to specialize in law and politics. When he returned to China he served as chief compiler of the Hanlin academy and the imperial tutor. After the establishment of the Republic of China he paid no attention to politics and became a lay Buddhist practitioner. He was selected as the vice-president of Sichuan's Buddhism association. He excelled with calligraphy and was also a disciple of the Huai Xuan school.

Hu Jun

(1870-1909) courtesy name Yu Lan, art name Zhen An, a person of Sichuan Hua Yang. In the 21st year of Guang Xu reign passed the highest imperial examination and was awarded a compiler position. Later served as the president of Sichuan's higher education institute. He then went to Japan to observe and study and upon his return formed the education research association and established exemplary elementary schools as well as specialized schools for politics, railway engineering and physical education. Once as Xi Liang was building the Chuan Han railroad[119] he went with him abroad on a fact-finding trip. His name can be seen in the list of names in 'Public Chariot Escalating a Letter'.[120]

---

[119] Chuan Han railroad had an initial plan to go from Chengdu Sichuan to Hankou in Hubei some 3000 kilometers.

[120] After the defeat to Japan in the first sino-Japanese war in 1895 Kang Youwei gathered a petition by 1200 scholars from around the country and remonstrated the humiliating terms that the Qing government agreed to. 'Public Chariot' is a term used since the Han dynasty describing when candidates successfully passed the provincial exam they would use a public chariot transporting them directly to the capital to sit for the pre-imperial highest exam.

翻譯言

劉沅，儒，師，醫，子，典型父，生于十八世紀末十九世紀初于四川。劉沅篤信於消弭人與人之間以及宗教之間的差異，並致力闡述人性本善，如隱晦則需喚醒人性深處根本之善。其生平摘錄於本冊尾篇。

在劉沅眾多著作之中，此冊採用几部經典著作點其核心。其學說表示為善是自然而然的，后人稱之槐軒學說。

此冊於不同時間地點的文章翻譯事件專欲難成，功于解除語言和文化的差异，甚至由舊思想傳承至新思維。許多例子顯示，古今風俗不同，甲語言的巧妙用法在乙語言中完全不合用。此當帶給譯者和讀者不少困難。槐軒學說提倡人心中善，即仁也。其超越文化疆界之差異，為各地仁人所有。然而，槐軒需透過當時當地之民情風俗，淺顯易懂的語言和想法才能達到教導多數人為善的目的。

克服語言和文化的困難后，此思想結合古今之精髓大放異彩。于學說里它描寫生命存在於物質和心神，有形和無形之間。此道理的核心為尋求中庸之道，亦即實際上理解與落實何謂適切及不妥。日常練習便可達到長壽和發展和諧的結果。

尋求中庸久久能達到浩然正气，消除心中所有私欲造成的障礙。成功尋得中庸便能作善而不累。能作善不累的功夫其淵源叫做天理。是一种無限能量推動本心的善意，也叫做良心。劉沅將其並稱為天理良心。

本冊獻給劉沅之曾孫劉伯谷，因其寬厚無私傳播此善。槐軒學說于現今，解釋前輩的文字，推進濟世活人，翻譯者于此頓首拜謝。

集冊槐軒非可與一般著作相提並論，故所有翻譯之缺漏均為譯者之不足。無可奈何望成就良冊希冀讀者原諒。

于康州 2016 年夏

孟亞倫

俗言

目录

俗言序

一、第一要敬天地父母也。

二、守身为先也。

三、修身先须正与诚也。

四、欲诚欲正必先戒邪淫也。

五、何以一犯邪淫便是禽兽也，

六、何以一犯邪淫便要短命绝嗣也。

七、断绝邪淫必从父母师友，慎所习也。

八、戒淫根本既端，又当从事大学之道，始能以礼节情也。

九、大学之道，不止全人道之当然，且希圣希天，却病延年，免饥寒困苦也。

十、大学诚意正心，必先畏天命，故不必禁祸福鬼神之说。

十一、道本中庸，因二字被先儒说得不明，人遂高视圣人，远视大道，而希圣希天之学旷世无人行矣。

十二、事父母也——兄弟附

十三、父母并尊，不可轻重，父一而母不一，孝父自然孝母前人误解礼经，不可不明辨也。

十四、事君也。

十五、出处大节，士与取士必以此为先，乃有真才也。

十六、三纲不正则五伦亦不正，故为上者当自修也。

十七、君相不可不以圣人自命也

十八、培植人才，礼贤下士，有国有家者皆当急务也

十九、道在日用伦常，而能尽道者希。分心性事功为两途，世俗圣贤不相合也，当明辨而力行之。

二十、教必先养，而后世养最难兴。必因时制宜，其权在君亲师也。

二十一、君亲之责固重，而师尤为先。非行大学之道，师固难求也。

二十二、有圣贤之师，自多圣贤之徒。圣贤固非甚难，先儒过为高远，使后学畏阻而废，切勿为所误也

二十三、道不外乎人情物理，故人人可能，但须以天理权衡之，即合时中矣。

二十四、人情物理不离世俗，切勿是古非今，薄视俗人俗也。

二十五、格致便是内外交养之功。说向外去，教人物物穷理，便有知无行，逐末忘本矣。

二十六、养气不动心，即大学之正心。此理不明，故辟佛老者以其伪罪其真，而明心见性修真养性一概抹杀，心与气之相关，正与诚之迥异，无人知矣

二十七、万事起于心。万理统于性，存心养性，然后伦常克践。佛老之正者不外心性，辟之而并失其存养之实，非也。

二十八、心性之功，乃人伦日用根本。错解《大学》格、致、诚、正，故不知佛老之正者亦同于儒，而歧杂多途，异端纷起。经不正，庶民何以兴也。

二十九、忠孝固德行之首，而古今错误亦多，必以孔孟之义为主，然后死不徒死，忠孝全其大美也。

三十、求忠臣必于孝子之门，而史册所载忠或不孝，孝或不忠，必明辨之，始免人疑忠孝之相妨也。

三十一、直道不明，乡愿太多，自古国家乱亡必由乎此，宜亟正也。

三十二、大学之道，包一切，埒一切，易知易能。在上以此立教，在下人人共行，天下无事矣。

三十三、道惟时中，人人可能，高视而贻害于家国，古今皆然。可叹也。

三十四、文以载道，道傲于文，必本躬行而著为言语文字，道乃不芜也。

三十五、有情世界四字人所共知，但须明辨而力行之，不然，则大悖道也。

三十六、圣人千言万语止是一理，理者，天人所共也。

俗言序

圣人不以著书立说自名也，或在上，或在下，随其职分所当为，自修其身，间或著为语言，训诱人群，人竞宝之，于是乎有典谟、训诰、易象、诗、书等籍。自羲农至文武，圣人之制已全，生民之法已备，孔子更修明折衷之，而曾、思、孟衍其绪，范围古今，后有作者莫能尚矣。而世儒纷纷著作，欲自成一家，遂使孔孟遗规危乎欲坠。愚无知也，因读书多年，颇有所见，故详释孔孟遗书，名曰《恒解》，以其为天之常道，地之常经，人人所知能之常事。而儿辈苦其繁也，不得已，又为《子问》、《正讹》、《下学梯航》、《古本大学质言》四端，使其易晓。而卷帙既多，弥增之惑，乃复撮其大要更为此编。所以谆谆而不惮词费者，为家庭授受计耳，岂敢以问世哉。大雅君子尚其恕之。

咸丰四年岁在甲寅正月止唐书时年八十有七

道原在乎力行，不在言语文字。因书籍太多，力行太少，不得已而为此篇，非与前人争辨，亦非有一毫求名之心，年耄而儿辈犹稚，不得已付之以为遗嘱耳。止唐自志。

俗 言

双江刘沅 著

自羲农至孔孟皆圣人，而其事不同者，何也？所值之时，所居之位，时俗尤不同也。圣人因时俗而为之节文，在上则有礼、乐制度，在下则有言行，皆适得乎中正，故能裁成天地之道，辅相天地之宜以左右民。自秦火以后，书籍贵而书籍亦日多，其发明圣道者固不乏人，而支离汗漫滋之，惑者尤众，以其未得圣人之真，徒推尊圣人而不知圣人只是人情物理通达之至耳。人情物理不尽合道，圣人以天理折衷之，不随俗亦不戾俗，合乎中正，即为时中，岂得谓世俗皆不可从哉。俗云一世人身万劫难，与孔子曰天地之性人为贵一理，有此人身，便要全此天理，才算得人。寻常人说要存天理良心，天理良心即人之所以异于禽兽者也。禽兽与人之分只争此些须，故曰几希，庶民去之，便是禽兽，君子存之，便是圣人。下文舜、禹、汤、文至孔子，都是存几希的人，便是圣人，可见圣人才算得人。天理良心人人皆有，人人可为，则圣人个个学得了，故曰：人皆可以为尧舜。因先儒说道太恍惚了，说圣人太高了，书传太多，人无从问津了，故愚不得已而以俗言示子弟如左：

一、第一要敬天地父母也。

《书》曰："天地万物父母"，俗云：人身一小天地，是天地父母之恩，人人都知道的，如何存心行事又不顾天理良心。父母生我之身，天地予我以人理，非天地固不能得此人理，非父母又何从得此人身，故天地父母名为四大。自古圣贤事天如事亲，事亲如事天。一念之邪，可以欺堂上父母，而不能欺覆载之父母，翘首见天，俯首见地，违天理便如违悖父母一般，父母必责子不孝，天地岂不责无天理之人乎。文王小心翼翼，昭事上帝，孔子曰："知我其天"，不是妄想妄言，只是视天地如父母耳。世人不知天人一气，谓天道高远，神明恍惚，一念之欺不知敬畏，久久而念念皆然，辜负天地父母生成之恩，失却为人正理，日沦于禽兽，而人心坏，风俗恶，天下亦纷纷多故。天理良心四字乃为人根本，世界污隆分界之原，不可一日而不讲也。《大学》、《中庸》言"慎独"，言十目十手，相在屋漏，便是要人体贴天理。先儒恐人废民义而谄鬼神，乃讳言鬼神，止说恐怕人知。然鬼神者阴阳之灵，天地为阴阳之宗，则敬鬼神仍是敬天地，所谓畏天命也。若任心而行，以天为无知，鬼神恍惚，安能有敬畏之心，又如何能收放心！或疑信鬼神便要讲祸福，讲祸福则凡事避祸求福，当为者亦不为，所以先儒不言祸福，不知敬天地不是求免祸得福也。凡事由心而起，心不敬、不诚，见于言行，又安能有善无恶。心之所思，人不能知而神天知之，故一念之起必去恶从善，方可对得头上天地，堂上父母，然人为天地父母所喜，又何有贫穷困苦不得其死者乎。天地主祸福之权，则免祸得福，亦其常理，故曰：惠迪吉，从逆凶，积善馀庆，积不善馀殃。天人一气相感，由其止同此一理，而奈何以俗见妄解大道也。

圣人念念克已，恐得罪天地，如不敢得罪父母一般，必如此而后可合天理，可以为人，不因祸福起见也。而其诱掖后人，则未尝不以祸福立教。《周易》一书全以吉、凶、悔、吝教人，夫子更多申言其理。儒者不知天人一贯之义，不思夫子栽培倾覆之说，徒忌讳鬼神祸福，只以道理教人，而事父母如天地者鲜，事天地如父母者更鲜。本原既错，修身立德更何处临保帝谓，视于无形，听于无声耶。故欲为人、欲无非分之灾患，必以敬天地父母为先。

二、守身为先也。

孔子言大学之道，壹是皆以修身为本，孟子亦言修其身而天下平，圣人之学，除却修身更无二道。然苟不得明师，则必错误，不特僧道失佛老之真，生许多邪妄，即儒生亦非孔孟之正。盖修身本末之功备于《大学》，宋儒窜改《大学》，私心妄言，而人益用惘然矣。修身必先守身，孟子曰："事孰为大，事亲为大，守孰为大，守身为大，不失其身而能事其亲者，吾闻之，失其身而能事其亲者，吾未之闻也"。孔子曰："天地之性人为贵"，"父母全而生之，子全而归之，可谓孝矣"。一举足而不敢忘父母，一出言而不敢忘父母，皆同此一理。守身之道，念念天理，事事谨慎，保身修身皆在其中，曾子之战战兢兢，临深履薄，凡绝嗜慾、去声色、崇德修慝，一切皆在其内。用功之实，不外动静交养，本末交修。能从事《大学》得守身之义，其上希圣希天，其次亦可希贤益寿，延年却病。后人以为奇异者，皆守身之义耳，故"仁者寿，大德必寿"，夫子所以云然，何不思之？自圣学失传，偏于养心者不知立命事天，偏于摄气者不知践形尽性，于是僧道之徒以守心为佛法，以运气求长生，而儒者亦效之，又欲从而自远之，或得其肤壳，昧其本原，不知守身之义，又安能更求诚身。夫人之受气至不齐矣，智、愚、修、短，自古异趣，因材而笃，天固无心，然覆载深仁，不无缺憾。圣人以修身之学教人，补天地生成之憾。道故至尊至贵，学故不可须臾或离，而圣人所以为天肖子。自先儒误解，而圣道几同画饼，为圣为贤，无能挽回造化矣。噫！

三、修身先须正与诚也。

天地止此一理。理气凝结，万古不穷，以其无贰、无杂、无盈亏绝续，名之曰诚。人得天地正理正气而生，能实全此理于身，名曰诚身。诚之至者圣人也，名曰：天下至诚。寻常人不欺心悖理，即是诚身之法，但必先讲明义理是非，合义理者为正，不合义理者为邪。理正了，真心去做，便是诚身。凡人心多邪妄，若心入于邪妄，更如何修身，故当力行非礼无视四句、关夫子存好心四句，刻刻奉行，久久方可去邪望正。关圣之所以为圣人，亦止光明正大，不欺不诈耳，勉之！勉之！

四、欲诚欲正，必先戒绝邪淫也。

孟子曰："人之所以异于禽兽者几希"。几希者，天理良心也。良心天理是个总名，大凡合义理之事做了，心中安乐，便是良心不昧。不合理事勉强作了，或不知而为，或明知而强为，既作之后，寤寐静思，必心上不安，便是良心难昧了。这个良心不安的念头，便是人种子未绝，为圣为贤的根基。趁此念头动处，痛心改悔，以后再不如此，一事如是，事事如是，渐渐做去，久久习惯，自然喜善而恶恶矣。但别样恶念或容易删除，惟色慾二字是血气上带来的，最容易丧心蔑理，亦最难斩断。然为人、为禽兽便在此处分界，切须发一片勇猛心，念天地神明在上，父母如在目前，人之妻女，如我姊妹一般，不看不想，何况敢乱为。将不好念头一刀斩断，便不入于禽兽了，便可望为孝子、忠臣，享富贵福泽了。世人一念不戒，丧天良为禽兽，且因一念之差，短命绝嗣。贫穷、疾厄、困苦皆色慾所误，所以子弟十六七岁便当切切教戒防闲，断了首恶，方为贤父母师长。下文详言之。

五、何以一犯淫邪便是禽兽也。

人为倮虫之长，当混沌之初，人物并生，无衣服遮身，无宫室蔽风雨，不知何物可食，旱死、冻死、饿死、毒死的不知若干人。无衣服便与禽兽一般，食草木百物遍体生毛。天生圣人制为衣服，然后与禽兽不同，又为宫室栖身，五谷养生，然后人得安全。因男女是阴阳正理，但容易苟合，为之婚礼，使各有夫妇，上继祖先，下延子孙，故《礼》曰：人道以大婚为大。圣人教人五伦，男女曰有别，盖禽兽亦有雌雄、牝牡，亦能生子，但无别耳。《礼》曰："无别无义，禽兽之道也"。《传》曰："男女无别，是禽兽也"。《礼》曰："夫惟禽兽无礼，故父子聚麀"。非自家夫妇与之苟合，便成禽兽。天地父母生我，成就一个人身，乃因一点邪欲失了人身，是为大不孝，何以立德立功，为世间不朽之人乎！何面目见父母先人，何以对妻子乎！古人云：不戒邪淫，便是猪狗，必遭屠割之惨。大兵大劫，每由邪人太多，可不悚惕之欤！

六、何以一犯邪淫便要短命绝嗣也。

人之所以为人，全是天理良心四字。犯邪淫之人只图一时快乐，全不想我有姐妹、有妻女，如我的姐妹妻女被人玷污，我甘心否！那玷污我的姐妹妻女的人，我容得他否！就是我的姐妹妻女行路有人注眼看他，我尚且不容他，况坏我亲眷的人，我安肯饶他！恨他杀他都是该的。把这念头翻转来想，我犯人妻女还是人否？天地神明肯饶恕我否？所以犯邪淫人往往短命少亡，否则绝嗣，即或前生修得好，祖宗尚有余荫，勉强过了一生，而子孙断无好处，甚或妻女子孙酬偿。试以世人考验之，便知毫发不爽，奈何不早收心，要犯邪淫，甘心种无限祸根入于禽兽也。

七、断绝邪淫，必从父母师友慎所习也。

　为父母者必先明义理，正其身心，节欲修身，虽自家夫妇亦不苟言、不苟笑，闺房衽席间言语动静亦有规矩，不露狎亵。儿女七八岁便防闲之，教训之，不许男女杂坐，外人引诱。凡有廉耻及端正、慈、良、恭、敬等事，细细训导。到了十四五岁更要留心，将人与禽兽不同道理说知，古今正人君子详示，教他实心体贴。出外从师，必选端正明理之人，不许小人同居、同游。女子谨守闺门，亲戚妇女有不正者，不许同之居处。择壻婚男必求忠厚、仁慈、有礼义之家，不可以贫富贵贱而论。父母正矣，又教子女以正，方才自幼习惯，久而自然。今人十六七岁便要婚娶，便要生男生女，为父母者虽眼前日用道理亦不知道是非，如何为父母、教儿孙，此世风所以日坏，人心所以难回也。孔子曰："知为人子，然后可以为人父"。子孙不肖，父母岂得辞责哉！至于师者与君亲并重，无论何业俱必有师，师不端正，虽好子弟也被他教坏了。且师既不正，则同学之人亦必不正，每日聚处乱说乱为邪僻之事，一言难尽，子弟见见闻闻，被他习染入于不肖，终身败坏不能挽回。为父母者只说儿子不肖，不知其为己过也。故凡人伦大义修身处世一切道理，若非明师教导，断不能明白。而择师必由父母，父母不正，子弟安能自择明师。何为明师？孝、弟、忠、信、礼、义、廉、耻八字讲得明白，又能自家行得有规矩、有良心便是。是故父母、师是人生善恶祸福根子，为父母师长者，不可不自修自愧也。孔子曰："苟正其身矣，于正人乎何有？不能正其身，如正人何？"孟子曰："身不行道，不行于妻子。使人不以道，不能行于妻子。"后世君亲师多侈然自是，不修己身，徒责臣子忠孝，在臣子之贤者固甘心致死无怨，而枉屈亦已多矣，若不肖者则为祸不可胜言。世人习而不察，三纲不正，犹欲五伦各得其所，有是理，有是事乎！

八、戒淫根本既端，又当从事大学之道，始能以礼节情也。

自古圣人以礼教人，不是全靠规矩法度，必从身心上用功。唐虞以前书缺有间矣，孔子删书，断自唐虞。《尧典》篇首颂尧之德曰："钦明、文思、安安"。钦、敬也，敬于内静养此心，敬于外检制言行，久久志气如神，道理明白，故曰钦明。人心不能无思，思多则妄，妄则不安。尧之钦明，心正身修矣，凡有所思，自然条理秩如，合乎时中，故曰文思。安安者，安而又安，从容中道也。此六字已将圣学言明，圣人千言万语，其根本止在于是，《大学》"诚意、正心、修身"即此之谓也。春秋道衰，孔子仅私语其徒。为君相者不知其义，遂纷纷多途，功利、刑名、词章，博杂之学日多，大学之道将坠，孔子虑后人莫得其传，故为圣经一章以语曾子，曾子又恐人不知入手之要，又从诚意释之，衍为五章。秦汉以降，孔孟之书大行，此书知尊，从者亦多，特不能深明其义耳。宋儒重此书而不得其功效之实，以一偏之见改窜原文，真西山从而推衍之，朱子大学遂行于时，夫子原书反无人讲求。《钦定礼记义疏》仍存《古本大学》，诚不敢没圣人之真也，愚为恒解及《古本大学质言》，细细指出用功次第，但朱子改本，士人久已遵行，则见愚所言，必然诧异鄙弃。然圣人之书原是讲明义理，使人有所遵循，欲学圣人者不遵依大学之道一一用功，又何能修其身，身不修了，又何能成己成人，无施不可。况圣言天，口所言莫非天理，其遗文岂可妄为改窜，将圣人之书妄改、妄解，天下人要想学圣人如何有用功处。愚今故特言明，将《大学》所言再细细言之，庶人知以道修身，不忝与君亲。修身之道如何？格去物欲以清心也，研究义理以致知也。清心寡欲，常常静心养神气、求放心而收藏有密，所谓"止至善也"。心易浮动，最难得静定，必须平时持敬，言行动静皆求合理，不合则克治之，合理则扩充之，从一点念头动处便不自欺、自恕。如此久久，然后善气多而志气清，孟子所谓"集义生气"也。曾子所以从诚意章作传，将夫子许多言语、道理尽纳入诚意中。诚意者动察也。无事则收心于中，一念不生，万缘屏绝，至虚至静，使神气相依，湛然无欲，此便是艮止之功，执中之道，静存也。《书》曰："安止"，《易》曰："艮止"，《诗》曰："静止"，夫子则曰："止至善"。止善者，天地之中。人身与天地同，识得此窍，能宅心于此，由有诸己而化神，便知天之所以为天。子思曰："天地之道，可一言而尽"，正谓此耳。而自古圣人不敢直泄者，以其为天地之奥，恐人亵视，且非得明师言之，亦无益也。孔子于坤曰："君子黄中通理，正位居体，美在其中而畅于四肢，发于事业，美之至也。"于艮曰："止其所也，时止则止，时行则行，动静不失其时，其道光明"。皆止至善之义理功效。孟子曰："充实之谓美，充实而有光辉之谓大"。盖人之所以生者气也，神为气之主，而心乃人之神明，所以善心难而恶心易者，气质累之也。有气而后有质，有质而气亦困。心者气血之灵，气血不能无暇，人心安得纯乎理哉，故必养浩然之气，久久始不动心。浩然之气不外于血气之气，而实非血气之气所同，其功用至神，孟子喻之以"刚大"，而曰"浩然"，以其功用言之耳，而其本体则无声臭之可名，故佛老曰："虚无"，元气虚无言其本体，浩然言其功用，非有二也。儒者讳言"虚无"二字，然不显之德同乎於穆，惟上天之载可拟。德何以不显所谓穆穆也，穆穆者深远之意，无可名状，则"虚无"矣。文之穆穆与天之穆同，以其纯乎天理，不可得而见者人心也。德在于心，又如何可见，所以名之曰："不显之德"。谓心德必见于事物才是，则夫子"知我其天，人莫我知"，岂非妄语乎。况养心之法，非虚无涵养，则懂懂往来者不止。大学所谓"定、静、安"三字如何得知实际，故必知止而后能"定、静、安"。朱子将至善说在事物上去，然事物之至善即知得了。如何便得"定、静、安"，此事理之明白易晓者，奈何曲从朱子而悖孔子乎。惟知天地之中求放心而止于其所，持其志无暴其气，久久而后，心始少纷扰为定，定久而后神安气寂为静，静久而后身心泰然为安，安则私欲日少，天机日生，凡穷理之事易于明辩，而后能虑，能虑则心不蔽于闻见，事不足以扰心，言行动静可合礼仪，是为能得。夫子以止至善为大学之要，特地指出次第功效。如此分明而误解之，使人逐物而求，谓物物穷理，久久便豁然贯通，心之全体大用无不明。内无养性之学，外恃耳目之明，如何便可"定、静、安"，又如何还要虑、还要得？即如忠孝是至善，谁人不知，而能忠孝者几人，定、静、虑又如何说得去？课之身心不可行，使人务外无终极，圣言竟为画饼矣。人心难制，道理难明，非止至善则无以存心，非虚无亦无以生浩然之气，欲去其邪心，归于义理，断断不能。故欲戒邪淫，知守身诚身等事，必从事大学之道。大学之道，人人可知、可能，不外此身而求，岂专为读书人言哉，亦岂欲人借此以鸣道学哉！

九、大学之道　不止是全人道之当然，且希圣希天、却病延年、免饥寒困苦也。

人得天地中正之气，是气即是理，理气之元即太极也。得此太极，在未生以前，一团神气无名无象，浑然粹然，所谓"天命之性"。子在母胎本无声臭，未具百骸，全是一团理气，故孟子曰："性善也"。及形骸已具，出离母腹，九窍开，七情发，先天中气散而难聚，分而难合，于是浑然之性变为纷纭之心。然其本体固存，不过气质之欲，物感之来，引之而失其正耳。故孔子曰："性相近"。圣人以学教人，格去物欲，致其天理之明，内而存养则止于至善，外而省察则诚其好恶，以存神养气为主。神即心也，神为气主，故必持其志无暴其气。但气乃先天浩然之气，非口鼻呼吸之气，心乃知觉运动之灵，亦不是先天之性。存心养性者，存其有觉之心，养其虚无之性。此间义理至精至微，非明师不授。儒者避羽流之言，讳言神气，不知人非神气不能生，天非神气不能立，但神气有先天后天之分，不容不辨耳。先天之神气，即天之所以为天，人得之以为性。日月星辰，天地之神光也，风云雷雨，天之真气也，然乃神气之散著者，其神气之元则不可得而窥，所谓上天之载，无声无臭。然则道在天地，至虚无者乃其本，形形色色者乃其用。人得天地之理而生，所以生者亦止神气。心即神也，人不能自见其心，天理在心又如何可见。存其心养其性者，一元之气久久充实而渐化神，非空空无着者也。儒者不言神而但言心，然心非神乎！理非虚无者乎！理宰乎气，气载乎理。离气，理于何有。是故无声无臭者，道之本。虚无养静者，致中之功。清净者，天理纯粹一私不杂之意。寂灭者，寂然不动私欲全无之谓。佛老之真者，何尝外理也，僧流误解而儒者不察，不知其为养心之法，而以为废弃伦常，岂不诬哉！惟心性止是神气之灵，故存心养性即存神养气，神气强固，奚不可延年。集义生气亦非如羽流但养凡神凡气，内而存养，外而伦常，本末交修，浩然之气塞乎天地，乃可以当之，故寿考即在其中。夫子曰："仁者寿，大德必寿"。又曰："天之所助者，顺也"。德行纯粹，神动天随，自天佑之，吉无不利，何至穷苦愁困，不能免无妄之灾哉。孔子曰："天生德于予，桓其如予何！天之未丧斯文也，匡入其如于予何！"此理至明，惜前人不达天人之理，而必区区避佛老之言，觉吉凶、悔吝、余庆、余殃等义，圣人皆为妄言，不亦惑乎。

十、大学诚意正心，必先畏天命，故不必禁祸福鬼神之说也。

天只一理，理无形而气有迹。理气之灵，名曰鬼神。天苍苍耳，地块然耳，其主宰理气，变化不测者鬼神也。人在天地匡廓之中，此心此理得天地之正，为天地心，一念之动合乎天理即顺天心，悖乎天理即逆天心，积之久而善恶迥不同矣。顺天者昌，逆天者亡，天亦何心，合理而与之亲则福，不合理而天与之远则祸。鬼神天地之灵，主宰理气，以善求天，如石投水，以恶求天，如水投石，自然之理，岂为奇怪事哉。故祸福止自求诸身心，不是违理而媚祷神天。《周易》一书以吉凶悔吝教人，因畏祸求福者，人情也，以祸福之由来示之，使知吉凶生于善恶，为善即有福，为恶即有祸，乃是教人为善，不是教人求福。不为善而求福，如入山而求鱼，入水而求薪，不惟无益，且必遭谄渎鬼神之罚。世人往往求福得祸，以为为善无益，不知其所谓善者非善也。譬如有人于此，爱人敬人，而父母淡漠将之，不刻刻思慕父母而爱敬他人，可谓善否？轻财好义，而于兄弟却计较财货，分别尔我，甚且坐视其困而不救，可谓善否？知神天首重者孝弟，爱敬者人之天良，天良以父母为根，不爱敬父母，天良已亡，又何能爱敬他人！孝子必友弟恭兄，念及父母疼念儿女，有不仁让者乎。爱敬始于孝悌，而后推此天良，仁民、爱物都真切不二，方才算得是善，方算合得天理。如此而不得福者鲜矣。但人心多妄，爱敬之心人人有之，或知而不为，为之而不真、不长久者，何也？放肆懒惰也。问何以怠肆？以为不如此亦可无妨，而不知爱敬者，人心天理之良，不爱敬父母兄弟便没了天良，天地神明便不喜欢了，尚有何好处。鬼神司天地之功化，天地不喜，鬼神即降之殃。故君子必畏天命，一念不存天良，即刻斩除，便是事天实学。不然，则孔子所谓"小人不知天命而不畏"，"小人而无忌惮也"，尚安能正心，又安能有福哉。世人无不求福避祸，且多事神求福，而不知鬼神不取祭祷，专取孝善之人。福泽原不难求，止在正心，正心先要诚意，诚意要慎独。《大学》《中庸》言慎独功夫曰："十目所视，十手所指，相在屋漏"，岂非敬畏天地鬼神乎。先儒一偏之论不合孔子，致人肆心蔑理，可叹也。或曰：夫子何以不语神？曰：夫子非不语也。凡语神必以人道实之，如云："鬼神体物不遗"，而以"神之格思，不可度思"，教人敬鬼神而远之，必先务民义，不是说鬼神荒渺，是说止此天理。天理近在吾身，反身修德而畏天命，天地鬼神即应之，"某之祷久"，"知我其天"，即此意耳，其或邪神野鬼为祟者，皆其人无德，而正神不佑之也。

十一、道本中庸，因二字被先儒说得不明，人遂高视圣人，远视大道，而希圣希天之学无人行矣。

战国时异端渐多，圣人之道将灭，子思乃述孔子《中庸》二字，衍以成书。何为中？凡事无过，无不及，做到恰好处也。何为庸？平常也。无过不及之中，人人可能，但不诚、不敬、不恒久耳。子思正恐人以道为难、为奇，故标此二字反复言之，奈儒者太说得精深，于是孔子、子思之心没矣。今试浅言之。所谓中者，合理而妥当耳，如饮食不可过饥，亦不可过饱，是中，亦是庸。凡事合理，做得恰好，人心是安的，便觉快活，可见中庸之理是天生与人的。又如酒、色、财、气四字，圣人亦不能离，但圣人饮酒不及乱，自家夫妇亦以礼寡欲，若外人子女便不看不说，并不敢一毫妄想了。凡人若知得此理，便是中庸，便是圣贤。士、农、工、商各有职业，能勤慎节俭，不肯荒惰，又能念念不欺不苟，常常顾着天理良心，便可渐渐合乎中庸。中庸之道，天理也，合了天理，上天自然保佑，何至饥寒困苦。平常二字人每忽略，平者如路坦平，不虚险也，常者如布帛、菽粟，不奇怪也。人生所以养生，止宫室、衣食、男女数事，所以成己成人经天纬地者，不过五伦，人人所有，人人所同，岂非至平至常。然而宫室、衣食、男女，愚人以此丧心蔑理，入于禽兽，君子以此修己安人，参赞化育。所以然者，义理之是非。不从一念检点则不诚意，久久习惯自然，欲不为小人不可得矣。故人伦日用及自家身心之事至平常，理实通乎天地。时时检束身心，谨言慎行，以忠恕心行仁义事，便可合天心，有何奇怪，有何难能哉！试更以浅近之理明之如左。

十二、事父母也—兄弟附

古今言孝理者甚多，劝人孝者亦不少，而卒少能孝者，何哉？父母少教训，长大为物情所惑也。凡孩子能言能行，稍知事务，便要教以亲爱恭敬之意，如父母尊长前不许乱说话、乱作事，尊长言语要恭敬听从，作事要留心，不许笑谈訾议，常常随侍父母，昏定晨省，问寝视膳，出告反面。眼前道理要日日遵行，不许放肆懈怠，久久习惯自然，便有不忍远离父母的念头了。到了长大，又选明师教训之，好朋友劝戒之，不许与小人相交，总要时时在父母之侧，完婚之后依然如此。明师益友将父母恩养之心细细讲示，又将婚配缘故讲明，父母与我婚配，是怕我外想邪淫，犯了首恶，故与我娶妻，免我胡思乱想。且男女是人生大伦，上接祖宗香烟，奉养父母，父母年老，内外操持家务，不致父母勤劳。若弟兄便是与我同骨肉的人，一样儿女，父母是个个心疼的，若一毫不知和气，父母便心疼怀恨，便是大不孝的。凡孝子未有不爱弟敬兄的，弟兄不合便是不孝，不孝不友之人安有好处，试看只重妻子，薄父母兄弟的人，未有不子孙消灭者。兄弟不和，止是为财为气，怕自己穷苦，又性燥不忍气，遂至不和。何不思人生衣禄全靠天祖，我厚待弟兄，天地神明祖宗父母都爱我了，何愁衣食不足，就是朋友亦有千金相赠之时，如何骨肉弟兄却忍心不顾。至于言语不合，行事不和，也是小事，外人笑我骂我凌辱我，君子且三自反，不与他较量，况自家骨肉有何不可忍让耶。孝弟孝友是一串事，不可分看，故言孝必言友弟恭兄。二事认真了，以爱敬行之，即是富贵寿考根苗，切须勉之。古来孝子只是不忍别离父母如孩子时一般，故瞻依二字是人子大根本。作孩子时，离父母一刻，便啼哭不安，长大贪恋外事，忘了父母，孟子言慕少艾、慕妻子、慕君等，人人知之，如何却不戒绝之。幼时非父母不生，长大不顾父母，良心天理何在！舜为大孝，只是如孩子依亲，至死不变耳，故曰："终生慕父母。"若父母有难，便"窃负而逃，遵海滨而处"，天子也不要。孝子心肠，被孟子说完了。父母爱子，无时不挂在心头，为人子的，也时时把父母挂在心头，自然瞻依父母，不忍不尽道了。父母为儿女费尽心血，始得成人，到得儿女成人，父母已是衰老，不是多病，便是多愁，若不得好儿女服侍奉养，怎得起居平安。生我父母该敬道爱敬，不待言了。又有过继与人为子者，抚我之人名曰养父、养母。凡过继必是同宗之人，虽有亲疏远近，总是一个祖人传下来的，我的生父生母念祖宗一脉，将我出继，是父母的大孝心。抚我的父母因自己无子，不得已抚我为子，那心中何等凄惨，惟恐我不孝顺，便枉费辛苦了，所以能孝养父养母人，其功德更百倍。愚友张如山，其父平生孝爱养父养母与生父母无异，生二子，长如山由乡贡服官至州牧，次虚堂为孝廉方正。其他凡推爱诚之心以爱敬养父母者，无不荣显。可见圣人制礼乃天心所在，不可不讲明也。孝子不但得亲之欢，更要谕亲于道。何为谕亲于道？父母一言一行、一动一静，善则曲成之，恶则谏阻之。盖我望父母康强福寿，还要父母自修，父母有善，天乃佑之，有不善，恐损父母之德，便损父母之福了。孟子曰："不得乎亲不可以为人，不顺乎亲不可以为子"。得亲，亲喜悦我，顺亲，谕亲于道也。愿父母为圣人又要父母欢心，二者相妨，事亲之道所以难尽，惟舜得亲、顺亲兼尽其道，所以底豫而为大孝。世上父母喜儿子承顺，儿子亦以承顺为孝，不知善可顺从，不善而顺从，陷亲不义，反为大不孝。所以孔子曰："恶有从亲之令可以为孝者乎！"事父母有几谏之法，即是不忍父母为不善也。然自己义理不明，又安能谕亲于道，非孝爱之至，又安得委曲周全。善用其术，使父母欢喜从谏，所以夫子言："不诚乎身，不能事其亲"。诚身之道，必从事大学之道，一时不能即诚，只要爱敬二字十分周到，亦必于亲有益矣。

十三、父母并尊，不可轻重，父一而母不一，孝父自然孝母。前人误解礼经，不可不明辨也。

父母天地也，地统于天，故母统于父。然屈于夫，断无屈于人子之理。犹地卑天尊似有低昂，然天生地成，地生天成，生成万物，实天地同功，可分彼此轻重乎？前人误解夫死从子、父在为母服期年之语，致世人重父忽母，犯不孝之罪者甚多，愚于四子六经尝辨之，今更赘说于此。妇人无外交，言不出于阃，虽正位乎内，亦与正位乎外同功，而外应总非妇人所得应酬，夫死则外事安得不属于子。然从子者，谓不能身任外事，非谓不得与闻也。为子者禀命于母，不得遂自专主。或夫亡子幼，则外事亦母主之，不过不身自越阃，其主持家政，养教儿女，必兼父道而行，古来贤母甚多，皆由此选。近世不孝之子，父没妄为，母不能禁，旁观亦以从子之说为凭，不罪其子，甚或致母吞声饮恨，愁怨终身，岂非言礼者贻之咎欤！孔子曰："父母之丧无贵贱一也，"安有父三年而母止期年者哉。盖古人父母之丧常服衰绖，饮食起居俱异于常，期而小祥，始不常服衰，除去首绖、练冠、縓缘，始食菜果，然要经仍不除，不食稻衣锦、不作乐。若父在则小祥衰绖皆除，衣食起居不纯用丧礼。所以然者，父为妻服期，小祥则父服除矣，虽夫妻情重，亦可渐渐忘怀，若人子仍以丧服侍侧，必触动父之哀情，饮食不甘、起居不适，反为不孝了。故圣人制礼，父在子不纯素，以便侍养于父，即笑语承欢亦可从权，非忘母也，为慰父之心不得已也。然不在父前，则哀念于母，食旨不甘、闻乐不乐，仍尽其心丧。是故父在为母期年乃恐伤父之心，岂薄母而厚父哉！圣人不止体人子之心，使得尽礼于父，亦且禁父私情，不许伤人子之意，故古礼妻死夫服虽止期年，而必俟人子三年丧毕然后续娶，亦体人子之心，子尚居丧而即续娶，恐子思母而增悲也。且父行吉礼，子何得不从吉礼，岂有吉礼事父事继母而尚为守三年丧礼者乎。先儒不知而妄解，以贻名教之害，不可不辨。是故父母一也，罔极之恩同，礼制安得不同。生母不待言矣，其他凡为父妻妾者皆母，即皆当尽孝。继母继吾母而育我，其同母不待言，庶母亦母之轮，其侍父也，母所为者代之，母所未为者亦为之，愁劳更倍于母。子不云乎，父母之所爱亦爱之，父母之所敬亦敬之，父母器重且必珍重爱惜，而况庶母乎。礼有八母之称，推孝父母之心以及于诸母，有爱敬之天良者断无不在在尽道，为民上及为亲为师者，其可不明以示人，本身以立教哉！

十四、事君也

君亲并重而君更大于父母,盖无君则弱肉强食,难保身家,尚无父母,何有于我哉。然事父母自幼至老不离,事君则择君而仕,待时而出,何也?事君者分君之劳,非徒爵禄,君代天理物,臣代君治民,亮天工而安海甸,岂为安荣利禄哉。若有德有才,君不知我,即或知我而不信任,则虽仕无益君民,宁别求执业亦可,何必窃位而误国、误民,良心抱愧也。自古圣贤不肯轻仕,或已仕而君不倚任,礼貌或衰,稍有疑贰,即见机而作,如孔子燔肉不至,孔明三顾始出,岂自重而慢君上哉,信任不专则不能行其道,久且有意外之虑。孔子曰:"以道事君,不可则止"。孟子曰:"无罪而杀士,则大夫可以去"。故已仕者不当苟禄,未仕尤必审几。一官有一官之事,一事有一事之理,自揣胜任然后致身,则上不负君,下不误民,不然宁贫贱可矣。如或亦有才德而不尽优为,必虚己下贤,求人自辅。自周公吐握、孔明集思是其前师,否则自矜自用,误国误民,其咎更重。古人询事考言,论定然后官之,任官然后爵之,随其所长而授以职。士亦自量其才,所以无弃才,亦无废事。后世不然,以词章取士,已不能知其平生矣,一登仕版,事理多疏,而凡夤缘瞻徇,苟且之径尤多。朝廷难以收得人之效,士子不复修廉正之行,何望郅隆乎。夫子不克家,必坏父母之事,臣不忠君,岂是天泽之宜。忠君者一片肫诚,惟恐一毫欺贰,恪恭将职,此心必自事亲时力行,然后可以移孝作忠。至于体用之学皆全,为大臣则格君心之非,小臣则随事尽职,盖非可望于庸人,又在君相平日培植之功。《大学》之书果人人践行,庶修己治人均可不愧,但不可从宋儒改本转入歧途耳!

十五、出处大节，士与取士者皆必以此为先，乃有真才也。

圣贤之学，成己即欲成人，岂不思济世徒尚孤高哉，然而非有知音必不苟仕。非自高也，相信不深则必不专心委任，君子岂肯苟图利禄。后世喜恭顺之臣，实能致身尽职者未得，而谐媚之流进矣。人主喜其易于驱使而不知其身家念重，欲求精白乃心，固已不能，且取士不慎，荐举则或误信，金壬科条则但防干进，束缚之，驰骤之，以不肖待君子，圣贤豪杰遁于山陬，以荣名诱士林，无识浅夫并为弊窦，是上不知气节为忠孝之本，高尚多骨鲠之流也。至于学者束发受书即以位禄为荣，第知肥其身家，罕有真爱君国者，且并无实学，才德经济不堪自问，而侥幸求进，使之佐理，不特无功，且必偾事。老莱子云：可荣以爵禄者，可随以刀锯，凡富贵利达之徒，未有能忠君爱民至诚不变者也。高尚之士不一，有志趣清高不乐仕途者，有慕清高之名一意肥遁者，皆非中庸之道。惟实有道德如孔、孟、伊、吕，乃实能自修其身，亦惓惓于天下，必使君为尧舜之君，民为尧舜之民，如或不遇则甘心乐道，不枉己以徇人，视万钟如敝履耳。若非贤君，则必以为孤高自恃，而不知其忠爱之诚，悲悯之志，有百倍于常人者，如孔孟未尝干进，用世切切于怀。盖有圣人之道者，自然不遗其亲，不后其君，为上者安可不逾格忧崇也。人主知此，必重育才之道，世人知此，必少苟贱之行，吾是以揭而言之。

十六、三纲不正，则五伦亦不正，故为上者当自修也。

道在五伦，五伦以三纲为重。重之者，非重其名分，重其责任也。惟天子兼君亲师之任，其尊如天，其于民如父母，爱养之、裁成之，故师道亦在其中。上天爱民，不能自为养教，乃亶聪作后，使代其功，为人君者，可佽然自足，不体上天之心哉？孔子称尧则天，非但誉尧，明为君必心如天、道如天始可也。天子而下，百官皆分天子之任，即皆有君亲师之责，若但享荣禄、负君恩，即得罪于天，所以明良交泰，乃成祥和。世之为父母者，第知责子不肖，而不知积德贻后、又善诱教，乃为父母之道。孔子曰："子也者，亲之后也，可不敬欤"。祖宗有积累之仁，然后子又生孙。不念父母之恩，徒以己为父母，便可责望于子孙，其小言行心术无以为法，其甚荡检踰闲，多生罪咎，而乃佽然纷然责备于子，岂知己先罪于父母乎。故孔子曰："知为人子，然后可以为人父，"不慈便是不孝，此理罕人知之久矣。孟子曰："中也养不中，才也养不才，故人乐有贤父兄也。如中也弃不中，才也弃不才，则贤不肖相去，不能以寸"，"身不行道，不行于妻子，使人不以道，不能行于妻子"，为父母者其亦思之否乎。夫妇为人伦之首，孔子曰：有夫妇后有父子、君臣、上下，男女正，天地之大义。人道以大婚为大，故礼必冕而亲迎。子思曰："君子之道，造端乎夫妇"。自古圣人莫不有贤配，夫子删诗，二南首列后妃，诗至五篇之多，馀亦多妇女之什，其训世之意可知。而后儒误解经义，谓《易经》抑阴扶阳，妇人惟酒食是议，不知阴阳相济乃成造化，造化之功莫大于五行，而天生地成，地生天成，互为其功。"地道无成而有终"，无成者，承天而时行，非坤元资生不如乾元之始也。斯干之诗，作室落成，祝居者攸芋攸宁，生男生女，男君王而女柔顺，嫁夫得其人，宜室宜家，无有非议之事，亦无俟威仪文饰，但时以酒食相乐，乃颂祷之词耳，岂谓妇人但议酒食而一切家政俱不与闻哉。果尔，则圣人正内、正外、阴教、阳教之义又何以通。自儒者误解此诗，令后世人民贵夫贱妻，或身不修而暴虐其妻，或妻本不贤而无以教化，上则无以事父母，中则无以和兄弟，下又何以成家教子孙哉！间有重伉俪者，又徒以情欲相亲，不问义理之是非，遂牝鸡司晨，百为乖舛，其害尤不胜计。夫妇女生长闺中，不闻外事，安得皆圣贤之徒，全赖丈夫为纲，有以整齐教化之，贤者敬之、不贤者善教之，必在我者一言一行皆可为法，徐徐渐染而化导之。如愚悍不法，则屏斥之，毋使得与家政而已，否或另置贤妾，或竟归之母家，无可归者亦置之别所，养之如旧以终其年，万不得已而后出之。使夫果仁贤，不能变化者亦少，是在人之自勉而已。至于师者，所以辅五伦、维风教，凡忠孝、仁义等事，必需明师导之。故曰：父生之，师成之。民生于三，事之如一，乌有心性伦常之理，无贤师而能臆测者乎。自古圣人皆必有师，自先儒谓圣人为天授，不须师承，而学者诿资质以自安，视师道为易事。为师者德行道艺未必信心而侈然自足，为弟者人伦日用俱不力行，而但务文字，其他百工技艺，身心不端而妄居师范者更不少，世安得有全才哉！故就臣子、妻与弟言，则君、亲、师与夫即未必贤亦不可一毫非议；而就君、亲、师与夫言，则必求问心无愧，然后伦纪修而人才出。此名教之大关，世运污隆之根本，不可不察，不可不勉也！

十七、君相不可不以圣人自命也

生民之始,人物杂居,无宫室、无衣服饮食等制,与禽兽无异也。天生圣人为之君相,使人别于禽兽。唐虞以前,其君如今酋长,各居其土,各子其民,有德如尧舜则人乃归之,然不过羁縻统属而已,故曰:天下归往谓之王,亶聪明作元后,元后作民父母,惟天惠民,惟辟奉天。不体天德以为德,不体天心以为心,何以能代天理物,化民成俗哉,故孔子表尧则天,以为世法。而尧舜体天以治世,且不以天下为私,必择贤而与之,非矫也,知君上非圣人莫能胜任也。顾圣人不常有,而国不可一日无君,于是乃有世及之典,其父为圣人,则必能以圣道教其子孙,即或久未必然,而有贤臣夹辅,亦可匡扶乂安,如禹之有启,汤武有伊周。其创业者本无利天下之心,天亦从而护佑之,继世不能即有桀纣,且培德深厚,作育有方,此三代所以享国久长也。后世以天下为利禄,有德而民归之者固已寥寥,又不知体天爱民,选贤图治,徒欲巩固河山,常保宗社,然而德既不厚,臣亦罕良,安得不祸生旋踵。夫天生蒸民,为之君长,必非无故而诞降,然聪明首出,亦必藉乎善教。从古圣王本身作则,可为后人倡,而谕教世子,必选大贤,如周之文武以圣人之资而有圣人之父,虑无不率家训而绍先型矣,然且以鬻熊、太公为师,咨虞访虢,周召毕荣,贤俊济济于廷,其后嗣亦安得而不贤智哉。故开创之君固当积功累仁,旁求名世,继体之君,亦必省身寡过,虚己求贤。昊天子天子,天子子天下,事天如事亲,爱民如爱子,天人有不翕应者乎。至于人臣分君之职,亮天工而抚元元,亦与君同其责备。未从事大学之道,诚其意,正其心,则虽有才能,必多遗行,况不以天亲视其君,不以仁义治其民,而窃位苟禄,甚且奸欺百端,世何以臻于荡平,天岂不降大戾乎。

十八、培植人才礼贤下士，有国有家者皆当急务也。

为君无不望有良臣，为父无不望有贤子，而不能者，培植之道不讲也。培植之道安在？修身而已。修身之道非一，以忠恕之心，行仁义之事，念念不忘诚敬而已。天理良心为仁，行之而善为义，仁义始于孝悌，推诸百为。凡一念之起，必求于心安，于理顺，以至于念念皆然，事事不苟，则德懋矣。即未能然，知时时检点心术，恐于心不安，于理不顺，亦可以久久而成德，传教子孙。为君者有裁成天下之权，其易培植人才不待言矣。为父者养教子孙，木本水源，亦可自主。本身立德，必求一毫无愧于心，尤必力行仁义，爱敬至诚，虚心集益，自返无怼，已足为后人楷模矣，而又交游俱善，子弟目见耳闻，如入芝兰之室，久而自化，岂患其越畔哉。自古及今，生而不肖者无多人。盖为君为父者不知此义，故家不成其为家，国不成其为国，是以不得已而揭言之耳。周家后稷教稼育民，功配彼天，自公刘以下皆圣人，宽仁厚德如大王迁岐，文王服事，其大著者酝酿祥和已久，而本成已以成人，至于中林野人，俱为干城腹心，若非文王寿考作人，武王、周公封建八百，安得许多贤士而用之。孟僖子称夫子曰："吾闻圣人有明德者，其后必有达人，今其将在孔某"。即此二端，有国有家者之由来可推，不然而欲求忠孝、贤圣，必不可得矣。

十九、道在日用伦常而能尽道者希，分心性事功为两途，世俗圣贤为不相合也，当明辨而力行之。

日用者何？一切言行事也。人生所赖以生者，不过宫室、衣服、饮食、男女四事，而常人以之蔑礼丧心，圣人以之事天立命，何哉？以礼节情，不离俗亦不徇俗，即妙矣。宫室可避风雨，饮食可免饥寒，男女承先启后。端其心术，修其职业，以天理良心为主，四者即可如意，不至困穷，此天人感应一定之理。若纵欲无度，非理营求，则反致灾患。世人于此处关键不明，所以无者妄求，有者倾覆，可叹也！五伦之事即在日用间，但道各不同。君友以义合者也，子曰：以道事君，不可则止，忠告善道，不可则止，故此二伦只好自尽其心于道，难以期其必相投合。若父母、兄弟、夫媳，则人人有之，不能外此而生，外此而有道。夫子系《易》曰："父父子子，兄兄弟弟，夫夫妇妇而家道正，正家而天下定"。家正耳，何以天下便可定哉？无人不有三伦，能各尽其道，各正其家，天下更有何事。自古圣王亦不过本治家以治国，日用伦常，安能外此而为道。父子兄弟夫妇至亲至迩，而其常变顺逆情事万有不齐，欲尽其道，必须明其分谊之当然，竭其天性之自然，勿任其心情，善全其事变，而后可以无愧。父母者天也，竭诚尽慎奉养瞻依终身，不待言矣，尤当明善诚身，谕亲于道盖人子欲亲福寿，仍须父母自修，若言行心术一有不合，即为父母之累，故得亲、顺亲，必兼尽其道焉。兄弟手足同以父母为根本，想到父母爱子个个一般，未有兄弟不相爱者，故孝友、孝弟一串而言，不友、不弟，即是不孝，纵有他事好处，根本先亏，神天祖先亦不眷佑，戒之！戒之！为兄者如舜，为弟如王览便得法。凡兄弟不和，为财、为气、听谗言三事而已。天要我穷，怎得饱暖，天要我富，怎得饥寒。然天何故爱我，必死守天理良心，乃合天意而得福也。银钱原是公共使用之物，朋友相好，尚且千金赠之，何况弟兄。我怜爱弟兄，惟恐其受饥寒，天地、神明、祖宗、父母便多欢喜了，安有尚穷饿之理。试看天下人宽让疏财者未有不昌达，刻薄弟兄者未有不消亡，奈何不急急回头！至于义理是非，辨明之者以修身也，弟兄之间则断断不可讲理，只以相亲相爱和睦为主，即有不是，亦徐徐劝化，不可骤发，不可执固。若平日相处，一分别是非，便起争竞了。或兄或弟言语行事不合，以痴聋待之，慢慢再劝化，不可化亦宽让，勿记于怀。如此责己、仁让，则妻妾及外人谗言自然不入耳了。夫正其纲，善教妻子，勿贪色欲，勿不修身，勿虐使其妻，一切言行不愧，方才可以为人夫、为人父，切勿侈然自足，不正其身而徒责妻子。如此则父父子子，兄兄弟弟，夫夫妇妇矣。人伦之道修，日用一切事为自然俱当乎天理。世俗不践人伦之道，而徒求嗜欲养身，富贵名世，固非义矣。儒者高谈性命而不从世俗之事使人切近奉行，诚敬孚之，遂致言理入于空幻，言道不屑世俗，岂知心性伦常内外一原，必本末交修随时处中哉。自古圣人德同而事不同者，随其时俗为之节文也，外世俗而言道，谈性命而无事功，于道何当，于世教何裨。戒之！勉之！

二十、教必先养，而后世养最难兴，必因时制宜，其权在君亲师也。

圣人治世亦止富、教二字，人人免于饥寒，人人为善去恶，天下有何事哉！惜人心难治，俗云：饱暖生淫欲，饥寒起盗心。穷则邪僻，富又骄淫，人心难治，将奈何哉。周制人皆有田，士皆学道，可谓周密矣，然而世官世禄，久遂骄横兼并虐下，在上者已然，在下者人人有田，无饥、困、流离之忧，久而放纵。至春秋时，便有许多不堪之事，废井田，去封建，虽商鞅之为，亦岂非天意哉。人心易肆，非经一番困苦，罕有能自淑者，即曾经困苦，一旦亨通，尚多奢纵，况生长富贵乎。为君上者严为立法，善为裁成，宫室衣食一切制度，齐民不得等于士大夫，士大夫非有德不能幸进，以大学之道育士，以六德六行登贤，凡民多财无所用之，则天下可群趋于仁义矣。为士者农、工、商、贾各执一业，但能端心术、修品行，以勤俭持家，亦何患不免饥寒。是在君亲师善为养教之，不然而苟求富贵，不循天理，得则欣欣、失则戚戚，吾未见有能久者也。朝无贵而不德之人，野无不义而富之士，则庶几焉。

二十一、君亲之责固重而师尤为先，非行大学之道，师固难求也。

《礼》曰："师无当于五服，五服弗得不亲"。大学之道，诏于天子，无北面。所以然者何哉？父母不尽圣贤，有圣贤之师而后知道、行道、全乎为人之理。及其成功，事亲必孝，事君必忠，凡成己成人之业无不可为。即为君、为亲，亦必有师而后成德，所以于君亲并重也。自古圣人无不有师，黄帝师广成、帝尧师务光、文王师鬻熊、武王师尚父、孔子师老聃。孔子师老聃，儒者不以为然，下赘言之，兹不赘。若王季，文王，皆圣人也，而必有师以诲其子，岂故谦下哉，身心性命之理，日用伦常之道，至平、至常、至精、至粹，非亲炙圣师，朝夕追随，亦趋亦步，岂易精微毕贯。以圣人为天授，不待于师，此不知道之言，彼于天人性命一以贯之之义，固未实践渐臻，故以一得之知谓为止境，而使后世学者高视圣人，轻视师表，谓资禀不逮，谓道可凭心臆测，其为害可胜言哉。夫子曰："吾闻老聃博古知今，则吾师也，吾将往而学焉"。从老聃助祭，聃呼其名，临别再称为犹龙。子夏对魏文侯曰："仲尼师老聃，窃比于老彭"，即老子也。朱子初注亦以为老子，后因人辟异端改为商贤大夫，然商贤大夫即老子矣。在商为守藏史，名钱铿，在周为柱下史，因长年恐惑人，故屡改名。百工技艺皆有师，何况圣人之学，立命事天，继往开来，为孝子，为纯臣，襄皇猷，明教泽，其道至大，其用至宏，而其功夫次第尤非可以一朝尽，岂容无师而能知之、行之哉。但师有圣人之德者旷世难逢，其次品端心正，实践伦常不欺、不苟，亦已可矣。又其次优于才学，稍知敦品，否则才艺可以节取。然苟大本不修，则无以造就人才，俾家有贤子，国有忠臣。夫子温故而知新可以为师，人罕知者，姑附于此。故者，天理也。天理无所不包，凡人伦日用以及天地民物，无小无大皆是，而其原具于心性，此理人独得之于天，与生俱来，故名曰故。圣人教人为学，全是欲人葆此天理，果能复其天命之初，则心纯乎仁，行合乎义，尽人性、物性，皆由己性而推。温者如火暖物，喻时习之功，内有以固其神明，外不稍惰其志气也。以养气言，则孟子所谓有诸己而充实浩然之气，睟然盎背，四体不言而喻。孔子秋阳以暴之，子思云形著动变，温温恭人者，外著形神，太和翔洽者，内存之德行。中庸言凝道功夫，特述孔子之言，非养浩然之气至于充实而有光辉，未易知温故之义，又安知如何知新，可以为师哉。道流言温养亦此意，惜为后世所乱，喻神为火，喻气为药，以神养气为以火练药，持其志曰武火烹练，毋忘毋助，听其自然曰文火温养，实则存神养气之别名耳。人之神气与天地通，圣人与天合德，止是心纯乎天理，但凡人心多妄，则不得为天性。圣人尽性，心纯乎天，即与天合，而究其实，则志气如神，浩然者塞乎天地。心即神也，为气之主，气，人身所以生，言理而不言神气，空空言心性，心性何所寄哉。性乃天理，称为元神浩然之气、乾原之气。知觉之心非性，以口鼻之气为气，力避佛老，而不知全祖，告子已失圣人之真。不得于言，勿求于心，或知其非，不得于心，勿求于气则不知矣。天命之性是理即是气，理气之宰曰神，岂容外视哉。不明孔孟之道而欲为师，孔孟所以叹人之患在此耳！

二十二、有圣贤之师自多圣贤之徒，圣贤固非甚难，先儒过为高远，使后学畏阻而废，切勿为所误也。

孔子言：生、安、学、利、困、勉，惟困而不学，民斯为下，果能学、问、思、辨、笃行，虽愚必明。孟子言："人皆可为尧舜"，因道止是天理二字，人人有天理则人人可为圣贤。天理者何？良心也，性也，明德也，如木果之有仁曰仁。性为全体之仁，义、礼、智、信皆所以行仁。孔子淳淳以仁望人曰：苟志于仁，无恶，有能用力于仁，未见力不足者，以良心天理人人易知而易行也。修身以道，修道以仁，仁者人也。孟子曰："仁也者人也，合而言之道也"，圣贤成己成人，除却此四字，无道不合，此四字便为异学。自汉儒错解子罕言仁章，宋儒因之谓人道甚大，夫子罕言，然则《论语》所记门人问仁，夫子言仁不一而足，其义何居？谓孔子以礼教人，然夫子曰："人而不仁如礼何"，"礼云礼云，玉帛云乎哉"，又是何意。弊由错解礼字，谓孔子之礼是寸步不离成法，而不知夫子动容周旋中礼，乃仁熟而义自精，从心不逾矩，凡一言一行，一动一静，莫非天理之自然，即莫非事物之当然，非拘拘文武周公之制也。故曰："无可，无不可"，"动而世为天下道，言而世为天下法，行而世为天下则"，岂必墨守前人规矩始为礼哉。后儒误认《仪礼》一书为圣作，并拘牵汉儒诸礼书，是以不得孔孟真诠而生反，反古迂窒之患兴矣。观子路与祭大反前事，而夫子称之曰："谁谓由也而不知礼乎"，则子之时中可见一斑。况三代下一切法制均非古人，而以古礼教人如泥塑木雕始为儒者，岂不谬哉！故礼者天理之节文，本天理良心而节其过、文其不及便是礼。守王制亦学圣贤，纯俭可从，拜上不可从，无一定，亦未尝不一定。仁熟自然义精，无智愚皆可能，则皆可以修身教人也，师道亦何患不立哉。道之大者在五伦，其理皆自心性而具，从事大学之道，格去己私，致其本体之明，先从诚意、慎独、去恶、迁善，再止于至善，静养天性，内外交养，本末交修，即不能十分纯全，亦可免为禽兽。夫子所谓：苟志于仁，无恶，有能用力于仁，未见力不足也。自先儒将大学古本改坏，希圣功夫模糊，影响千有余年，更从何处有名师乎。孔子曰：有教无类，虽愚必明。今则谓圣人为天授，读书学道亦难希圣。孔孟之后，仅数人知道耳。嗟乎！人皆有天良，圣人亦不过全乎人理，而谓凡人不可为圣、为贤，必如某某道学规模，岂不冤哉！天地所以生人，圣人所以教人，人之所以异于禽兽，一概抹杀，试平心思之，可乎不可。

二十三、道不外人情物理，故人人可能，但须以天理权衡之，即合时中矣。

亘古此人，亘古此心理，故圣王不易民而治。人情嗜好不同，然所以养生，止宫室、衣食、男女四事，不足者营求，既有者贪侈，而蔑理丧心种种邪妄作矣。圣王治世，所欲与之聚之，所恶无施，有以养其生矣。即于所欲所恶之事，为之礼制，人情乐而趋之，习久安于固然。故人情物理外，生人便无生理，圣人亦无事功。但人情物理不尽合乎中正，必以天理为主，折衷弃取，不合乎礼即断断不为。礼只是人情物理之事，不太过，亦不不及，不是一定拘拘要行古人之制。先儒不识天理良心四字便是大道，教人循循古礼，至于大反世俗，显悖王章，方斤斤焉以为理学，是以人迂而置之，畏而远之，中庸之道遂不明矣。王安石屡谒濂溪而不得见，忿然曰："吾独不可返而求诸六经乎"。司马公卒，程伊川治丧，用冒笼束全身，东坡曰："尚少一事"。伊川问："何事"？曰："当书字一幅题曰：右公文一角仰阎罗大王开折"。朱子慢客，客曰："斗酒只鸡，山中未为乏也"。遂来伪学之禁。明儒拘礼，记男子不死于妇人之手，屏绝妻女，身死而家人不知其何时。故不通人情物理而言道远，不特难以施行，且阻人以学圣，是以必当明辨而体行也。

二十四、人情物理不离世俗，切勿是古非今，薄视俗人俗事也。

五帝殊时，不相袭礼，三王异时，不相沿乐，时势不同，人情风俗变易多端，生其时，从其俗，酌人情物理而合中正，凡圣人皆然也。孔子曰："斯民也，三代之所以直道而行"，"吾非斯人之徒与而谁与"，纯俭可从，拜上不可从，曷尝外世俗而别为道哉，但去其非存其是焉耳。是故随时处中，人人可能，如夏本炎热，大雨亦必加衣矣，冬本严寒，日暖亦或减衣矣。由是而推，凡事皆然，不外乎理，不过乎中即是。后世风俗人情迥殊，前代儒者徒读古书，高言古礼，不知变通，以之修己治人，无一可者，是以孔孟之言等于画饼，而修齐治平难望咸宜矣。大学之道只是教人真心术以敦人伦，其功夫人人可能，无古今之异，而果得其理，即随时可以处中，无如被先儒改坏古本，遂莫能知所从事矣。

二十五、格致便是内外交养之功，说向外去，教人物物穷理，便有知无行，逐末忘本矣。

圣学不外静存动察两途，本非难能之事。凡人应酬万变，皆赖此心，而心不尽善，以人心私妄太多也。人心何以多私？有此气质，便有耳目口体之欲，此欲是人所以生，即人心也。人不能外气质之欲而生，安能去人心而可以为圣。然圣人竟与人异者，何也？曰：人心皆听命于道心耳。道心者何？曰：性也。性岂在心之外乎？曰：否。然则一心何以二名？曰：心之所以灵者气，气之禀于生初者无不纯，故曰：人性皆善。得天地之理气而为人，以其分天地之正气而有性。性存于太虚之中，人得其光英之照，父母以形交，而理气以虚无混合有此身，有此心，此实而可验者也。而性之本与虚无与天地通，为理气粹者，岂可名言哉。大学之教，使人静养其未发之中，以清其源，动审其中节之和，以善其用。非静何以知动，非浩然之气有基，又何能力持其动。故格物而志气清明，致知而是非不惑。其格物也，去人欲而保清明也。其致知也，学问思辨而别是非，是则扩充，非则克治，动察之一端耳。然人心私妄最是难尽，若非养乾元之浩气，必不能去气质之疵累。孟子养气不动心乃自古圣人实功，因世益衰，乃不得已而揭言之。不知其理，安知大学格致诚正之义。先儒未解道心人心之由来，又不识养气何以不动心，而中庸之道，康庄变为荆棘矣。读书学道，欲为圣贤，无如人心何，安得不视圣贤如天人，随世俗而湮灭哉。

二十六、养气不动心，即大学之正心。此理不明，故辟佛老者以其伪，罪其真，而明心见性，修真养性一概抹杀，心与气之相关，正与诚之迥异，无人知矣。

三代以前，无异端之名，以君上作则于上，师儒教授于下也。周制大司徒以乡三物教万民，而宾兴之六德、六行、六艺，自天子至庶人皆同此学术，知仁、圣、义、中、和。后世所谓万难之事而当时万民咸肆习之，盖其理本人人所有，则其学亦不患不能行耳。周衰，礼教渐湮，夫子乃有攻乎异端之叹，然当时所谓异端者，不过不遵六德、六行之人，其实子之最恶者，在上则鄙夫，在下则乡愿耳。至佛在孔子之前，老子与夫子同时，且从而学礼，未尝谓为异端。秦始皇无道，金人破户使往西方求佛，老子则青牛西隐。中夏之尚佛老也，以儒修不正，奸乱日生，人厌恶之，避而趋清净耳。汉兴，民苦烦虐，以淡朴为安，故萧、曹为相，有画一清净之歌，而说者遂以为黄老，然黄帝垂裳，德同尧舜，老子知礼，赞以犹龙，曷可谓为异端。佛自秦时肇起，两汉犹鲜僧徒，魏、晋以下篡乱，大道将湮，佛教始盛，而达摩东来示以真谛，亦恐传之太伪，误世亦诬佛耳。不料数传以后，果失其宗，虽高明之士亦有得真诠者，而俗僧异术日以益多，学老子者亦然。佛之明心见性，所谓尽其心者，知其性也，而但学其空空，以心为性；老之修真养性，即所谓闲邪存诚也，而以为别有奇怪之术。不知心性外无圣人，又安有佛老，而必痛加排斥者曰废人伦。然佛有妻、有子。废人伦者，四裔旧俗，非佛导之，中华佛寺以养穷民，不得不禁蓄妻子。老子之不废人伦彰彰矣，赵宋始禁道士娶妻，则以废伦罪之亦不可。凡僧道之伪妄者，皆愚民惑众求新，无不身罹法网。禁其伪者，存其真者，以庵观寺宇养无告之穷民，盖理势不得不然者矣。必贬斥佛老，谓道止日用伦常，而不知其理必由心而发，存心养性清其源，日用伦常习其事，圣人然，佛老有何独不然。佛曰：一切佛田不离方寸，老曰：多言数穷，不如守中，是内而存心养性同也。渡尽众生，方能成佛，堂上父母两尊大佛，三千阴功，八百德行，人道尽而仙道始立，是外而日用伦常实践也。僧羽之妄，岂可以罪其本始哉。今将静心则曰禅也，将养气则曰玄也，避禅与玄之名而不从心性用功，欲践伦常断断不能，夫是以反复而赘言之。若忌虚无玄空，则养气而心憧憧，持志之义不明矣。

二十七、万事起于心，万理统于性，存心养性，然后伦常克践。佛老之正者不外心性，辟之而并失其存养之实，非也。

天止一理，人得之以为性，圣人不过尽性。佛曰明心见性，道曰修真养性，则知其所谓空与玄者，只是养性之时一私不杂之意耳。致其中而浑然无物曰空，悦诸心而天趣陶然曰玄，岂谓废人伦日用哉。今天下僧流所谓禅定者，六祖坛经也，以养知觉之心为性，慧悟者亦多，然实非佛之全功。周濂溪得其法于寿涯，程朱衍之，遂以为圣学，而又必辟佛老以附于孔孟。天资之优者，心中私欲较少，静坐之久，便觉智慧明通，亦可立身立业，为世名流。质之钝者不能也，去而之他，反不如僧道犹多守清规，甘澹泊，则以不知虚无清净四字乃养心之法也。除却四字，放心必不能收，止至善而定静安亦不得其解，大学之道功夫次第无从践行，徒攘斥佛老何益哉。盖后天之心不纯乎性，存虚无之心，乃生乾元之气，气充实后内外交修，大而化神，然后可不动心也。

二十八、心性之功乃人伦日用根本，错解大学格致诚正，故不知佛老之正者亦同于儒，而歧杂多途，异端纷起。经不正，庶民何以兴也。

　　道莫大于五伦，五伦止是天理，人人皆有天理，如何罕有忠孝仁义之人？只因心中私伪难除。凡耳目口鼻四支之欲随感而动，逐物而迁，虽千牛难挽，久久习为固然，人与禽兽亦不复顾，以礼束之，以法禁之，视如无有。古今事变不忍言者，皆自人心不正为之也。若非急急力行大学之道，将如何靖人心而敦五伦哉。先儒只知辟佛老，尊圣人，而实未践行圣人之学，教人不过静心而已。常常省察克治，便欲气质之私不行，则原思何以不得为仁；凡事物物穷理求其明白，则圣人一贯又何以不由多识？圣人心性之功次第浅深一概不知，而曰上继孔孟维持大道，其心是，其人是，而其所学不是。《大学古文》一改窜，而心性之功无从入手矣。无正心修身之功，古今亦有名臣宰辅，忠孝节义，然大抵皆天资高明，至性不同流俗，所以慷慨激发从容就义者不一而足，孔子所谓仁人志士，孟子所称豪杰之士，其争光日月，维持人伦，天间世而一生，不欲正气遂泯耳。若由下学而上达，全德者甚少。父师作则，示以静养其中，动履其和，上者即可入于圣神，其次亦不至无仁、无礼、欺君亲而祸民人，所以圣人云：有教无类，知之一，成功一。自先儒以心为性，觉义理不能贯通万事，改窜《大学》，以物物穷理为要功，使人疲耳目，役心志，穷尽天下之物，无益身心，而不遗其亲，不后其君，反少人知之。曰：道不易明，心不易正，而不知其存养心性者无本也。孔孟后非无真传，被文人自恃闿尽，不知万事万理本于心，而但知日用伦常。日用伦常之理何一不本于心，心不正，意不诚，求名求利，嗜欲纷纭，曰：此日用伦常也，而不知任心而行，徇欲悖理，往往皆是名利薰心，忠孝不能实践，而徒斥佛老，是名为不废人伦亦虚耳。佛老之伪者诚为乱民，其正者未尝无清高绝俗之士。古今所传，不可诬也，奈何不辨黑白混而同之，鄙而弃之。佛老有妻子室家，不废人伦，其教人曰：一切佛田不离方寸，多言不如守中，是以心性为主矣。又曰：渡尽众生方能成佛，三千阴功八百德行，是修道以仁之义，不外日用伦常而修身矣。举世隐忍不言，若再无人言，其误世何极，故愚特违众而饶舌也。

二十九、忠孝固德行之首，而古今错误亦多，必以孔孟之义为主，然后死不徒死，忠孝全其大美也。

凡事皆以圣人为师，而况人伦之大乎。君亲当忠孝，人人知之，不忠不孝者无足道，已知忠知孝而不得其中，则亦不合圣人，虽无伤于忠孝，然人争效之，则反误后来，如泄冶之忠，申生之孝，岂得谓其非哉，而人之多辟，无自立辟，君子已为泄冶伤之。为吴泰伯不亦可乎？狐突早为太子劝之，即情势万难挽回，君亲欲其死，亦当审于义理之安，况奸人陷害，君亲一时被欺，宗社所联，徒死有伤祖德，岂可不慎。孔子曰："以道事君，不可则止"，曾子芸瓜被斥。孟子不枉道而仕，言孝则曰得亲顺亲兼全，言忠则曰格心成善。故杀身成仁，必其势已穷，君父死而义不独生，或受重寄而不终其事，乃必死耳。若谓忠孝必以死为贵则非。微、箕、比干皆贵戚之卿，与国同休戚者也。而微子远遁，箕子佯狂，不与比干同死，孔子皆以为仁，则比干之谏非欲其死，而特出于不幸也。焚廪捐阶，舜可以死而不死，卒底豫而全大孝。死而无益，与君亲徒死何为哉。且君亲一时之怒，安知其不悔心，留其身以有待，或君亲憬悟，忠孝以终，岂不妙乎。或被斥逐，君亲危亡，以身赴救而安之尤妙，若不能救，君亲亡而己不独生，此时一死岂不可贵。君亲同恩同尊而出处不同，未食君禄者不必死徇，然亦不事二姓。若子道必先谕亲于道，或亲不从而至危亡，必以身徇，间有不必徇者，无后及宗社无人，或当雪耻者也。故死忠死孝人生大节，当死而尽善者亦难，非力行大学之道至于仁熟义精，安能辨哉。徒以死为贵，或陷亲不义，无益君亲，且君亲悔悟，恨其无及，岂不遗憾九原乎。所以圣人之行，孔孟之义，不可一日不讲也。

三十、求忠臣必于孝子之门，而史册所载忠或不孝、孝或不忠，必明辨之，始免人疑忠孝之相妨也。

忠孝之所以通者，为其天良真切，不欺亲，自然不欺君也。但父母生我养我，自幼至老终身与父母相依，非若事君必择君而事。有世受禄养者、有世托宇下者、有初委赘、有膺特达之知及委任大小职分不同，孟子言所就三、所去三之类，或出、或处、或止、或速，有许多斟酌，非可苟且而就。故观臣者必观其事父母何如，能竭诚尽慎，不欺、不苟，则必亦不欺于君，不苟于仕，此所以求忠臣必于孝子也。君有严威，令人可畏，君有爵禄，令人可贪，故事君而恭敬者多，事亲而诚敬者少。爱亲爱君之心至者，其敬恭服事处于天性之自然，且事亲必谕亲于道乃为大孝，事君亦引君当道乃为良臣，孝而又忠毫发无疵者，非上智不能也。事父母终身在膝下，事君则自揣其才何如，始可授职。若为贪而仕，抱关击柝可以免饥寒已足，否则为苟禄。凡才德兼优者，虽江湖亦不忘君，而又断不枉道徇人，岂薄视君哉。仕则以身许君，有死无二，虽父母亦不能兼顾，然忠于君即是孝于亲矣。所以受君之禄，必君实能信任，可以有益君民而后可，此乃伊、葛之流，非可以望于寻常之辈。三代下仕宦者大半好爵是縻，非实有致君泽民之略，又言扬行举虽取士之成法，然有言者多，有行者少，文章华国，以吏为师，在上者无由知其修于家者若何，又乌知其心于君者奚似，是故忠与孝分途，出与处异致，而忠者未必孝，孝者不能忠，所以同原者晦矣。古之孝子惟知有亲可乐，虽天下亦如敝蹝，曷尝欲舍亲求荣，而苟君信用之，亦必一毫不欺，故忠臣必先不遗其亲，未有忍违亲而犹效忠于君，欺其君而犹能笃孝者也。世变日甚，大学之道不明，忠孝两全之道知者甚希，则史册所传或忠或孝，取其天性之过人、捐生之苦志可矣。然古今之事，有忠孝至诚，哀感行路，而其君其亲若罔闻之者，则大道不明，人伦不正，又岂独臣子之咎哉。

三十一、直道不明，乡愿太多，自古国家乱亡必由乎此，宜亟正也。

子曰："人之生也直，枉之生也幸而免"，"斯民也，三代之所以直道而行"。皋陶九德，以直为先，孟子直养无害为养气根本，此一字人往往忽略，遂使义理是非颠倒混淆，为国家大患，治日常少，乱日常多，可叹也！直非偏直、刚直、孤直、峭直、一切不明义理、任性施为者可托。所谓直者，秉天理而行，是是非非毫无枉屈，亦非负气孤行，不谐世俗。夫子之言达也曰："质直而好义，察言而观色，虑以下人"。以直为直，如木有干，天理是非辨之明、守之定矣，而又不敢自恃，博采义理，虚心从善，则理虽直而处世应酬，温、良、恭、俭、让全焉，所以为盛德之至，无施不可。世俗所谓直者，大都义理不明，悻直自用，或稍有所见，便抹却众人，或出或处，偾事贾祸者不一而足。于是人以直道为讳，曰：敬让者立身之本，和光同尘，君子之道，而似是实非，乡愿遂接踵于天下矣。不辨义理是非，不问事理轻重大小，一概以摸棱行之，恐得罪于君父，阿意曲从，则忠爱之心日薄；恐得罪于权贵，则承颜望色，莽、操之势以成。推而至于居家处世，在在惟恐得祸，具臣所不从者亦从，贩竖所不屑者亦就，天下尚安得有正气哉！诗曰好是正直，斯为靖共神听，锡福必由乎此，岂非以天理民彝是非之公，不可一毫枉屈哉。直必以正，非正不得为直，正直二字不行，则忠孝目为金壬，权奸推为仪范，其弊何可胜言！孟子言孔子思狂狷，恶乡愿，而终之以反经则无邪慝，解者谓邪慝杨墨之徒，而不知孟子所指乃乡愿也。杨墨之弊，识者犹多不为，若乡愿则外托于谦恭，内习为柔顺，同乎流俗，合乎世，众皆悦之，君父不察，以为忠孝，群众不察，以为贤良，而不知是非颠倒，直道全亡，新莽奉以伊周，曹魏居然禅让，非不直之人附和，安得而成篡逆乎。孔子曰："举直错诸枉则民服"，罔生为悻免，目乡愿为贼，示人以不直即宜死亡，贼害人心，莫此为甚。惜乎世情好谀恶直，宁使是非不明，不肯得罪宵小也。

三十二、大学之道包一切，扫一切，易知易能，在上以此立教，在下人人共行，天下无事矣。

自圣人之师罕有，儒者所学浅而欲语高深，纷纷妄说，致人以学道为难事，以圣人为天生，而康莊化为荆棘矣。不知天下古今虽万有不齐，而其要止在人心。人心一正，则无论何事，天理良心不坏，则一切礼、乐、法、制俱易知能，俱为有用实学。若人心不正，任百般才能，必用之不得其正。心如何而正？实行大学之道而已。格物、格去物欲，致知、致其义理之知也。欲寡则心清而义理易明，又以学问思辨之功致其知，凡日用伦常动静语默之理，俱细细讲明是非，明白了则笃实行之，是为诚意。诚意者，从一点动处便检点是非，非者即刻斩除，是者实心去做，不忍为不仁，不敢为不义，不欺、不苟、不怠、不肆，由一念以推于念念，一事以推于事事，善日积而恶日消，则本源清矣。而由是泽之以诗书，广之以闻见，父母督率之，明师友裁成之，行之至真且久，上焉者可以希圣希天，其次为君子、为善人，即至下亦不肯为昧良心事。所以大学之道为圣人辅相裁成大用。且人生无论智愚，所欲者不过饱暖安全而已。饱暖安全，其权操于天地，赏善罚恶，馀庆馀殃，天理万古不变。能行格、致、诚之功者，必畏天命、守天理，便与天意合了，而又不纵情恣欲，凡保身养生之术亦必能行，孟子所谓守身为大也。大学之道，守身诚身并行，愚前已言之，人人可知，人人可行，寿世仁民，即此其道，奈何本迩而求诸远，本易而求诸难，使人人失其固有，逐于歧途也。

三十三、道惟时中，人人可能，高视而贻害于家国，古今皆然，可叹也。

孟子以孔子为圣之时，后人遂谓时中止有孔子，大误也。自羲农至孔孟皆圣人，而事业不同者，何哉？五帝殊时，不相袭礼，三王异世，不相沿乐。孔子曰：尧授舜，汤放桀，武王伐纣，时也，君子而时中。凡君子皆时中，何独孔子。因圣人而不得位，自孔子始，人罕知之，故孟子极力推崇孔子。孔子一介布衣耳，言行事业无异常人，而实综括前圣，恰得时中，孟子表其为圣之时，使人学孔子，岂谓孔子一人时中，五帝三王皆不然乎。且时中二字并非难知难行者，如暑天忽凉则加衣，寒天忽热亦易服，凡起居饮食随时增损，不一而足，愚夫愚妇皆知，何至学圣人而遂高视二字，甚至于治国治家，亦不知时？父子济恶，绍圣贻殃、曷胜浩叹。夫一家之中，父耕桑而子簪组，子匹夫而父公卿，遭遇亦惟其时，但能立德修身，则穷达虽殊，皆为作述之美。自王安石变法祸宋，后人遂以变法为讳，不解三年无改之言有为而发，且不思道字之义。夫子因有父善而子不善者，故特言无改于父之道，若父不合道，则子必速改为孝，成亲之美，始为大孝，岂以阿意曲从为孝哉。虽圣人之法亦无久而不敝，所赖随时匡救，以道维持，归于至当。古圣贤干蛊者不具论，如文武同德，非有可革之政也，而夫子称武周为善继述。凡先人善言善行，固宜不愆不忘，而时异势殊，亦有当变通之处，况非纯善无疵。而斤斤受旧，至于流弊昭然，危在旦夕，尚不更张，其害彰彰在史册中，但非有修身立德，硕辅名贤斟酌尽善不可耳。明太祖不许宦官干预，而燕文设锦衣卫贻祸子孙，己以亲藩篡位，制亲王不许典兵，而末季子孙罹福禄酒之惨。不当变而变，当变而不变，均为非宜，有国有家者当如何培忠厚、育贤才，以为久远乎。尧舜不以天下私其子，选贤而与，子孙与三代相终始，爱子者无如此矣。周武王不以天下为私器，封建而使各自为治，后世无人谋其子孙之位，永世亦莫加于此矣。时中二字，小有小效，大有大效，要在人善为审慎行之，非有贤父师诲以大学之道，未易言也。但以时俗显然之弊而论，更张不难，亦必不可缓，而狃于不敢变法，驯至不救，不能不为长太息耳。

三十四、文以载道，道敝于文，必本躬行而著为言语文字，
道乃不芜也。

自书契兴而斯文阐，人伦庶物，无事不赖文字，夫子亦曰斯文在兹，匡人其如予何，则文之重可知矣。然而才智之士，学不深而逞私见以妄作，反为害道，夫子已有不知而作之叹，则无实德而务虚名，欲以词华见者，其来久矣。孟子曰处士横议，若非秦火一炬，洙泗遗文岂能敌异端邪说之多乎。焚书、禁书、不许读书，奇事奇闻，自古未有，然由后而观，未必非文字芜杂，天心恶之，假手于秦皇。经毒焰之凶残，壁中丝竹乃贵。斯文兴废，关系世道人心，孔孟之学大行，实由秦火之故。自汉至今书籍日繁，而惑世诬民之说亦日众，又理学、儒林、文艺等各标一帜，文与道若不相蒙，知与行不必兼到，天人性命之学日入于渺冥，日用伦常之事但趋于浮杂，而文日多道日晦焉。朱子云读书便好，然书岂可尽读哉，即圣人之书亦岂徒诵读求荣哉。大道不过伦常，智愚皆可知行，孩提知爱，稍长知敬，贤父母善养善教，毋使失其天良，明师益友更加切磋，则不忍其亲之心日长而日坚，推之兄弟宗族无不然，忍悖其君者寡矣。笃敬其长之心日增而日慎，推之于州里蛮貊无不恭，敢慢其君者又何有乎。孟子曰："亲亲仁也，敬长义也，无他，达之天下"。盖人皆有所不忍，达之于其所忍为仁，人皆有所不为，达之于其所为曰义，此岂难能者哉。读书明理，明此而已，为文阐道，阐此而已。士人读圣贤书而天理良心忽焉不讲，凡名利所在，即忘身以徇之，求不忍为不仁、不敢为不义者寥寥。而

著为文则居然义理，遂使圣人明伦察物之意竟成虚文，而以之名世者不乏，是文字反为大道之蠹，岂不可伤哉！有志维风者亦欲自张一帜，不入窠臼，而实践未深，名为卫道，实乃晦道，如王通僭经，子云拟《易》，人知非之，而孔子之书亦不阙疑，任意改窜，则不可解矣。圣人之言皆天理，故畏圣人之言，即是畏天命，外天理而有言，外圣人而立说，自以为得，实似是而非。圣人之道不明，岂非文字多岐乎。夫文章者道德之华，凡可以经理人伦庶物、有益民生者，皆为不可少之言，否则蛙鸣聒耳，使人心风俗日趋于浮伪，而身心性命之理、日用伦常之道不实力体行，且内外交养、本末交修分为歧途，贻误来学，文亦何贵也！

三十五、有情世界四字，人所共知，但须明辨而力行之。不然，则大悖道也。

性情二字，天地人神皆有之，不可忽也。情统于性，性者理也。天理之无声无臭者不可窥而成象成形，著为万象，则天地之情可见。人心之存主者不可测，而喜、怒、哀、乐发为言动，则邪正之情亦了然，故情字不可轻视。然情者性之用也，而亦性之贼也。其几在乎正与不正之间。夫人之情亦安得而遂正哉？非养性之功已纯，中有所主，七情统于一性，安能有正无妄。常人欲正其情，必学、问、思、辨以明其理，笃行以诚其身，知止于至善。静存有主矣，又于一念之起不欺、不苟，一言一行必诚、必敬，始而勉强，久而自然，然后邪妄日少，好恶之情可正，岂曰任意而行，快心悦体即为有情世界之正哉。人生适意之事不过衣食男女数事，圣人亦不能外，而凡事义理节文之，故情正而性亦日坚，若一失其正，则情荡而性又何存，故惟圣罔念作狂，圣人亦必允执厥中。情七而性则一，以性节情，不可任情乱性，孟子所谓旦昼梏亡违，禽兽不远者，岂不由于七情之妄乎！君君、臣臣、父父、子子五伦各有其道，以至诚行之，曲尽其道，则至情所钟，即至性所存，推之于仁民爱物，本一心以通亿万人无不攸宜为有情世界之实义。自大道罕行，世人以嗜欲之私为性情之正，凡可以快心志者无不为，而天性日薄，伦理日乖，甚至诗书中人荡检踰闲，自不知咎，反演为诗文、杂说，自诩风流，所以一二愚民厌而旁趋，求一清净之方，于是学为僧羽之出家矣，惑于邪学之神怪矣。使诗书中人皆服习中庸之道，内而正心，外而饬纪，不入于风流放浪之行，天下人则而效焉，何患异端邪说易以炫乱乎。故情之一字正而心无不正，安得人人皆践格致诚正之道哉！

三十六、圣人千言万语止是一理，理者，天人所共也。

天地人神一气相通，以其本一理相贯。人为三才之主，尽人合天之学只是全其为人之理，不愧于天地，又何愧于父母乎。乃歧视天地人神，致人以中庸之道为身外之物，岂不可叹，可惜！圣人亦人耳，孔子何以曰知我其天？文王何以同天之于穆？孔子曰："人者，天地之心"。孟子曰："万物皆备于我"。天地一父母也。人道全是天道，尽人道，合天道，与天合德，如儿子学父母，与父母一般圣贤而已，非奇怪事。在天为天理，在人为良心，天理良心人人有之。念念不离四字，大则希圣希天，小亦全忠全孝，所以读圣人书，学圣人之行，畏圣人之言，止是要全此四字，方不愧为人。奈先儒支离其说，高自位置，谓道非常人所能，遂使圣道如烟雾矣。天地人一贯，神明之正者，皆天地正气之灵，司天地之功化，为民生之主宰，儒者一概斥为诬罔，则夫子体物不遗之义皆罔矣。且俗儒谓鬼神荒渺，然则祭如在，祭神如神在，孔子亦是愚人，可乎！不知天地无心、无言，而夫微之显，诚之所布濩者，鬼神明著其几，如大风拔木，惊霆腾空，岂得以为不见不闻者虚诞乎。及风霆寂然，万籁无声，前之震惊骇听者归于何处，岂非微之显费而隐者欤。乃闢虚无二字，止就见闻事为上言理，岂知不显之德潜虽伏而亦昭，与上天之载同夫无声无臭者，所谓于穆也，不显之德，文王之德之纯也。天道然，人道亦然，所以天人合撰。此义不明，佛老之正者以邪视之，而学佛老者悖佛老以求奇，异端邪术纷然并作，儒者极力攘斥，而卒不能禁，岂非儒修之实未得其真，修已治人亦不得其反经之义哉。

下学梯航

刘沅 编著

《下学梯航》叙

道犹路也，止此一理，天地人神所共由，故曰道。人之异于禽兽者几希，天理而已。全之则人，无之则物。存几希者皆圣人，则圣人亦只全乎所以为人焉尔。孔子曰：人者天地之心，困勉成功则一。孟子曰：人皆可以为尧舜。未尝谓道必择人而为。即德至圣人，亦生人之恒事，磻溪钓叟、版筑佣工，即终于匹夫，岂非圣贤？前人误解大德受命，致人不敢为圣，其将安于下愚而后可。夫圣人者，人伦之至耳。人不能外五伦而生，安得不师圣人之敦伦？今圣人在上，百度维新，陶淑天下，无非欲其不愧为人；而惮于自修，甘于暴弃，则以言圣人者多失之太高，不知圣与人同，但力行中庸之道也。中庸之道，至平至常，亦至神至奇，惟其神奇即在平常之中，所以为中庸。愚老矣，及门多有问难者，酬答维艰，不得已命儿子松文、梽文等，书愚管见，以告来者。一家之私言，垂老之愚见，不堪为君子告也，聊代刍荛。原其心而恕其妄，幸甚！幸甚！

道光三十年 岁在庚戌重九日 双流止唐刘沅书时年八十有三

下 学 梯 航

天理良心

天之理而人得之以为心之良,即所云天命之谓性也。性字从忄从生,是人得天中正之心。天之理即天之心,太极也,诚也,人得此理为性;万物皆天所生,而人独得天中正之理,故曰德。未生以前,得诸天者曰明德;既生以后,七情扰而嗜欲纷,非复受中之本然矣,复性而全其所得之理,亦曰德。以其为天地生生之本,于人为万理从出之原,如木果之有仁,故曰仁。诚者实有此理,乃实可以为人也。道如大路,人所共由,故天理良心,人人所有。圣人止是全此四字,遂与天通。本四字而行之,则合天理矣。但恐其或过或不及,节之文之曰礼,无过无不及,行之恰得其宜曰义,智者知之真,信者行之诚且久,故五常止此天理良心四字。天理良心,人人知之,不能行之。岂无良哉!父师之教不端,见闻习染误之也。今撮其存天理之意于左。

一、静存

心浮也,而使之沉;心显也,而使之潜。沉潜二字,即收心之法也。《中庸》曰:"潜虽伏矣,亦孔之昭。"君子之所不可及者,人所不见。人所不见之地,非有密乎?洗心退藏于密,知止而后有定矣。孔子曰为仁,孟子曰养气。存心养性,《大学》止至善也,《中庸》致中也,皆在其中。盖静者动之本,静而后知其动,致中乃能致和。不然,出入无时,莫知其乡,心放而不知,即克治亦不能强制也。《易》曰:

"憧憧往来，朋从尔思。"凡人后天之心皆如是。存其有觉之心，养其虚静之性，非如但养知觉之心者比，愚屡言之矣。

二、动察

心不可见也，动而著于言行，乃有是非。其是者美矣，其非者即所谓恶。恶著于外，其恶易知；恶藏于心，其恶更甚。故崇德必先修慝。一念之起而是焉，扩充之可也；一念之起而非，必克治之。于其几之动，而即自觉之，自禁之，不可使其即逝，大学所谓诚意也。然孰是孰非，不先知之，何以能诚意？朱子所以补格物，而特所谓物者，浩无涯涘，则非圣人之本旨也。孔子曰："不明乎善，不诚乎身。"欲诚其意，先致其知。致知之道如左。

三、师授

上二条静存动察，先儒亦言之行之，而惜所谓静者，存有觉之心而已，不知圣人洗心有密之实；所谓动察者，研穷事物之理而已，不知理以心性五伦为要。天下之物，不可胜穷，天下之事，亦安能皆知？圣人一以贯之，只是内养其心者极熟，念念无非天理，所谓仁也；外察于理者至精，事事皆合其宜，所谓义也。仁熟然后义精，义精必由仁熟。养浩然之气，由有诸己而充实，渐至化神，非明师不授，非恒诚不几。知者知其理、践其功，所谓明善者，明此而已。明乎一念之非，而百为皆谬，则邪妄杂念所必芟；明乎一动之非，而伦理不洽，则仁敬孝慈所必践。凡人莫不有天良。为恶之人，其始不过一念之非、一事之失，因无贤亲师为之作则，为之诏示，故习惯而驰。故静存动察之功，有明师指授，则是非得失，观感熏陶，即易明白。况四子六经，昭昭人寰，圣世规模，炳炳垂训，熟而玩之，力而行之，有何不可入德？若夫广见闻、慎交游，亦致知之要者，而要无非择别善恶二字。见贤思齐，见不贤内省；三人行必有师。实践夫子二章之言，则致知易矣。外此名物象数、技艺百家，有益于心性伦常者取之，否则弃之。夫子所以言学问思辨，有弗学问思辨者，致知不外此四端，非教人尽天下之物知之。奈何不为其易，而为其难哉！

四、改过

人孰无过？但恐安而就之，愧而匿之，则过遂成恶。过出无心，改之即为无过，固不待言；即有心之恶，苟豁然醒悟，翻然自责，毅然不再犯，更久久积善，亦可晚盖矣。常人惟恐人知己过，是以惮于改之，不知圣人所以为圣人，止是日日改过而已。孔子假年学易，始无大过，何况凡人？成汤万方有罪，在予一人；武王百姓有过，在予一人。天下之过，且引为己过，而以身之过为讳乎？若不改过，便无学圣根基。戒之！戒之！

五、笃行

夫子言以三达德行五达道，其学之之目，学、问、思、辨、笃行。学问思辨，所以致知；笃行，所以行也。而又曰有弗学云云，以有所弗为者多，盖事物不胜穷，惟切于伦常日用者为要，不可不以五者勉之耳。笃之一字，该宏毅二字在内。曾子曰"士不可以不宏毅"，为其任重而道远。任何以重？曰仁； 道何以远？曰死。自俗人观之，鲜不以为迂矣。不知仁者天理，外天理即非人。不为仁将不愿为人乎？但为仁之功，非朝夕可了，亦无一息可懈，故须宏毅。宏毅即笃之谓也。人生所以适意者，不过宫室、衣服、饮食、男女四事，圣人亦不离此，而以理节情，不恣嗜欲，久久习为固然，则上承宗庙，下教子孙，不负天地君亲生成之念，内而存养，去人见天，外而省察，改过迁善，至死不渝，斯德成名立矣。达则伊周，穷则孔孟，是为天地间不可少之人。若不自贵其身，而纵其情欲，外于礼义，富贵亦不过豢养形骸，贫贱更形同草木。孟子曰："舍正路而弗由，放其心而不知求，哀哉！"所以哀者，不可不知也。夫人生不过宫室、衣食、男女，而仁圣贤人，天必福之，安有饥寒困苦而死者？夷齐之饿，忠孝节义之捐躯，仁也、义也。全而受者全而归，与天地日月同休，不为凶祸，然亦不幸遭遇之穷耳，岂仁圣必如此哉？此义不明，将藉为口实，曰为善无益。辨之，慎之。

以上五条，大要已得，惟致知一事，颇难枚举。四子六经，义精而文繁，史传群书，博杂而难辨。今就世俗共知之言列后，勿以为诞妄肤庸，是者行之，非者革之，即可以进德矣。

孔子四言

非礼勿视

心之精神全在于目,目所视而心即驰,正则天理,邪则禽兽。色欲一事,少年尤易入邪。于美色而视若姊妹,于邪物而视如豺虎,此求放心第一要功。

非礼勿听

耳通性海,入于耳而乱于心,邪思妄想以成,不待言矣。自天子至庶人,不明义理,为谗邪败德致祸者尤众,故当切戒。

非礼勿言

言以达其心。凡五伦浃洽,必由恩谊周到;力行仁义,岂不赖言宣畅谐和之?至于阐道德,述圣谟,解争讼,需言之事尤多。但必平日素有修身之学,烛理之明,始能随事告语,曲尽其义。常人任心而谈,不知返己自课,不特妄言恶言、败伤伦类者不足观,即自负才能,言行不相顾,亦可羞怍。故夫子屡屡教人慎言,大抵多言不如少言,有言不如无言。非其人而言,非其礼而言,不自责而言,皆非也。

非礼勿动

动兼内外而言。外而一动一静,必准乎理,内而一念之非,必除其根,乃是。

关夫子四言

存好心，行好事，说好话，交好人。

心之所存，见于事与言，而必先自其存心慎之，兼上文动静之功在内。好话必以圣言为师，好人则节取之、全取之，该亲师取友三人行章义在内。

豫誠堂家訓

刘沅编著

天理良心，人之所以為人；寬仁厚德，覆載所以長久。昧良悖理，不得為人；褊心小量，安能合天？得天理以為人，天地故為父母；父母才有我身，父母故同天地。欺堂上父母易，欺頭上父母難。一念欺天，即為不孝；一念欺親，得罪于天。修道以諭親，尊父母如天地也；盡性而參贊，事天地如父母也。孝在修德，德在修心。移孝可以作忠，只為不欺不肆；靜存始能動察，必須無怠無荒。犯了邪淫，便是禽獸；喜歡勢利，定成鄙夫。保養作善，即守身誠身之義；知非改過，為希賢希圣之門。人生如夢，修善修福方長；大道難逢，父教師教為本。自心抱愧，說甚夫綱父綱；作事不真，怎樣為臣為子？治天下無多術，養教周全；學圣賢有何難，恕道便好。勤職業，修心術，何患飢寒？貪財色，亂人倫，必戕身命。弟兄以仁讓為主，正家以夫婦為先。飽暖平安，是為清福；溫良恭儉，到處春風。讀書要讀好書，凡事必宗孔孟；作人要作好人，時刻敬畏神天。善為儿孫積財，莫如積德；多行巧詐害己，安能害人？先代格言甚多，在乎身体；圣人事業何在？必先正心。私欲去而聰明始開，致知故先格物；念頭好而是非分明，實踐乃為誠意。養心養气，小效亦可延年；成己成人，功夫全在大學。道須深造，功在返求。在上不正其趨，人才從何而出？倫常本于心性，故曰一以貫之。學業騖于浮華，所以万事墮矣！戒之勉之，庶乎不替祖訓。

学圣人局量

刘沅编著

大慈悲心

慈悲仁也。仁人心也。天理良心也。凡人必有仁。然后念念事事。惟恐不知人好歹。一言一动。惟恐得罪于人。至于忠孝友悌。大伦所在。其不忍一念相欺。不敢一念怠肆。更无待言矣。仁也。而曰大慈悲者。由一念以及于念念。由一事以及于事事。俱是此不忍人之心。所谓昆虫草木不可伤。尽其性以尽人性物性。参赞化育。皆以此为根本。

大广大心

广大谓度量也。古人云。有大量者。始有大福。量小者。居心狭隘。见理不明。气质刚躁。止知有己。不知有人。止徒利己。不顾损人。自恃而不服善。自私而不谅人。自小而不容人。能有度量。必自平日反躬自责之人。一言一行。惟恐不合乎理。损伤于人。刻刻检点自己不是。虽外人怒我詈（lì）我。十分亏我。多不理他。止是自家反躬自问。问心无愧了。任他无理相加。都全然不理。至于君父大伦所在。以及弟兄朋友。犯而不校。更不待言矣。

大方便心

方便者何。敏于事也。勇于义也。人世相与同居同游。同往来晋接。无非五伦中人。五伦中人。有尊卑大小。贵贱亲疏。贤否远近之不同。如君父母。至尊至亲。竭诚竭力。敬慎服事。君亲而贤。能象其贤。君亲而不贤。匡救谕谏。能干其蛊。做得十分周到。至使其君亲为圣人。忠孝事业。做到无古无今。此臣子分内之事。不足为功。凡事君事亲。十分周到。不得言方便也。此外。弟兄朋友。其中亲疏厚薄。贤愚是非。断不能一同而视。事兄爱弟信友。先自家各尽其道。爱之敬之。不欺不苟。久久不变。不管他说我是非。我止尽其心。尽其道。求无愧于我心。若他有事。止要不悖义理。则真心代劳。尽心尽力。委曲成全好事。此便是方便之道也。但事有难易。境有丰啬。时势有常变。顺逆不同。虽当方便。也要斟酌义理情事。必不可一概冒昧而行。至于从井救人。危身辱亲尤非。所以古人云力量做得来的。尽其力量。力量做不来的。亦必用心周到。此所言者。谓事情大理所关也。若夫平日检身修德。一言一行。一步一趋。随身方便。其事难以枚举。其功亦简而易行。止要肯留心。不怠不肆。便可处处方便。如行路。见一木一石碍脚。恐妨人行。去之。饥寒困苦。一切不佳之事。惟恐人有。饱煖安全得意之事。惟恐人不周全。一日之内。斗室之间。无处不可方便。此两字实心奉行。仁义二字。都在其中矣。

大清静心

如何清静。见财不贪。见色不爱。一念一事。不纵情悖理皆是。止知安分守己。劝职业。修心术。念人生万事。终由天命。天之爱人者。止此天理良心。我念念不失天理良心。事事体贴而行。无论德行道义。择一合义理者为之。如耕读商贾。专心学习此艺。勤而不懈。俭而不奢。廉而不贪。专而不分。又念念检点。不肯一毫亏损天良。如此。无论何事。俱可以谋生度日。此即俗所谓靠天而行也。人心妄想无穷。不可任心行事。止要一生不受饥寒。仰事俯蓄。可以粗足。便是第一美境了。至于富贵荣华之人。彼有积累善德。上天方才赐之福禄。我无他积累。如何妄想与他一般。果然存心恬退。时时芟除妄想。则久久习为固然。无论贫贱困苦。都安心住下去了。此乃寻常人刻持私心。勉强学为清净之法。若夫读书明理之人。能存心养性。履仁蹈义。内而涵养有功。久久。鄙俗之见自消。外而动循礼义。久久。美恶之情浑忘。则必有静存动察。始终本末之功。圣人非道非义。一介不取予。万钟千驷弗视。由斯道也。此清净二字。上之。则希圣希贤。皭羅天下。中之。则有守有为。行藏不苟。下之。亦云水心情。无处不可自适。是在人自为之。而自勉之耳。

大柔和心

和者。恩谊浃洽之谓也。以其上而言。修于身者。喜怒哀乐皆中节。是天下之达道也。措诸世者。天下中国如一人。是覆载之宏深也。此和之至者。非圣人不能。以其次而言。五伦之内。各尽其道。各得其所。恩明谊美。情义不相乖离。此和之切要。不可无。亦人之所当尽者。再次。则不忍为不仁。不敢为不义。小心敬慎。平心静气。惟恐伤人。惟恐偾事。惟恐取祸。谦虚忍让。纵有大不平。大不堪之事。大可恨。大可诛之人。也置之不问。将自家好胜好强。刚躁之气。极力柔服下来。故曰柔和也。宽柔以教。不报无道。君子居之。此之谓也。不然。柔之一字。乃不好字面。善柔也。柔奸也。柔弱也。柔佞也。柔靡也。安得而为之。凡人不能忍辱谦让。俱是血气刚强。心情躁暴所致。故柔其气以从理。和其情以同物。然后伦谊可以浃洽。动履可以无灾。右五言。本佛道书中语。而其义理。实与圣人之道无殊。圣人言行。不外乎此。即四子六经。名贤议论。亦不外乎此。但世人忽而置之。迂而笑之。甚且以为异端而辟之。是以学圣学贤。无从入手。愚尝举以训门人。谓此五言。乃学圣之局量。必先有此五言心思。实行五言义理。然后可以希贤希圣而希天。惜乎遵行者罕。今老矣。不得已。书示儿曹以为一家之授受云尔。

刘沅生平

出于槐轩概述：川西夫子刘沅与槐轩学说

吕笑龙编辑

双流传统文化研习会

第一节 明末迁蜀世居双流

刘沅（公元1768-1855年），字止唐，一字讷如，号清阳居士、碧霞居士，生于清乾隆三十三年（1768年），四川双流云栖里人（今属彭镇羊坪村）。先世祖居湖北麻城孝感乡，明季不纲，远祖刘朝弼（字棐忱），于正德、嘉靖年间，为避世乱，举家来蜀，定居在四川眉州南隅岷江之畔。六世祖刘宇舟（字峤云），明朝武将，封为建义将军，明亡守节，弃官归隐。高祖刘坤（字后菴），在四川眉州蟆颐山中坝长洲下，以教授五经课徒为业；明末战乱，先避乱峨眉，后栖身温江县东关董村，后因家口繁衍，移居至双流县云栖里，至今尚有部分刘氏族人居住在此。

曾祖刘嘉珍（字玉函），少弱多疾，尤耽典籍，喜读两汉书，工小楷。祖刘汉鼎（字君谟），有德行，好读《易》，曾著有《易蕴发明》一书，常言"俭于己，功于人，暗于才，懋于德"，立为庭训。

父刘汝钦（字敬五），幼承家学，洞澈性理，精通《易经》，壮年从军，曾随岳钟琪辗转岷嶓间，金川之役亲与其事，专办粮秣，后退伍还乡，深居简出，以课子设帐训蒙自娱；刘汝钦性喜读书，乐善好施，在乡享有豪士之名，著作仅存诗一首及《玉皇尊经》注三卷，《玉皇宝忏》注一卷。

附：

（一）清代大学者、文学家纪昀（字晓岚，乾隆年间进士。官至礼部尚书、协办大学士）亲撰《敬五公墓志铭》摘录：

"天佐明德，祥鸾奋翼，忠孝克家，与世无既，郁郁佳诚，卜以千亿，于昭报施，善人其永，视此铭碣。"

（二）清代嘉庆帝师朱珪亲撰《敬五公诔词》：

"易朽者，形也；不敝者，神也；而不依形而立者，形与神可以并寿。敬五之生也，孝拟祥览，义匹鲁周，捐旧怨于王生，明冤狱于蒋姓，完党敬之婚，焚千金之券，皆为人所不能为，而平居笃亲睦族，谦己济人，盛事不可枚举，是诚豪杰之士欤，余庆何可圉也。讃曰：云雨翻覆，世态仓皇；疏亲弃旧，不狂为狂；惟公令德，慨当以慷；千金一掷，二酉余香；笃生俊乂，观国之光；太乙驻节，辉映瑶阊；出无入有，肖此昂藏；琅函玉笈，终荫此堂。

大兴朱珪 顿首拜撰"

兄刘濖（字芳皋），幼时入邑庠，乾隆五十九年（1794年）举于乡，嘉庆元年（1796年）进士，在京由钦点翰林院庶吉士散馆，该授刑部主事，官广西郁林州知州。芳皋公曾题弥勒佛联曰："开口便笑，笑古笑今，凡事付之一笑；大肚能容，容天容地，于人何所不容。"读之足拓心胸。

第二节 科举登仕辞官为师

刘沅先生幼年体弱，但颖悟向学，聪敏过人，七岁能文，有神童之誉。垂髫之年，与兄刘濖在乡云栖里中元寺就读私塾。逾年，有古淳者，字鹤峰（县中名士，乾隆年间双流岁贡，曾出任过天全州教谕，工书画，耽吟咏，著作有《鹤峰诗集》，今大英博物馆收藏有其画。）致仕后，还籍牧马山，于板桥梓地方文昌宫，开馆训蒙。刘沅弟兄久慕鹤峰先生道德文章，相率负笈于此，执弟子礼，后成为古淳师最为器重的门人。若干年后，刘沅弟兄虽早已跻身士林，仍不忘故乡山水，重经板桥，留下多首怀念求学时代生活的诗，其中一首最为脍炙人口。诗曰：

归雁声中去路遥，读书事业壮怀飘。

八千里外多知己，三十年前旧板桥。

曾向鸡群留雪爪，更无凤侣共云霄。

此来惹得江山笑，前度儿郎发已凋。

解放前，双流黄水板桥梓文昌宫西墙，曾有一通高约一丈的大石碑，上面镌刻有"儒林刘止唐弟兄读书处"（清翰林伍肇龄书）十二个鎏金大字，光灿夺目，可惜毁于十年动乱。

刘沅先生十八岁离开文昌宫入县学，清乾隆五十年（1785年），以冠军入为双流县庠生，乾隆五十二年（1787年）食饩为廪生，乾隆五十三年（1788年）选拔为明经，又于乾隆五十四年（1789年）因文行兼优而选拔为贡生，乾隆五十七年（公元1792年）由拔贡中试举人。清乾隆五十八年（1793年）、乾隆六十年（1795年）、嘉庆元年（1796年）三次参加会试皆不中，刘沅先生念及高堂老母，形孤体弱，加之家境贫寒，遂无心仕途。被选拔为贡生后，在家乡云栖里朝阳庵小庙著书讲学，所得束脩用来孝敬母亲，或贴补家用。其兄刘濖中进士后，刘沅先生曾言"显扬之事，兄已遂矣，犬马之养，愿得身任之"，遂留守在家侍奉母亲。

第三节 偶遇隐士初窥道源

清嘉庆元年（1796年），刘濖中进士出任翰林院庶吉士散馆，刘沅先生随其兄作伴北上，弟兄二人途经陕西紫柏山留侯庙时，刘沅遇到了他一生当中的第一个奇人——隐居于此的静一道人。静一道人与刘沅相谈甚契，为他讲解了修养之道，临别还以吕纯阳所注的《道德经》相赠；刘沅"讶其与吾儒同"，发现道家养生与儒家修养之道颇有相通之处，初步窥探到两者之间千丝万缕的学术联系。这次巧遇，对即将而立之年的刘沅无疑起到了潜移默化作用，可以说为刘沅一生的学术奠定了重要的基调。刘沅日后留心道学，自成一说，在学术上开辟了一条"以儒为宗，旁及佛道"的道路。

第四节 拜师野云修身养性

刘沅先生在京逗留期间，家中发生两起悲愤之事，先是家兄刘芳皋的第二个儿子死去，接着自家坟地被豪邻侵占，母亲因此忧愤发病。刘沅先生不顾旅途劳顿，急忙返家，因奔忙操劳，诸事不顺，加之苦读体质孱弱，导致身心疲惫不堪，病卧床榻，年纪轻轻就已像七、八十岁老人一样，担心自己命不遐长，难以为母亲养老送终，于是愈加悲观。

嘉庆二年（1797年），刘沅先生偶然在本地彭家场集上，遇到一位卖药老人，"形容殊异，心爱敬之，求示延年之方"，这就是野云老人李果圆。野云老人给了刘沅治病药方，还向他阐示"仁者寿，大德必寿"、"人生自有长生药"等圣贤之言，"示以穷理尽性、内外本末之功"，嘱咐他"存心养性""返而求诸身心可也"。刘沅先生见老者不凡，顿有所悟，遂拜其为师，自此在老人指导下服药调养，修身养性。不到两年，刘沅羸弱的病体完全康复，且日趋强健。野云老人所传要旨为"存神养气即存心养性"，其实质是儒道两家性命修养之学的融合，刘沅虽身体力行，颇有成效，亦有所领悟，但因生计和俗务牵挂，尚未对其进行理论性的总结。

嘉庆九年（1804年）初夏，与刘沅朝夕相处的野云老人辞去，期间教导刘沅时间将近八年。此后刘沅先生对修身养性功夫更加励志勤修，身心日益健旺，从六十岁至八十岁生八子，年近九十岁才辞世。后来他感慨说："回思平生，辛苦备尝，几如再世，使不遇野云老人，早归大暮。"野云老人成了对刘沅一生影响最大的决定性人物，使"李实孔师"、"儒道一体"等直承老孔的大道文化思想，成为槐轩学说的重要思想来源和学术特点，并在其学术思想中占有极其重要的地位。

第五节 开馆授徒道重儒林

自清乾隆五十一年（1786年），刘沅先生从双流县柑梓乡三圣村（旧名云栖里）开始训徒讲学起，至嘉庆十二年（1807年），刘沅奉母命迁居成都南门淳化街（又名三巷子，1959 年修建锦江大礼堂时拆除殆尽），自建房屋，新立门户。因云栖里旧宅有庭槐近二百年，移宅省城后，纯化街新宅院中又有三株老槐树，浓荫掩映，雍穆恬静，刘沅遂名宅曰"槐轩"（清翰林伍肇龄曾亲书"儒林刘止唐先生第"）。此后，刘沅先生一直在成都淳化街设馆讲学，专心致力于学术研究和教育后学，门生弟子遍布西南各省，世称"槐轩学派"。

道光六年（1826 年）礼部下文，刘沅选授湖北天门县知县。奉檄后，刘沅宦情淡薄，力辞不赴，托词说要在家丁忧受制。在北京逗留数月，朝廷念其孝诚，不敢夺情，授以文职正二品资政大夫（散阶），改授国子监典簿而归。清《国史馆儒林传·刘沅本传》说他"安贫乐道，不愿外任，改国子监典簿，寻乞假归，遂隐居教授"，即指此事。

从辞别乡居，移居成都，此后四十八年，刘沅在成都淳化街设馆讲学治学，直至八十八岁谢世。他有教无类，教学报酬不计多寡，家贫学子，无钱一样可以就学。教学内容，除了传统经史书籍之外，还传授学生静养之道，以强健身体。常年求学的学生达三百人以上，前后师从学习的有数千人，刘沅先生也因此被誉为"塾师之雄"。据清《国史馆儒林传·刘沅本传》记载："成进士登贤书者百余人，明经贡士三百余人，薰沐善良得为孝子悌弟，贤名播乡闻者，指不胜屈"。其生徒中既有农工商贾，亦有科甲仕宦、社会名流，学业者无不以槐轩门人自矜。

刘沅先生在世之时，其学术已经远播他省，被尊为"川西夫子"，因其门生弟子遍布省内外，桃李满天下，世称"槐轩学派"，亦称"刘门"（如孔门、程门一样的学术团体）。刘沅先生辞世后，其子及门人将他毕生著述详加整理考订付梓，总其名曰《槐轩全书》，刊行流布于世。

先生取妻彭氏，篷室陈氏，继配袁氏，"俱贤淑，善理家政，故先生无内顾之忧，钻研训诲，至老不倦。"（刘芬《止唐先生墓志铭》）。子嗣中，有的官居京华，或翰林，或部员；有的恬居梓里，或举人、或乡贤，乐静守成，潜心治学，属文属史，咸以大器期之。

清咸丰五年（1855年）十二月十九日子时，刘沅先生仙逝，享年八十有八。次年十月初二日葬于双流县西十里彭家场云栖里墓祠之右。墓碑题"清国子监典簿刘沅 青阳居士"，先生大弟子刘芬撰并书丹"清处士刘止唐先生墓志铭"。先生墓地搬迁后，由其玄孙刘恒壁（字东父）将墓碑重题为"清处士刘止唐之墓"。处士之称，亦为刘沅先生自拟。

清光绪三十一年（1905年），翰林院编修、成都尊经书院山长邛州伍肇龄（嵩生）和华阳颜楷、胡峻等，通过四川总督锡良启奏朝廷，恳请将刘沅一生事迹付史馆立传，奏由"为故绅学行可风，恳恩宜付史馆立传，以励潜修"。同年十月二十四日，清廷御批："着照所请。该衙门知道。钦此。"由此名列清《国史馆儒林传·刘沅本传》。

清四川总督锡良

（1853—1917），字清弼，拜岳特氏（巴岳特氏），蒙古镶蓝旗人，同治十三年进士。1903年（光绪二十九年），锡良调任四川总督，1907年3月（光绪三十三年）调任云贵总督，他为官三十七年，以正直清廉、勤政务实而著称，是晚清时代一位政绩颇佳，贡献较大的历史人物。

伍肇龄

（1826-1915）字嵩生，进士出身，晚清翰林、教育家。四川邛州（今邛崃人）。回乡后主讲成都锦江书院多年。工书法，善古文。

成都锦江书院有联云："有补于天地曰功，有益于世教曰名；有精神之谓富，有廉耻之谓贵；原乎始之谓道，得于己之谓德；不屑鄙陋斯为文，不涉傲慢斯为章。"

---摘录于《遗训存略·卷上》

颜楷

（1877-1927）字雍耆，学者、书法家。四川华阳人。1905年被清廷派往日本攻读法政，归国后任翰林院编修加侍讲。民国后不问政治，信佛为居士，被选为四川佛教会副会长。擅长书法，亦为槐轩学派弟子。

胡峻

（1870-1909）字雨岚，号贞庵，四川华阳人。光绪二十一年进士，授编修。后总理四川高等学堂，曾赴日本考察，归后，设教育研究会，立模范小学，创法政、铁道及体育诸专校。曾因锡良创筑川汉铁路，随同出国考察。"公车上书"之举亦列名其中。

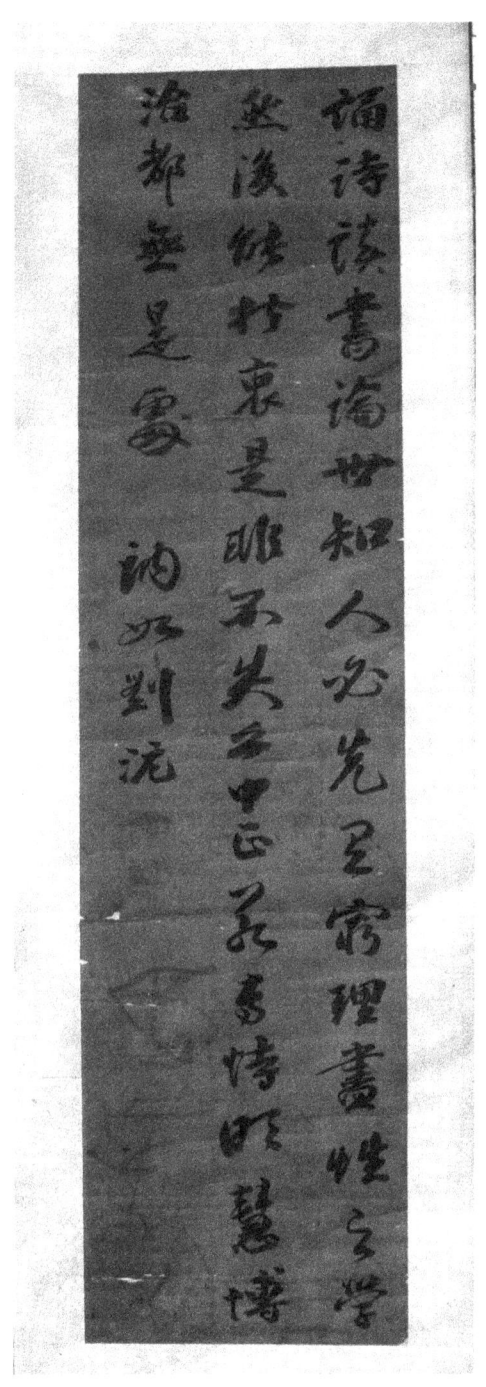

Liu Yuan's Calligraphy

www.ingramcontent.com/pod-product-compliance
Lightning Source LLC
Chambersburg PA
CBHW050634150426

42811CB00052B/815